Race, Religion, and Black Lives Matter

BLACK LIVES & LIBERATION

SERIES EDITORS

Brandon Byrd, *Vanderbilt University*
Zandria F. Robinson, *Rhodes College*
Christopher Cameron, *University of North Carolina, Charlotte*

BLACK LIVES MATTER. What began as a Twitter hashtag after the 2013 acquittal of George Zimmerman for the murder of Trayvon Martin has since become a widely recognized rallying cry for black being and resistance. The series aims are two-fold: 1) to explore social justice and activism by black individuals and communities throughout history to the present, including the Black Lives Matter movement and the evolving ways it is being articulated and practiced across the African Diaspora; and 2) to examine everyday life and culture, rectifying well-worn "histories" that have excluded or denied the contributions of black individuals and communities or recast them as entirely white endeavors. Projects draw from a range of disciplines in the humanities and social sciences and will first and foremost be informed by "peopled" analyses, focusing on everyday actors and community folks.

RACE, RELIGION, & BLACK LIVES MATTER

Essays *on a* Moment *and a* Movement

EDITED BY

Christopher Cameron *and*
Phillip Luke Sinitiere

Vanderbilt University Press
Nashville, Tennesee

Library of Congress Cataloging-in-Publication Data

Names: Cameron, Christopher, 1983- editor. | Sinitiere, Phillip Luke,
  editor.
Title: Race, religion, and Black Lives Matter : essays on a moment and a
  movement / Christopher Cameron and Phillip Luke Sinitiere, eds.
Description: Nashville : Vanderbilt University Press, [2021] | Includes
  bibliographical references.
Identifiers: LCCN 2021007082 (print) | LCCN 2021007083 (ebook) | ISBN
  9780826502070 (hardcover) | ISBN 9780826502063 (paperback) | ISBN
  9780826502094 (epub) | ISBN 9780826502100 (pdf)
Subjects: LCSH: Black lives matter movement—Religious aspects. | African
  Americans—Civil rights. | African Americans—Religion. | Civil
  rights—Religious aspects. | Race relations—Religious aspects. |
  Religion and social problems—United States. | United States—Race
  relations.
Classification: LCC E185.615 .R21325 2021 (print) | LCC E185.615 (ebook)
  | DDC 323.1196/073—dc23
LC record available at https://lccn.loc.gov/2021007082
LC ebook record available at https://lccn.loc.gov/2021007083

Contents

Acknowledgments

We would like to thank Vanderbilt University Press director Gianna Mosser for supporting this project from the beginning and for shepherding its progress through a particularly challenging pandemic year. Her wisdom, insight, and good cheer improved this book. We appreciate her long-time support of both our scholarship and the African American Intellectual History Society (AAIHS). It is truly an honor to work together again. We are grateful to other Vanderbilt University Press staff who helped to bring this book to fruition: Joell Smith-Borne, Betsy Phillips, Jenna Phillips, Cynthia Yeager, and Brittany Johnson. We are also pleased that this book is part of the Black Lives and Liberation Series. Thanks also goes to the two anonymous readers; their suggestions helped to refine the book's argument and strengthen the connections between and across the chapters. Finally, we are immensely grateful for the opportunity to collaborate with so many brilliant scholars whose chapters comprise this volume. Their excellent work has shed new light on understanding of BLM, its history, and its ongoing significance.

Introduction

Christopher Cameron & Phillip Luke Sinitiere

The Black Lives Matter (BLM) movement began in 2013 when a Florida jury acquitted George Zimmerman of Trayvon Martin's murder. Yet the movement symbolizes far more than the moment of Martin's death. It signals a new moment of opposition and insurgency against white supremacy's intended goal of disciplining blackness and Black people. Perhaps ironically, BLM emerged against the backdrop of the Obama era, during the tenure of African American attorney general Eric Holder, and in the midst of a vast expansion of the surveillance state, a long-standing tool of anti-Black repression. The early twenty-first century's saturation with neoliberalism often renders even some purportedly progressive people and/or movements resolutely complicit in structures of exploitation, extraction, and violence. Given such realities, BLM demands recognition of the dignity of Black life while it mobilizes protest for policy change, including the reorganization of resources for a more just and equitable world. It requires the apprehension of police brutality and insists on justice for state actors who perpetuate, fund, and support anti-Black violence.

BLM's genesis as a hashtag by Alicia Garza, Patrisse Cullors, and Opal Tometi marks the historical moment of its creation as an organization and as a movement in the digital era. At the same time, BLM has deep roots in struggles for Black liberation and in one regard extends the Black Power movement of the 1960s and 1970s. BLM, like its predecessor movements, embodies flesh and blood through local organizing, national and global protests, hunger strikes, and numerous acts of civil disobedience. Chants like "All night! All day! We're gonna fight for Freddie Gray!" and "No justice, no fear! Sandra Bland is marching here!" give voice simultaneously to the rage, truth, hope, and insurgency that sustains BLM. If BLM's contemporary presence connects politically to earlier eras of Black liberation struggles, then it follows that religion is a key variable in the movement's overall work and history.

BLM has generously welcomed a broad group of individuals whom religious institutions have historically resisted or rejected. Yet, contrary to general perceptions, religion has been neither absent nor excluded from the movement's activities. For example, BLM co-founder Patrisse Cullors practices a West African Yoruba religious tradition known as Ifa. She has found in the tradition's spirituality a source of existential strength in Black freedom work. "When you are working with people who have been directly impacted by state violence and heavy policing in our communities," she states, "it is really important that there is a connection to the spirit world." Drawing a connection between religious ideas and religious practice in the context of activism and cultural production, she said, "People's resilience, I think, is tied to their will to live, our will to survive, which is deeply spiritual. . . . I don't believe spirit is this thing that lives outside of us dictating our lives, but rather our ability to be deeply connected to something that is bigger than us. I think that is what makes our work powerful."[1] Opal Tometi also uses the language of resilience and love in conjunction with what she calls "faith practices" from the Christian context in which she was raised. Her father, a Nigerian immigrant, is a pastor in Arizona at a church called Phoenix Impact Center. Tometi cites religion as one of the inspirations behind her activist work on behalf of immigrants and for people of color: "I'm a believer, I believe in Jesus as a revolutionary person . . . that's my grounding."[2] Growing up, Alicia Garza identified with her stepfather's Jewish heritage.[3] More recently, she described the act of writing as a spiritual experience. For Garza, spirituality expressed through this form of creative labor is corporeal, it is embodied. "I tingle, my body electric with a spirit that moves from my chest, down my arms, into my fingers. . . . For me, writing is a spiritual practice. It is a purging, a renewal, a call to action I am unable to defy."[4] Tometi, Garza, and Cullors's comments show that BLM is not a wholly secular movement; aspects of institutional religion and faith commitments commingle with spiritual practices of material experiences. This suggests that scholars of history, politics, race, society, and culture should explore critically and analytically the place of religion in BLM-era activism.

This volume has a simple but far-reaching argument: religion is an important thread in BLM and has indelibly shaped and impacted the movement.[5] To advance this claim, *Race, Religion, and Black Lives Matter* examines religion's place in the movement through the lenses of history, politics, and culture. While this collection is not exhaustive or comprehensive in its coverage of religion and BLM, it selectively anthologizes unique aspects of Black religious history, thought, and culture in relation to political struggle in the contemporary era. The chapters aim to document historical change in light of current trends and current events. The contributors analyze religion and BLM in a current historical moment fraught with aggressive, fascist, authoritarian tendencies and one shaped by profound ingenuity, creativity, and insightful perspectives on Black history and culture.

This book adopts a capacious rendering of "religion" that includes everything from subjects that address religious ideas and religions in practice, music, and visual art to topics of irreligion, humanism, atheism, and beyond. It defines "religion" as broadly as possible by drawing from the fields of religious studies and history. Combining religious studies scholar Anthony Pinn's work with scholarship on American religious history, we define religion as the quest over time to make meaning in response to and/or in relationship with life's material conditions, and the attempt to address life's circumstances through text, image, sound, music, ritual, or other instrument in order to fashion individual identity, create existential purpose, and cultivate community.[6] Thematically, the book considers the intersection of race, religion, and BLM with gender and sexuality, space and place, cultural production, social media, state surveillance, theology, and more. This essay collection's wider conception of religion also embraces multidisciplinary assessments of BLM. It recognizes how historians, theologians, humanist activists, atheist educators, sociologists, and ethnographers collectively explore the multitudinous dimensions of religion and its connection to race and BLM.

These different aspects of the Black religious experience speak to another central theme in this collection, namely the religious pluralism exhibited in the Movement for Black Lives (M4BL). While evangelical Protestantism is still often presented as the normative expression of African American religion, this book follows the lead of scholars such as Yvonne Chireau, Anthony Pinn, and Judith Weisenfeld to display the rich diversity of Black religious traditions that comprise BLM. As Pinn notes in his foundational work *Varieties of African American Religious Experience*, "both 'theistic' and 'nontheistic' forms of religious expression and experience are religion because religion, simply understood, spreads beyond traditional boundaries of Christian formulations."[7] Like the BLM movement, many of these traditions are nonhierarchical and led by women who advance intersectional social justice and theological agendas. In the same way that the M4BL emphasizes political participation and the leadership of those on the margins, a group-centered approach that Barbara Ransby notes is "very much akin to the teachings of Black Freedom Movement icon Ella Baker," so too do religious expressions and institutions that grew out of the movement emphasize a radical democratic approach to both religion and politics that is inclusive and responsive to local needs.[8] These religious expressions increasingly exist outside of traditional religious and educational institutions, in much the same way that the M4BL does.

Relatedly, since race and religion are not static, this essay collection considers the entanglement of race and religion to examine how religious ideas, beliefs, and practices fostered or intersected with political commitments to justice. Simultaneously, the volume explores the ways that racialization undergirds religion in the United States to explain how religion has also historically served the arguments and actions of white supremacy. In other words, by exploring the contemporary phenomenon of BLM, this book seeks to contextualize how race and religion reinforce each other's presence in ways that over time have produced and reproduced oppression and have generated ideas, practices, and policies grounded in justice, dignity, and freedom.

This volume's unique overlapping analysis of race, religion, and BLM threads together several strands of historiography while it is in most direct scholarly conversation with the fields of history and religious studies. First, as a book about BLM, this work has benefitted from synthetic examinations of the movement's origins, practices of resistance, achievements, failures, aspirations, and intellectual frameworks by writers, journalists, and scholars such as Jordan Camp, Jelani Cobb, Angela Davis, Amanda Nell Edgard, Eddie Glaude, Christina Heatherton, Marc Lamont Hill, Andre Johnson, Christopher Lebron, Wesley Lowery, Johanna Luttrell, Barbara Ransby, Keeanga-Yamahtta Taylor, Tehama Lopez Bunyasi, and Candis Watts Smith. Despite the analytical variety and detailed coverage of BLM these works offer, none of them sufficiently address the role of religion in the movement. Christian theologians, pastors, and activists such as M. Shawn Copeland, Kelly Brown Douglas, Leah Gunning Francis, Wil Gafney, William Barber III, Jonathan Wilson-Hartgrove, Jim Wallis, Anthony Bradley, and Olga M. Sedura have authored important texts related to the movement as well, especially theological and spiritual exploration of liberation praxis. These advocacy-based books consider religious claims, religious ideas, and religious practices in light of the contemporary BLM era. However, while these studies indeed address religion and BLM, they do so primarily from the standpoint of theological scholarship and practitioner-oriented spiritual application.[9]

The scholarship on religion, history, and the Black freedom struggle is most congruent to the perspectives presented in this essay collection. In concert with current scholarly trends, this book uses religion as a lens through which to examine, investigate, and understand the ways it has been used to bolster oppression and the ways it has been deployed to expand liberation. Bridging the realms of ideas and popular culture, and exploring how the Black radical imagination has informed the work of social and political movements, Black intellectual history also shapes the critical scholarly framework this volume adopts. It examines diverse modes of intellectual production from both elite and proletarian perspectives and considers how the consequences of ideas shaped and reshaped society. The book also traces the contours of formal and informal intellectual networks. It follows the diffusion of knowledge across institutions and throughout the various creative corners of popular culture. This volume's orientation toward Black intellectual history focuses on the role of Black thought in fostering social and political change. It examines ideas produced by Black thinkers from diverse positions that stretch across markers of class, gender, sexuality, religion, and geography. It attends to the vigorous productivity of traditionally credentialed Black intellectual elites as well as those working in resonant and insurgent spaces elsewhere in society.[10]

The idea for this volume originated in conversations that the editors had at the 2017 African American Intellectual History Society conference at Vanderbilt University. As we discussed our way through the historiography on race, religion, and civil rights and the expansion of work on Black intellectual history, and examined the increasing number of publications on BLM, we sought to build a volume that uses historical and cultural analysis of a contemporary moment to elucidate its connections to the longer history of religion and the civil rights movement. To these ends, we asked contributors to answer the following questions in their essays: How does your chapter connect to BLM specifically? How does it illuminate the historical or cultural antecedents that help to explain the rise of BLM? In what way(s) does its historical or cultural analysis shed light on the contemporary era of which BLM is a part? In light of your answer to these questions—how does your chapter elucidate and/or advance understanding of religion and BLM; in other words, what new angles of understanding or nuanced perspective does it produce?

This volume consists of two sections: "Historical Foundations" and "Contemporary Connections." Section 1 begins with Matthew Cressler's "A Secular Civil Rights Movement?: How Black Power and Black Catholics Help Us Rethink the Religion in Black Lives Matter." He notes BLM is the largest and most significant civil rights movement since the 1970s and thus has invited numerous comparisons to that earlier movement. Many have claimed that in opposition to the civil rights movement, BLM is secular in orientation and thus is more similar to Black Power. Cressler complicates that easy comparison by noting that "religion" was not the opposite of "radical" in the 1960s and that many adherents of Black Power in the 1960s were traditionally religious. He does so by focusing on Black Catholics' role in the Black Power movement, a role, he argues, that should push scholars to rethink the very category of "religion." Kerry Pimblott's essay, "Beyond *De-Christianization*: Rethinking the Religious Landscapes and Legacies of Black Power in the Age of #BlackLivesMatter," also explores the ties between Black Power and BLM. Historians and other scholars of the civil rights movement have often posited a "de-Christianization" thesis whereby Black Power, a supposedly secular movement, contrasts to the earlier, church-led mainstream organizing tradition. BLM is envisioned in the same vein as Black Power, yet this "de-Christianization thesis has always been speculative. Scholars in the new subfield of Black Power studies, many of whom examine the movement in local contexts, are finding that thesis to be untenable and are challenging the teleological narrative that runs from Black Power to BLM." Pimblott joins this chorus of scholars in arguing for the critical importance of place in any analysis of religion and the Black Freedom Movement. Indeed, for Pimblott, place is even more important than ideology in analyses of the relationship of the Black Church to local protest movements.

While not specifically a part of the Black Power movement, MOVE likewise speaks to the historical ties between the Black Power era and Black Lives Matter in the present day. In his chapter, "MOVE, Mourning, and Memory," Richard Kent Evans explores the historical memory of the MOVE bombing in Philadelphia in 1985. MOVE, a small religious movement that emerged in the early 1970s, was founded on the teachings of John Africa, who argued the natural world had been corrupted by human beings. Evans notes that outside of Philadelphia, the bombing of this religious community's headquarters seems to have been completely forgotten, largely because most are unsure who should be mourned, a situation that authorities actively worked to bring to fruition. Since 2015, a new generation of activists has specifi-cally worked to raise awareness of this historical event, showing the powerful hold of history on this contemporary movement and the ways mourning has become a central component of BLM.

Carol Wayne White's chapter also links the historical Black intellec-tual tradition to contemporary ties between religion and BLM. Her essay, "Black Lives Matter and the New Materialism: Past Truths, Present Struggles, and Future Promises," addresses the absurdity of the contemporary juxtaposition of "all lives matter" to "Black lives matter" within contemporary discourse on race. Through the theoretical lens of religious naturalism, she calls for a reassessment of BLM as a compelling form of new materialism in which recent attention to the intrinsic value of Black lives becomes an important point of departure for understanding that all human lives are in fact sacred aspects of myriad nature. This section ends with Chris-topher Cameron's chapter, "The Faith of the Future: Black Lives of Unitarian Universalism," which explores the historical ties between the Black Empowerment controversy of the 1960s and the recent creation of the Black Lives of Unitarian Universalism Organizing Collective (Black Lives UU). The Black Empowerment controversy of the 1960s emerged in the wake of efforts of African American Unitarian Universalists to make the denomination more respon-sive to the demands of the Black Power movement. Members such as Hayward Henry created the Black Unitarian Universalist Caucus (BUUC) to help fund local organizing efforts in Black communities, an initiative that provided a model for the contemporary Black Lives UU movement, which has as its main goals tying together the faith perspective of Unitarian Universalism with the political perspective of Black Lives Matter.

The second section begins with Joseph Winters' chapter "Death, Spirituality, and the Matter of Blackness." Winters explores the con-nections between Afro-pessimism and Black Lives Matter. While many see these two as mutually exclusive, he argues that there are strong affinities, and productive tensions, between Afro-pessimism and BLM. To get at these affinities and tensions, he examines the "die-in" ritual and the general emphasis on movement within BLM.

Marjorie Corbman's essay, "'A Song That Speaks the Language of the Times': Muslim and Christian Homiletic Responses to the Black Lives Matter Movement and the Need for a Spiritual Vocabulary of Admonition," examines the lack of a rigorously self-reflective, self-critical, and repentant spiritual vocabulary in American religious communities as a major obstacle to the dismantling of white supremacy and the organizing against anti-Black, state-sanctioned violence in the United States. Drawing from four Christian sermons and four Muslim khutbas that Black religious communities have made publicly available, Corbman demonstrates how the birth of the M4BL, both within and outside of institutional religious communities, has cultivated a language of faithful anger and critical hope that could be crucial in transforming the religious imagination of American society.

Following Corbman's essay is Iman AbdoulKarim's exploration of gender and theology in Muslim women's BLM activism. "Islam Is Black Lives Matter" draws on qualitative interviews conducted in 2016 with Muslim women BLM activists and explores how Muslim women craft a religious identity that supports their intersectional activism in the BLM movement. Participants merge BLM's intersectional organizing strategies with Islamic mandates for social justice by utilizing prayer as a form of resistance; framing their activism as fulfilling a religious obligation to take direct action against injustice; and engaging Islamic texts to defend their activism and feminist politics as a reflection of Islam's community-centered approach toward social justice. In examining how participants' activism informs the meanings they assign to Islam and vice versa, AbdoulKarim affirms Islam's role as a Black protest religion, yet she argues that articulations of Muslimness as embodied acts of resistance to anti-Blackness are evolving alongside discourses on gender and sexuality in the BLM era. Thus, she notes, a full rendering of Islam's role in BLM must account for race *and* gender to understand the complex function of religion in the contemporary movement for Black life.

The final three chapters in this section all focus on the ties between religion, popular culture, and BLM. Alex Stucky's "The Need for a Bulletproof Black Man: *Luke Cage* and the Negotiation of Race, Gender, and Religion in Black Communities" explores the dynamics of race, gender, and power, arguing that all are foregrounded in Netflix's *Luke Cage*. Luke Cage (Mike Colter), he posits, struggles to save Harlem and finds himself battling not only against gangs but prolific state violence against Black bodies. Despite being a series named after its male protagonist, *Luke Cage* offers an introspective look at the role of women in Black communities. Additionally, questions about salvation for Black communities become a significant theme as scripture and religious motifs recur regularly. The Cain and Abel tale found in *Luke Cage*, Stucky argues, casts doubt about the role of religion in Black communities as Diamondback, Mariah, and other villains manipulate scripture to serve their villainous desires. Yet Cage's religious upbringing continually provides him with the strength to fight against systems of violence and apathy. In the wake of the murder of Black men, *Luke Cage* asks whether Black communities should find solace in religion as society expresses indifference to these murders or turn toward new heroes.

Alexandra Hartmann and Phillip Luke Sinitiere's essays link religion, music, and BLM. Hartmann's chapter, "The Sounds of Hope: Black Humanism, Deep Democracy, and Black Lives Matter," explores the ties between music and political protest in African American culture. Hartmann argues that Black humanism, a nontheistic orientation that rejects belief in the supernatural and centers the needs of human beings in this world, is foundational to BLM and that this Black humanism finds expression in the music of figures such as Beyoncé, Kendrick Lamar, John Legend, and Usher. These artists, she notes, hail from a long tradition of Black humanist intellectuals and artists, including James Baldwin, Zora Neale Hurston, Toni Morrison, and Cornel West. The influence between music and BLM goes both ways, she notes, as Black music has become more explicitly political since the rise of BLM. Moving from humanism and toward contemporary American evangelicalism, Phillip Luke Sinitiere's "Black Lives Matter and American Evangelicalism: Conflict and Consonance in History and Culture" investigates the cultural history and political meaning of Christians and hip hop, especially art that has been made, produced, and circulated during the BLM era. It analyzes the art and aesthetics of rappers and emcees who identify as evangelical: Propaganda, Sho Baraka, and Jackie Hill Perry. Each of these artists has not only made multiple albums during the BLM era, they engage rap and religion through other sites of cultural production (e.g., spoken word, lectures, books, podcasts). The chapter attends to the historical context in which art is made and spotlights art produced at the junctures of BLM, race, and the religious culture of Protestant evangelical Christianity. It probes the tensions of how an insurgent art form challenges evangelicalism's hierarchical (and often spiritualized) assumptions about race and culture, and how hip hop aesthetics expose evangelicalism's racial hypocrisy while disclosing the potential for rearrangements of power and material resources and a possible future of interracial solidarity.

It is impossible for one volume to address the complex questions that reside at the nexus of race, religion, and BLM, and the historical conditions that produced that nexus. However, by exploring the current moment of a contemporary phenomenon and documenting different facets of the movement, we aim to encourage further scholarship that will continue to provide historical perspectives on the links between race, religion, and BLM.

NOTES

1. Hebah H. Farrag, "The Role of Spirit in the #BlackLivesMatter Movement: A Conversation with Activist and Artist Patrisse Cullors," *Religion Dispatches*, June 24, 2015, http://religiondispatches.org/the-role-of-spirit-in-the-blacklivesmatter-movement-a-conversation-with-activist-and-artist-patrisse-cullors. See also the references to religion in Patrisse Khan-Cullors, *When They Call You a Terrorist: A Black Lives Matter Memoir* (New York: St. Martin's Press, 2018).
2. Rob Bell, "Opal Tometi from #blacklivesmatter," *The RobCast*, November 29, 2015, https://robbell.podbean.com/e/episode-52-opal-tometi-from-blacklivesmatter.
3. Jelani Cobb, "The Matter of Black Lives," *New Yorker*, March 14, 2016, https://www.newyorker.com/magazine/2016/03/14/where-is-black-lives-matter-headed; Jewish Women's Archive, "Organizers," https://jwa.org/powercouples/booth-garza.
4. Alicia Garza, *The Purpose of Power: How We Come Together When We Fall Apart* (New York: One World, 2020), 171.

5. This book will specify when its use of Black Lives Matter refers specifically to the BLM organization. Otherwise BLM refers to the BLM movement generally and the more expansive Movement For Black Lives (M4BL). Unless otherwise noted, references to BLM also encompass M4BL.

6. See Pinn's analysis of religion in his books *Introducing African American Religion* (New York: Routledge, 2013); *What Is African American Religion?* (Minneapolis, MN: Fortress Press, 2011); *The African American Religious Experience in America* (Westport, CT: Greenwood, 2006); and *Embodiment and the New Shape of Black Theological Thought* (New York: New York University Press, 2010).

7. Anthony B. Pinn, *Varieties of African American Religious Experience* (Minneapolis, MN: Augsburg Fortress Publishers, 1998), 3.

8. Barbara Ransby, *Making All Black Lives Matter: Reimagining Freedom in the Twenty-First Century* (Oakland: University of California Press, 2018), 3.

9. M. Shawn Copeland, "Memory, #BlackLivesMatter, and Theologians," *Political Theology* 17, no. 1 (January 2016): 1–3; Leah Gunning Francis, *Ferguson and Faith: Sparking Leadership and Awakening Community* (St. Louis, MO: Chalice, 2015); Kelly Brown Douglas, *Stand Your Ground: Black Bodies and the Justice of God* (New York: Orbis, 2015); Jim Wallis, *America's Original Sin: Racism, White Privilege, and the Bridge to a New America* (Grand Rapids, MI: Brazos, 2016); Wil Gafney, "A Reflection on the Black Lives Matter Movement and Its Impact on My Scholarship," *Journal of Biblical Literature* 136, no. 1 (Winter 2017): 204–7; William Barber III with Jonathan Wilson-Hartgrove, *The Third Reconstruction: How a Moral Movement Is Overcoming the Politics of Division and Fear* (Boston, MA: Beacon Press, 2018); Jonathan Wilson-Hartgrove, *Reconstructing the Gospel: Finding Freedom from Slaveholding Religion* (Downers Grove, IL: InterVarsity Press, 2018).

10. Some of the guides in our thinking about Black intellectual history, the Black radical tradition, and religion appear in the essays published in *Black Perspectives*, the blog of the African American Intellectual History Society (www.aaihs.org/black-perspectives), as well as related chapters from *New Perspectives on the Black Intellectual Tradition*, ed. Keisha N. Blain, Christopher Cameron, and Ashley D. Farmer (Evanston, IL: Northwestern University Press, 2018) and *Toward an Intellectual History of Black Women*, ed. Mia Bay, Farah J. Griffin, Martha S. Jones, and Barbara D. Savage (Chapel Hill: University of North Carolina Press, 2015).

FURTHER READING

Black Lives Matter

Bunyasi, Tehama Lopez, and Candis Watts Smith, *Stay Woke: A People's Guide to Making All Black Lives Matter*. New York: New York University Press, 2019.

Camp, Jordan T., and Christina Heatherton, *Policing the Planet: Why the Policing Crisis Led to Black Lives Matter*. Brooklyn, NY: Verso, 2016.

Cobb, Jelani. "The Matter of Black Lives," *New Yorker*, March 14, 2016. http://www.newyorker.com/magazine/2016/03/14/where-is-black-lives-matter-headed.

Davis, Angela Y. *Freedom Is a Constant Struggle: Ferguson, Palestine, and the Foundations of a Movement*. Chicago: Haymarket, 2016.

Diverlus, Rodney, Sandra Hudson, and Syrus Marcus Ware. *Until We Are Free: Reflections on Black Lives Matter and Canada*. Regina, SK: University of Regina Press, 2020.

Edgard, Amanda Nell, and Andre Johnson, eds. *The Struggle Over Black Lives Matter and All Lives Matter*. Lanham, MD: Lexington Books, 2018.

Glaude, Eddie S. *Democracy in Black: How Race Still Enslaves the American Soul*. New York: Crown, 2016.

Hagopian, Jesse, and Denisha Jones. *Black Lives Matter at School: An Uprising for Educational Justice*. Chicago: Haymarket, 2020.

Hinderliter, Beth, and Steve Peraza. *More Than Our Pain: Affect and Emotion in the Era of Black Lives Matter*. New York: State University of New York Press, 2021.

Hill, Marc Lamont. *Nobody: Casualties of America's War on the Vulnerable, from Ferguson to Flint*. New York: Atria, 2016.

LeBron, Christopher. *The Making of Black Lives Matter: A Brief History of an Idea*. Updated Edition. New York: Oxford University Press, 2022.

Lowery, Wesley. *"They Can't Kill Us All": Ferguson, Baltimore, and a New Era in America's Racial Justice Movement*. New York: Little, Brown and Company, 2016.

Luttrell, Johanna C. *White People and Black Lives Matter: Ignorance, Empathy, and Justice*. New York: Palgrave, 2019.

Ransby, Barbara. *Making All Black Lives Matter: Reimagining Freedom in the Twenty-First Century*. Oakland: University of California Press, 2018.

Taylor, Keeanga-Yamahtta. *From #BlackLivesMatter to Black Liberation*. Expanded Second Edition. Chicago: Haymarket, 2021.

———. "Five Years Later, Do Black Lives Matter?" *Jacobin*, September 30, 2019. https://www.jacobinmag.com/2019/09/black-lives-matter-laquan-mcdonald-mike-brown-eric-garner.

Race, Religion, and the Black Freedom Struggle

Blum, Edward J. *Reforging the White Republic: Race, Religion, and American Nationalism, 1865–1898*. Baton Rouge: Louisiana State University Press, 2005.

Chang, Derek. *Citizens of a Christian Nation: Evangelical Missions and the Problem of Race in the Nineteenth Century*. Philadelphia: University of Pennsylvania Press, 2010.

Chappell, David L. *A Stone of Hope: Prophetic Religion and the Death of Jim Crow*. Chapel Hill: University of North Carolina Press, 2004.

Cheah, Joseph. *Race and Religion in American Buddhism: White Supremacy and Immigrant Adaptation.* New York: Oxford University Press, 2011.

Clegg, Claude. *The Life and Times of Elijah Muhammad.* Chapel Hill: University of North Carolina Press, 2014.

Dupont, Carolyn Renée. *Mississippi Praying: Southern White Evangelicals and the Civil Rights Movement, 1945–1975.* New York: New York University Press, 2013.

Emerson, Michael O., and Christian Smith. *Divided by Faith: Evangelical Religion and the Problem of Race in America.* New York: Oxford University Press, 2000.

Finley, Stephen C., and Biko Mandela Gray. "God Is a White Racist: Imminent Atheism as a Religious Response to Black Lives Matter and State-Sanctioned Anti-Black Violence." *Journal of Africana Religions* 3, no. 4 (2015): 443–53.

Goetz, Rebecca. *The Baptism of Early Virginia: How Christianity Created Race.* Baltimore, MD: Johns Hopkins University Press, 2012.

Harvey, Paul. *Freedom's Coming: Religious Culture and the Shaping of the South from the Civil War through the Civil Rights Era.* Chapel Hill: University of North Carolina Press, 2005.

Jacobs, Seth. *American Miracle Man in Vietnam: Ngo Dinh Diem, Religion, Race, and U.S. Intervention in Southeast Asia.* Durham, NC: Duke University Press, 2005.

Marsh, Charles. *God's Long Summer: Stories of Faith and Civil Rights.* Princeton, NJ: Princeton University Press, 2008.

———. *The Beloved Community: How Faith Shapes Social Justice, from the Civil Rights Movement to Today.* New York: Basic Books, 2005.

Morales, Harold D. *Latino and Muslim in America: Race, Religion, and the Making of a New Minority.* New York: Oxford University Press, 2018.

Noll, Mark A. *God and Race in American Politics.* Princeton, NJ: Princeton University Press, 2010.

Pinn, Anthony, Joseph Winters, and Terrence L. Johnson. "Religion and Black Lives Matter." Forum at Georgetown's Berkley Center for Religion, Peace, and World Affairs, October 24, 2016, https://berkleycenter.georgetown.edu/forum/religion-and-black-lives-matter.

"Religion, Secularism, and Black Lives Matter," *The Immanent Frame,* September 22, 2016. http://blogs.ssrc.org/tif/2016/09/22/religion-secularism-and-black-lives-matter/?disp=print.

Slade, Peter. *Open Friendship in a Closed Society: Mission Mississippi and a Theology of Friendship.* New York: Oxford University Press, 2009.

Slade, Peter, Charles Marsh, and Peter Goodwin Heltzel, eds. *Mobilizing for the Common Good: The Lived Theology of John M. Perkins.* Jackson: University Press of Mississippi, 2013.

Williams, Shannen Dee. "The Global Catholic Church and the Radical Possibilities of #BlackLivesMatter," *Journal of Africana Religions* 3, no. 4 (2015): 503–15.

PART ONE
Historical Foundations

CHAPTER 1

A Secular Civil Rights Movement?

How Black Power and Black Catholics Help Us Rethink the Religion in Black Lives Matter

Matthew J. Cressler

The Black Lives Matter movement is, without question, the most significant and sustained movement for racial justice since the end of the "long civil rights era" in the 1970s. As such, it has become common to compare the movement to its predecessors. A particular conception of "religion," and its relationship to the politics of protest, has been key to these comparisons. Scholars and activists alike have debated whether Black Lives Matter is a *"secular* civil rights movement."[1] Working from the assumption that it is a secular movement, many have argued that the more apt analogue to Black Lives Matter is not civil rights but Black Power. This argument is an embodiment of what historian Kerry Pimblott calls the "de-Christianization thesis" in Chapter 2 of this book, which contends that as Black Power rose in the late 1960s Black churches moved to the margins of freedom struggles. The activist and public theologian Rahiel Tesfamariam seemed to echo this sentiment when she said of the Black Lives

Matter movement that, "If there is a model of revolution that these young people have mirrored most, it's not [Martin Luther] King's Southern Christian Leadership Conference, but rather the radical and countercultural beliefs of the Black Panther Party." She goes on to compare Black Lives Matter with the Panthers and contrast it with Black Christianity. "Like the Panthers," she continues, "they have unapologetically celebrated blackness, raising 'black power' fists, sporting afros and wearing T-shirts with African imagery. In contrast, the church hasn't typically been as radical in its rhetoric and tactics. King, for example, opposed the militant arm of the civil rights movement, noting that 'black power' carried 'connotations of violence and separatism.'"[2] There is certainly truth to Tesfamariam's comparison. Historian Hasan Kwame Jefferies has similarly argued that Black Power is a more appropriate point of comparison for Black Lives Matter. This is especially the case when one focuses attention on the Movement for Black Lives' official platform, which channels more Malcolm X than Martin King, more Black Panther Party than Southern Christian Leadership Conference.[3] Yet, as a scholar of religion and race, what interests me are the ways that, for Tesfamariam and so many others, "religion" in this formulation has come to be defined as an antonym to "radical." This essay aims to interrogate the assumptions about "religion" as a concept that operate underneath the surface of the argument that Black Lives Matter is a secular movement. It does so by offering historical perspective on religion in the Black Power movement, another so-called "secular civil rights movement" that preceded Black Lives Matter by almost four decades. First, it examines the contours of what constitutes "the religious" in discussions of civil rights, Black Power, and Black Lives Matter. Building on this theoretical intervention, this essay argues that the history of Black Catholics in the Black Power era can complicate our comfortable narratives of what religion and racial justice are supposed to look like and, consequently, challenge us to rethink what we mean by "religion" in the first place.

"This Ain't Yo Mama's Civil Rights Movement"

This provocative phrase was emblazoned on Rahiel Tesfamariam's black t-shirt as she marched with protestors through the streets of St. Louis, Missouri, in the summer of 2015. Her shirt paraphrased Tef Poe, the local hip hop artist and co-founder of Hands Up United. "This ain't your daddy's civil rights movement," as he put it, represented Tef Poe's rebuke to the well-established national civil rights organizations that tried to wrest leadership of the protests from the youth in Ferguson in the wake of Michael Brown's murder. His turn of phrase came to serve as a synecdoche of sorts for the Black Lives Matter moment and movement writ large.[4] Tef Poe, Tesfamariam, and others have rightly identified the political, tactical, and generational differences that separate Black Lives Matter protests from those that came before.[5] What Tesfamariam does more explicitly than most is articulate the religious dimensions of these differences. Whereas the civil rights movement tended to be "manned" by "well-dressed, respectable clergymen," the M4BL is unapologetically feminist and queer. While the civil rights movement relied on the respectability politics that governed Black churches, today's movement "encourages all to 'come as you are.' Natural. Bohemian. Rebellious. Tatted up. Provocative. Ratchet." "While the civil rights movement of the 1960s was characterized by nonviolent resistance strategies" Tesfamariam argues, "this movement has been much more confrontational." In other words, present-day activists are unwilling to play by the rules of "the Black Church," which tends to be more conservative in all senses of the term—in leadership styles, in protest tactics, in gender and sexual politics. This juxtaposition is at the root of Tesfamariam's identification of Black Lives Matter not with King's Christian resisters but with the Black Panther Party's Marxist revolutionaries.[6]

Oddly enough, critics of Black Lives Matter would likely agree with her to some extent. The use of the civil rights movement—or, more precisely, a particular and selective imagining of "the civil rights movement"—as a measuring stick against which to judge Black Lives Matter has been one of the most common ways to criticize contemporary protests. Martin Luther King—or, better yet, a willfully ignorant imagining of "MLK"—has proved a useful meme in this regard. When Ferguson and Baltimore exploded in uprisings, critics retorted, "King would never condone riots." When protesters block traffic with cries of "No Justice! No Peace!," critics reply, "King would never disrupt traffic." When righteous rage over Black death and non-indictments boils over, critics insist "King was never hostile or angry." Now, it goes without saying that this sanitized MLK is a lie. (This meme is what some writers have referred to as the "Santaclausification" of King and has been thoroughly debunked.[7]) Nevertheless, this particular imagining serves as one of the most effective strategies by which critics can delegitimize Black Lives Matter. It functions as a "myth," in religious studies scholar Bruce Lincoln's use of the term. It is "ideology in narrative form."[8] The narrative could be summarized as follows: Black and white Christians in the mid-twentieth century joined together in love and, arms linked and singing "We Shall Overcome," changed the hearts of the nation and peacefully brought an end of racism. MLK figures prominently in this myth, serving as a beloved salvific hero who died to inaugurate a post-racial era. When critics frame "the civil rights movement" in this way and deploy it against Black Lives Matter, a significant element in the critique is that Black Lives Matter lacks the religious-ness of the MLK-led movement. "Religion," in this view, is thought of as a particular mode of Christianity that is loving, long-suffering, and forgiving. This is why the myth works well when deployed against contemporary, confrontational protestors. The defanged fantasy Martin Luther King can be deployed against anyone upsetting the order of the status quo or calling attention to injustice.

Historian Nikhil Pal Singh identified and interrogated this "ideology in narrative form" almost a decade before the rise of Black Lives Matter. In *Black Is a Country* (2004), Singh coined the phrase "civic myth of civil rights" to identify the ways selective readings of the civil rights movement and Martin Luther King were used to buttress the aims of the US racial state and subvert ongoing struggles for Black liberation and democracy.[9] This civic myth of civil rights is the story rehearsed every year in celebration of America's progress toward Martin Luther King's dream of the day when children "will not be judged by the color of their skin, but by the content of their character." Thankfully, Singh is just one of a number of scholars who have challenged this mythic rendering that centers almost exclusively on the male-minister-led movement that fought segregation in the Jim Crow South through respectable nonviolent Christian protest between 1955 and 1965. We now know that Black activists fought for fair housing and equal employment in the urban North ten years before Rosa Parks sat down in that Montgomery bus; that nonviolence always coexisted, albeit in tension, with long-standing Black traditions of armed self-defense; and that Black women were instrumental organizers without whom there would have been no movement at all.[10]

The civic myth of civil rights operates as a declension narrative, which tells the cautionary tale of how the impatience and anger of Black Power activists undid civil rights successes. The Black Panthers, in this telling, serve as the pantomime villains that wasted the good will of well-meaning white people and inaugurated decades of repressive backlash. In this way, the civic myth of civil rights was weaponized to delegitimize Black Power protest decades before it would be deployed to delegitimize Black Lives Matter. Scholars such as Singh disabuse us of the misconception of this declension narrative. And yet, one myth has survived this demythologization. The civil rights movement still tends to be imagined as the religious antecedent to a secular Black Power movement. As Kerry Pimblott unpacks in her book and discusses in Chapter 2, both "popular and scholarly accounts of black power depict a movement marked by a profound *de-Christianization*." She further notes that this juxtaposition of religious (read: Christian) civil rights with secular (read: radical) Black Power contributed to arguments about the movement's declension, pinning the blame on "black power's abandonment of its spiritual moorings."[11] This is certainly the case in religious historian Charles Marsh's classic book *God's Long Summer* (1997), wherein he positions Cleveland Sellers and Black Power as the tragic conclusion in a cautionary tale about what happens when you put "the Gospel on the backburner."[12] While Singh is generally unconcerned with religion as such, he does inadvertently reinforce this same distinction when he contrasts the ways the civic myth of civil rights buttresses the US nation-state's "dominant and defining systems of belief: *Christianity*, liberal-individualism, and democratic-capitalism" with the actual anti-imperialist King defined by "more complex, *worldly*, and *radical* politics."[13]

Thus, an array of different people have bought into the idea that Black Lives Matter, and Black Power before it, differ sharply from a prior generation's civil rights struggles due to an absence of religion. They are, of course, making this case for different reasons. Tesfamariam is not only defending Black Lives Matter against its (Black) Christian critics, she is also forwarding a critique of the conservativism of Black-church politics in the hopes of remaking Black religion and radicalism for the twenty-first century. Critics wielding the meme-ified MLK are attempting to either dismiss or destroy efforts to upend the white supremacist status quo. Historians like Singh are hoping to recover the more radical legacies of Black freedom struggles that have been obscured by memory and subverted by the state. Nevertheless, despite their differences, all operate under the assumption that "radicalism" serves as code for "not religious." Scholars and popular audiences alike share the presumption that, for better or for worse, Black freedom struggles radicalized once they were freed from the restraints of religion.

Black Catholic history, to which we will now turn, seriously challenges this reading. Activists and scholars are right to criticize the Black Christian exceptionalism of civil rights scholarship that polices the parameters of "proper" protest by comparing all activism to King's Christian nonviolence. Yet we should not overstate the case in our attempt to reinstate Black Power in Black freedom struggle historiography. It is true that Black Power represented a significant critique of racial liberalism as an ideology and Christian nonviolence as a tactic. But it is also true that some Black religious communities, especially those in urban settings outside the US South, embraced this critique. By the end of the 1960s a small but growing number of Black Catholics did too. Black Power transformed Black Catholics, and Black Catholics, in turn, engaged the political and cultural nationalisms that defined the Black Power era.

Black Catholics and Black Power

The presumption that "religion" is synonymous with a particular mode of Christianity and that "radicalism" is, by its nature, secular pervades US Catholic historiography. Most histories of Catholics and racial justice focus on Catholic racial liberals, sometimes called "interracialists," who shared the presuppositions of racial liberalism writ large.[14] Interracialists understood racism to be an outgrowth of personal animus that could be ameliorated by breaking down the barriers that kept races separate. They argued that the best way to improve "race relations" would be to erase race altogether. Through organizations like the Catholic Interracial Council, interracialists fought hard for the dissolution of so-called racial parishes that separated Black, Irish, Italian, and Mexican Catholics from one another. They built relationships across both parish and racial boundaries through athletic associations like the Catholic Youth Organization. And they struggled to desegregate white (Catholic) suburbs. To tweak the motto of King's Southern Christian Leadership Conference, interracialists endeavored to "redeem the soul of Catholic America" and convince their fellow Catholics to live according to (what they took to be) the true precepts of the Universal Church. Catholic interracialists, in other words, fit comfortably into the concept of "religion" that Black Lives Matter era activists, critics, and academics have associated with civil rights struggles. There is no better example of this than the lament of one white priest who yearned for a "Catholic version of Martin Luther King," by which he meant a charismatic and respectable Black Catholic committed to the struggles of racial liberals, namely, interracial struggles for an integrated America.[15]

While these histories are important, the overemphasis on interracialists has tended to reinforce the idea that to be Catholic and committed to racial justice was to be engaged in the racial liberalism that dominated civil rights struggles in the first half of the twentieth century. In other words, this historiography operated in the framework of that civic myth of civil rights. The problem with this perspective is that it obscures the lives of those who struggled for racial justice but did not conform to the norms set by the Southern Christian

Leadership Conference, to take one classic example. Those looking for Catholic versions of Martin Luther King will be hard pressed to find them. But when we turn our attention to the decade after King's death, when we shift our focus away from racial liberals and toward Black nationalists and radicals—from civil rights to Black Power—we find that the assassination of Martin Luther King marked the beginning rather than the end of Black Catholic freedom struggles. Black Power galvanized Black Catholics and provided activists with the tools to transform the Church. When we stop searching for Catholic Martin Luther Kings, we can begin to see Black Catholic Stokely Carmichaels and Angela Davises.

On April 4, 1968, Martin Luther King was shot in Memphis and urban insurrections erupted in cities across the country. Less than two weeks later in Detroit, Michigan, on April 16, Black Catholic priests, along with at least one woman religious and one brother, gathered together in rage and grief. This marked the birth of the Black Catholic Clergy Caucus. Their inaugural statement sent shockwaves across Catholic America and, for our purposes here, is especially notable for how it challenged prevailing assumptions about what "religion" was presumed to look like when engaged in protest. It began by stating in no uncertain terms that "the Catholic Church in the United States, primarily a white racist institution, has addressed itself primarily to white society and is definitely a part of that society."[16] This phrasing was intentionally confrontational and rejected the standard liberal formulation that individual Catholics might be racist, but that the Church itself transcended race. No, the Caucus insisted, the Catholic Church is a "white racist institution." Counter to the common liberal commitment to interracial cooperation and integration, these Black priests called on the Church to recognize as legitimate "demands that Black people control their own affairs and make decisions for themselves."[17] Foremost among these demands was the insistence that Black priests be placed in positions of power at all levels. Finally, and perhaps most surprising of all, the Clergy Caucus pronounced nonviolence dead, "in the sense of Black nonviolence hoping for concessions after white brutality." The priests argued "that the same principles on which we justify legitimate self-defense and just warfare must be applied to violence when it represents Black response to white violence."[18]

Sister Martin de Porres Grey—present that day but prohibited by the priests from full participation—pinpointed this moment as the onset of a Black Catholic revolution, the commencement of "black consciousness for black Catholics."[19] In response to her exclusion, Sister Grey spearheaded the founding of the National Black Sisters' Conference in Pittsburgh, Pennsylvania.[20] Black women religious pledged themselves "to work unceasingly for the liberation of black people." They denounced "expressions of individual and institutional racism found in our society and within our Church" and declared them "to be categorically evil and inimical to the freedom of all men everywhere, and particularly destructive of black people in America."[21] The sisters' stated objectives included the eradication of "the powerlessness, the poverty, and the distorted self-image of victimized black people" and the promotion of a "positive self-image among ourselves, in our black folk, especially in our black youth," as well as the stimulation of "community action aimed at the achievement of social, political, and economic black power."[22]

These two national organizations, soon joined by Black Catholic brothers, seminarians, and lay people, demonstrated the depths to which Black Catholic activists were increasingly indebted to Black Power. As such, they complicate the stark contrast between a religious Christian civil rights movement and a secular radical Black Power movement. Rather than rejecting the revolutionary politics of the Black Panther Party, Black Catholics were embracing what historian Robert Self described as the shift in the precepts of the Black freedom struggles from "faith in law to faith in direct action; from faith in individualist remedies to faith in collective and community-based remedies; and from faith in American pluralism to faith in Black Nationalism and radicalism."[23] "Black Power" signified a constellation of ideas and practices that, generally speaking, were grounded on a critique of racial liberalism and entailed an embrace of Black self-determination. In calling for control of Catholic institutions in Black communities, Black priests shared in arguments for self-determination and community control popularized in large part by Stokely Carmichael (later Kwame Ture) and Charles Hamilton's *Black Power: The Politics of Liberation* (1967).[24] Rather than turning to the principled nonviolence of Martin Luther King, the Clergy Caucus paraphrased the famous aphorism of Malcolm X (Malik El-Shabazz): "I don't call it violence when it's in self-defense; I call it intelligence." Black sisters directly addressed the psychological wages of institutional racism in the Church. Their attention to improving Black "self-image," in particular, echoed the influence of Black nationalist women pioneers such as Amy Ashwood and Amy Jacques Garvey who, along with figures like Marcus Garvey and Elijah Muhammad, insisted that social and political liberation were impossible without emancipation from "mental slavery."[25] These sisters and priests were just the first of a generation of Black Catholics who initiated over a decade of advocacy and activism that came to be known as "the Black Catholic Movement."

Centering Black Catholics in our studies of religion and racial justice in the twentieth century challenges the declension narrative that positions Black Power as the anti-religious afterbirth of the "classic" Christian civil rights movement. This becomes even more apparent when we narrow our focus from the national to the local—a point Pimblott illustrates in Chapter 2 through her extended discussion of the significance of place in Black Power studies. A glimpse into the life of Father George H. Clements unsettles the stories we're accustomed to hearing when it comes to Black Power. Born in 1932 and ordained in 1957, Clements was only the second Black priest ordained by the Archdiocese of Chicago. His career as an activist-priest began when he travelled with his South Side parishioners to the 1963 March on Washington for Jobs and Freedom. He answered Martin Luther King's call for clergy to converge on Selma, Alabama, to march for voting rights in 1965. But Clements attributes his racial and political awakening to King's assassination three years later. In the years that followed, Father Clements came to be known as a "chaplain" of the Illinois Chapter of the Black Panther Party and proved instrumental in the founding of the Afro-American Patrolmen's League.

The Black Panther Party (BPP) often serves as a convenient symbol for the presumed secularity of the Black Power movement writ large, and for good reason. The BPP was indebted to Marxist anti-colonialism, not Christian institutions or theology. Huey P. Newton and Bobby Seale's Black Panther Party Platform, first published in 1967, combined a nationalist call for Black solidarity and a Marxist critique of American capitalism with an extended repurposing of the US Declaration of Independence. "What We Want, What We Believe" demanded Black social, political, and economic self-determination and exemplified the radical anti-imperialist end of the broader Black Power spectrum. But while the BPP did not emerge out of Black churches, this did not mean the Panthers were anti-religious by any means. On the contrary, the charismatic leaders of the Illinois Chapter of the Black Panther Party, Fred Hampton and Bobby Rush, were famous for forging coalitions with a wide range of allies, so long as they were committed to the cause of liberation of oppressed peoples. In this, Hampton and Rush bore striking resemblance to the pragmatic community organizing of Stokely Carmichael who, as discussed in Chapter 2, learned to speak the language of Black churches despite his personal atheism. Father Clements and Black Catholic Chicagoans were among the Black Panther Party's allies in Chicago. According to Clements, the Panthers called on him to mediate an internal dispute in 1968. When the priest successfully resolved the issue, he came to be known affectionately as their "chaplain" and became friends with Fred Hampton. The Panthers reciprocated soon thereafter, coming to Clements's aid when the archbishop of Chicago refused to promote him to pastor a parish. The first few months of 1969 witnessed Black Panthers standing vigil in the vestibules of Catholic parishes as concerned Black Catholics and their white allies engaged in pray-in protests calling for Black Catholic self-determination. By June, Clements and two other Black priests had won their promotions.[26]

The shared victory of Black Catholics and Black Panthers over the archdiocese was followed not long after by tragedy. Mere months after George Clements became pastor of Holy Angels Catholic Church on the South Side of Chicago, the Chicago Police Department and the Federal Bureau of Investigation conspired to kill Fred Hampton.[27] With Hampton dead, the remaining Chicago Panthers feared further assassinations. Police raided the apartment of the Chicago Panther's second-in-command, Bobby Rush, the following day, but by that point he was already safely in hiding.[28] As Father Clements later recalled in *The New World*, he played a role in protecting Panthers sought by the police. "Everyone knew that Bobby was next on the list. And he fled," said Clements. Where did he go? The new pastor of Holy Angels had introduced Rush to "a little known thing in the Middle Ages called the 'right of sanctuary,'" encouraging Rush to hide at Holy Angels.[29]

When Rush eventually surrendered himself, he did so under escort by Black Catholic police officer and ally Renault "Reggie" Robinson.[30] Robinson represented yet another Black Catholic-Black Power connection in Chicago. He was one of five Black members of the Chicago Police Department who banded together, in part in outrage over Mayor Richard J. Daley's order that police officers should "shoot to kill" looters in the aftermath of King's assassination and in part in response to the rampant racism that pervaded the majority-white police force. These officers co-founded the Afro-American Patrolmen's League (AAPL) in secret in the basement of a Catholic church, arranged by Father Clements, to avoid reprisal from their fellow officers.[31] Over the next ten years the AAPL confronted discrimination within the force and fought to transform the image of the Black police officer in African American communities, adopting the motto "Black Power Through the Law."[32]

Far from viewing Black Power as hostile to religiousness, Father George Clements and a national movement of like-minded Black Catholics, of which he was a prominent part, insisted that Black Power represented the last best hope to save the US Catholic Church from white supremacy. Clements's 1970 call for Catholics to "dream impossible dreams" captures this point perfectly. Referring to Jesus Christ as "that great man who dreamed impossible dreams and who got lynched on a cross," Clements imagined a Church "where there is no thought of closing inner-city, black Catholic schools because of money, while allowing suburban white Catholic schools to flourish; a Church where there are Catholic hospitals that give free medical care to the poor . . .; a Church where Martin Luther King Jr. is accepted as a saint as readily as St. Patrick, St. Boniface or Our Lady of Czestochowa . . .; a Church that sincerely attempts to bring about black [self-]determination."[33] These dreams of a Catholic Church that subsidizes inner-city education, provides free healthcare, honors Black saints, and supports Black self-determination were undoubtedly shaped by the revolutionary politics of the Black Panther Party. The BPP, after all, offered free food and medical care for those in need and fought for Black self-determination. This Catholic priest and friend of Fred Hampton, who eulogized Hampton at his funeral, knew that "a bullet is the answer that is given to many of our dreams." But, in an echo of Hampton himself who said one could kill the revolutionary but not the revolution, Clements did "not believe that anyone can really kill the impossible dreamer."

Rethinking Religion and Racial Justice

Father Clements and other Black Catholics in the Black Power era challenge the assumption that Black Power was essentially secular. A quick clarifying word is in order, though. The point of this historical intervention is not to insist, instead, that Black Power is essentially religious. I am not attempting to religi-fy Black Power. Scholars have served an important corrective by turning our attention to activists, organizations, and traditions beyond the bounds of what is often termed "the Black Church," and even beyond Black religion altogether. This move is one embraced by the editors of this volume, who have emphasized Black religious pluralism and embraced a capacious conception of "religion" that includes the nontheistic, atheist, and humanist. This corrective has been important for a number of reasons, not least of which are the significant problems with the opposite assumption; namely, that Black freedom struggles are always already religious. Religious studies scholar Barbara Diane Savage, for instance, demonstrates that the active role Black churches took in the civil rights era was the exception, historically speaking, rather than the rule. The Black Christian activism of the civil rights era has been retroactively read backward through history by scholars and popular audiences alike, rendering "the Black Church" as, in and of itself, an activist institution. Savage shows that the civil rights era was exceptional in this regard.[34] Religious studies scholar Curtis Evans, in a similar way, argues that Black religion has been overdetermined, burdened with the assumption that it is inherently politically progressive.[35] It is important to note that the majority of Black churches in the United States were not actively involved in civil rights struggles, just as it is important to affirm that many activist organizations were not explicitly religious.

The Black Panther Party was not founded by religious figures, it did not mobilize out of religious institutions, and it did not draw on religious ideas to develop its political ideology or tactical strategy. We should not forget this. What the history of Black Catholics in the Black Power era can do, however, is challenge us to rethink what we mean by religion and racial justice.[36] It does this, first and foremost, by inverting what is presumed to be the proper relationship between religion and politics. The civic myth of civil rights, with its emphasis on southern struggles and organizations like the Southern Christian Leadership Conference, emphasizes religious institutions, organizations, and people as the *origin* of activist politics, as the initiators and leaders of protest. Black protest emerges out of Black religion. But in the case of Black Catholics and Black Power, freedom struggles did not emerge out of churches. Instead, Black Catholics followed the lead of the activists rising up in the streets of Chicago and Detroit and Pittsburgh and elsewhere. Black Power inspired Black Catholics (and other Black Christians) to action. The same could be said of the Black Lives Matter era. Young people in the streets of Ferguson, Baltimore, Chicago, Oakland, Minneapolis, and Atlanta did not take their lead from women and men of the cloth. They took to the streets, and (some) ministers followed them. It is not true that Black Power and Black Lives Matter are somehow inherently secular. It is true, though, that Black Power and Black Lives Matter inspired religious communities to join the struggle for racial injustice, not the other way around.

Rahiel Tesfamariam expressed this sentiment and there are others like her, such as the activist, musician, and Pentecostal minister

Reverend Osagyefo Uhuru Sekou. In November 2014, in the midst of the one hundred days of protest that followed Michael Brown's murder, Reverend Sekou responded to fellow clergy who had criticized young protestors for not being Christian enough, for not playing by the rules of proper protest. His open letter bore a remarkable resemblance to Martin Luther King Jr.'s letter from a Birmingham city jail cell, which also called out clergy who preached caution and chastised protestors for being impatient and angry. "The Clergy's Place Is with the Protestors in Ferguson" inverts the presumed relationship between religion and politics in the same way Black Catholics in Chicago had decades earlier. Sekou positions the clergy as those who should follow protestors rather than lead them. "We are called to choose sides," he insisted. "Clergy must not only 'support' protesters. We are called to be protesters."[37] Just as a prior generation of Black Catholics were inspired to activism by the words of Malcolm X and the actions of Fred Hampton, ministers like Sekou have been activated by the activism of Black Lives Matter movement. As he put it in another interview, "I take my orders from 23-year-old queer women."[38]

Black Catholics in the Black Power era encourage us to think about the ways Black Power influenced religion. They also push us to develop a more expansive notion of what constitutes "religion" in the first place. The dearth of books on Black Power and religion testifies to the limitations of our current conceptions of "religion" and "racial justice." Most histories of religion and race frame "racial justice" as the quest to fully incorporate racial Others into the US nation-state with all the rights that membership entails. By and large, to borrow a phrase from classic racial liberal Gunnar Myrdal, they narrate attempts to resolve the "American Dilemma" of a nation that preaches freedom but practices segregation, whose ideals do not match reality. Black Power, historically and historiographically, interrupts this train of thought and poses other questions: What if there is no dilemma at all? What if unfreedom is not a flaw in the system but part of the system itself? Most religious histories of the Black freedom struggles precede from and reinforce the presumption that the US nation-state is capable of conferring freedom. Black Power calls this presumption into question. Kwame Ture (Stokely Carmichael) and Charles Hamilton argue "there is no 'American dilemma' because black people in this country form a colony, and it is not in the interest of the colonial power to liberate them."[39] Whether one agrees with their anticolonial assessment of the US nation-state is not necessarily the point. The point is that they frame "racial justice" itself in a very different way than many are accustomed to thinking about it in scholarship. They insist that we think of racial justice not in terms of achieving an unrealized but ever-present freedom, but in terms of liberation from colonialism.

Black Power has the potential to challenge the premises on which the US liberal democratic project is grounded—to which so much scholarship on American religion, especially scholarship on American Catholicism, has been in service. This is why, I would argue, Black Catholics and Black Power don't fit so neatly into our narratives of American Catholicism, why so many histories of religion and racial justice end in 1968, and why histories of Black Power have been left largely to "secular" historians. Black Power challenges the very myths on which US American religious and US American Catholic history rests. Black Power, at least in its radical anticolonial formulations, is not about incorporating Black people into the existing structures of the US nation-state, but about revolutionizing the structures themselves. Black Power is not about getting the United States to live up to its ideals or, in the context of US Catholicism, getting the Church to practice what it preaches. Rather, it names the US and the US Church as complicit in and constitutive of white supremacy on a structural level and thus in need of "a radical revolution of values," to quote the real and radical Martin Luther King rather than his meme. Black Power, in this reading, is about revolution and reconstitution rather than reform and incorporation. It sees the US not as the land of the free in need of being freer but as an empire whose freedom is constituted by its coloniality. It sees the Catholic Church not as a Universal and Mystical Body in need of truer members, but as an institution complicit in the construction of white supremacy and colonial conquest. All of this, I think, has the potential to make visible Black lives and Black freedom struggles that all too often remain invisible in American religious history. It also leads us to another way of conceptualizing what "religion" is.[40]

The civic myth of civil rights operates with the assumption that "religion" is a synonym for a particular mode of Christian respectability. With this working framework in place, Black Power and Black Lives Matter are understood as secular by default. There is no space for anticolonial movements, calls for armed self-defense, or talk of revolution in the "religion" encoded in the civic myth and embodied by the MLK meme that delegitimizes Black Lives Matter. Thus, it is time that we articulate a new one. This is what Reverend Sekou suggests to his fellow clergy in that letter. "There is a certain irony," he reflected, "in clergy calling upon youth to calm down to allow the system a chance to run its course. These calls for moderation are the hallmark of leadership too closely tied to the powers that be." Yes, people in Ferguson marching through the streets were angry. But this was not a problem for clergy. On the contrary, "We, too, should be angry; we, too, should be mad as hell. Our blood should boil at that fact that black blood is spilled with impunity in the United States." "We are called to be protesters," he concluded, "at once outraged and disciplined. By placing our bodies on the cross of a militarized police, deep infrastructural racial bias and a system that profits from human misery, a new way of being and seeing America and all its promise is being born."[41] Sekou called on Christian clergy to join Black Lives Matter activists in the streets. In a similar way, Black Power and Black Lives Matter movements call on scholars to come up with terms capacious enough to encompass the radical work they are doing to remake our world.

As this essay has shown, declarations that the Movement for Black Lives is a "secular civil rights movement" are not without consequence. Whether or not it is intentional, this positioning of the Movement both rests on a mythic imagining of the civil rights movement and reinforces a problematic conception of the category of "religion." In short, it equates civil rights struggles with southern Black Christian nonviolence and assumes religion, insofar as it relates to the politics of protest, is antithetical with radicalism, anticolonialism, and armed self-defense. Black Catholics in the Black Power era, by way of contrast, serve as a critical counterexample to this caricature. The inspiration they drew from Kwame Ture (Stokely Carmichael) and Malcolm X, not to mention the activist alliances Black Catholics forged with the Black Panther Party in Chicago, challenge narrow notions of religion and racial justice as synonymous with racial liberalism. This history, this essay has argued, can help us come up with more capacious conceptions of both the category of "religion" and the nature of "racial justice," as Christopher Cameron and Phillip Luke Sinitiere call for in their introduction to this book; ones wide enough to capture the creativity of the Black Lives Matter movement.

NOTES

1. Emphasis added; "Religion, Secularism, and Black Lives Matter," *The Immanent Frame*, accessed April 16, 2021, https://tif.ssrc.org/2016/09/22/religion-secularism-and-black-lives-matter. See also Ari Colston, "'Losing Religion': Black Lives Matter, the Sacred, and the Secular," Canopy Forum on the Interactions of Religion and Law, August 12, 2020, https://canopyforum.org/2020/08/12/losing-religion-black-lives-matter-the-sacred-and-the-secular.
2. Rahiel Tesfamariam, "Why the Modern Civil Rights Movement Keeps Religious Leaders at Arm's Length," *Washington Post*, September 18, 2015, https://www.washingtonpost.com/opinions/how-black-activism-lost-its-religion/2015/09/18/2f56fc00-5d6b-11e5-8e9e-dce8a2a2a679_story.html.
3. Hasan Kwame Jefferies, "Black Lives Matter: A Legacy of Black Power Protest," *Black Perspectives* (blog), African American Intellectual History Society, September 15, 2016, https://www.aaihs.org/black-lives-matter-a-legacy-of-black-power-protest-2. For more on the platform of the Movement for Black Lives, see "Vision for Black Lives," https://m4bl.org/policy-platforms (accessed May 20, 2021).
4. For another example of this comparison see Frederick C. Harris, "The Next Civil Rights Movement?" *Dissent Magazine*, Summer 2015, https://www.dissentmagazine.org/article/black-lives-matter-new-civil-rights-movement-fredrick-harris.
5. For more on the legacies of the Black Lives Matter movement and how it differs from previous generations of activism see Barbara Ransby, "Black Lives Matter Is Democracy in Action," *New York Times*, October 21, 2017, https://www.nytimes.com/2017/10/21/opinion/sunday/black-lives-matter-leadership.html; Keeanga-Yamahtta Taylor, *From #BlackLivesMatter to Black Liberation* (Chicago: Haymarket Books, 2016); Barbara Ransby, *Making All Black Lives*

Matter: Reimagining Freedom in the Twenty-First Century (Berkley: University of California Press, 2018).

6. Tesfamariam, "Why the Modern Civil Rights Movement."

7. See David Sirota, "Santa Claus-ifying Martin Luther King Jr.," *In These Times*, February 1, 2013, https://inthesetimes.com/article/santa-clausifying-martin-luther-king-jr; Ed Gilbreath, "The Angry Martin Luther King," *Christianity Today*, January 18, 2016, https://www.christianitytoday.com/ct/2016/january-web-only/angry-martin-luther-king.html; Zaid Jilani, "What the Santa Clausi-fication of Martin Luther King Jr. Leaves Out," *The Intercept*, January 16, 2017, https://theintercept.com/2017/01/16/what-the-santa-clausification-of-martin-luther-king-jr-leaves-out. For a comprehensive and incisive critique of the more general appropriation of "civil rights history" to political ends, see Jeanne Theoharis, *A More Beautiful and Terrible History: The Uses and Misuses of Civil Rights History* (Boston, MA: Beacon Press, 2018).

8. Bruce Lincoln, *Theorizing Myth: Narrative, Ideology, and Scholarship* (Chicago: University of Chicago Press, 1999), xii.

9. Nikhil Pal Singh, *Black Is a Country: Race and the Unfinished Struggle for Democracy* (Cambridge, MA: Harvard University Press, 2004), 17.

10. Scholars challenging the civic myth of civil rights would include, though not be limited to, Martha Biondi, *To Stand and Fight: The Struggle for Civil Rights in Postwar New York City* (Cambridge, MA: Harvard University Press, 2003); Robert O. Self, *American Babylon: Race and the Struggle for Postwar Oakland* (Princeton, NJ: Princeton University Press, 2003); Barbara Ransby, *Ella Baker and the Black Freedom Movement: A Radical Democratic Vision* (Chapel Hill: University of North Carolina Press, 2006); Thomas J. Sugrue, *Sweet Land of Liberty: The Forgotten Struggle for Civil Rights in the North* (New York: Random House, 2008); Danielle L. McGuire, *At the Dark End of the Street: Black Women, Rape, and Resistance—A New History of the Civil Rights Movement from Rosa Parks to the Rise of Black Power* (New York: Vintage Books, 2011); Charles E. Cobb Jr., *This Nonviolent Stuff'll Get You Killed: How Guns Made the Civil Rights Movement Possible* (Durham, NC: Duke University Press, 2015).

11. Kerry Pimblott, *Faith in Black Power: Religion, Race, and Resistance in Cairo, Illinois* (Lexington: University Press of Kentucky, 2017), 4.

12. Charles Marsh, *God's Long Summer: Stories of Faith and Civil Rights* (Princeton, NJ: Princeton University Press, 1997), 179.

13. Singh, *Black Is a Country*, 3 (emphasis mine).

14. For some substantial critiques of "racial liberalism," albeit from different angles, see Kimberlé Williams Crenshaw, "Race Liberalism and the Deradical-ization of Racial Reform," *Harvard Law Review* 130 (October 2017): 2298-319; Charles W. Mills, *Black Rights/White Wrongs: The Critique of Racial Liberalism* (Oxford, UK: Oxford University Press, 2017); Singh, *Black Is a Country*. Black Catholic historians are notable exceptions to this tendency in US Catholic

historiography. Notable examples include Cyprian Davis, *The History of Black Catholics in the United States* (New York: Crossroad Publishing Company, 1995); M. Shawn Copeland ed., with LaReine-Marie Mosely, SND, and Albert J. Raboteau, *Uncommon Faithfulness: The Black Catholic Experience* (Maryknoll, NY: Orbis, 2009); and Shannen Dee Williams, "'You Could Do the Irish Jig, but Anything African Was Taboo': Black Nuns, Contested Memories, and the Twentieth Century Struggle to Desegregate US Catholic Religious Life," *Journal of African American History* 102, no. 2 (2017): 125–56.

15. John T. McGreevy, *Parish Boundaries: The Catholic Encounter with Race in the Twentieth Century Urban North* (Chicago: University of Chicago Press, 1996), 90. For a select bibliography of Catholic interracialism, see David W. Southern, *John LaFarge and the Limits of Catholic Interracialism, 1911–1963* (Baton Rouge: Louisiana State University Press, 1996); Amy L. Koehlinger, *The New Nuns: Racial Justice and Religious Reform in the 1960s* (Cambridge, MA: Harvard University Press, 2007); R. Bentley Anderson, S.J., *Black, White, and Catholic: New Orleans Interracialism, 1947–1956* (Nashville, TN: Vanderbilt University Press, 2008); Timothy B. Neary, *Crossing Parish Boundaries: Race, Sports, and Catholic Youth in Chicago, 1914–1954* (Chicago: University of Chicago Press, 2016); Karen J. Johnson, *One in Christ: Chicago Catholics and the Quest for Interracial Justice* (Oxford, UK: Oxford University Press, 2018). For a general overview of the subject, see Phillip Luke Sinitiere, "Interracialism and American Christianity," *Oxford Research Encyclopedia of Religion* (Dec. 19, 2017), https://doi.org/10.1093/acrefore/9780199340378.013.499.

16. "A Statement of the Black Catholic Clergy Caucus, 1968," in *"Stamped with the Image of God": African Americans as God's Image in Black*, ed. Cyprian Davis and Jamie Phelps (Maryknoll, NY: Orbis Books, 2003), 111.

17. Ibid., 112.

18. Ibid.

19. Sr. M. Martin de Porres Grey, "The Church, Revolution and Black Catholics," *Black Scholar* 2, no. 4 (December 1970): 23.

20. The story of Sister Martin de Porres Grey's exclusion from the founding of the BCCC was told to me by Shannen Dee Williams, who has written extensively on Black Catholic sisters in the United States both in print and online. See Williams, *Subversive Habits: Black Catholic Nuns in the Long African-American Freedom Struggle* (Durham, NC: Duke University Press, forthcoming).

21. "The Survival of Soul: National Black Sisters' Conference Position Paper, 1969," in Davis and Phelps, *"Stamped with the Image of God,"* 114.

22. Ibid., 115.

23. Robert O. Self, "The Black Panther Party in the Long Civil Rights Era," in *In Search of the Black Panther Party: New Perspectives on a Revolutionary Movement*, ed. Jama Lazerow and Yohuru Williams (Durham, NC: Duke University Press, 2006), 36.

24. Stokely Carmichael and Charles V. Hamilton, *Black Power: The Politics of Liberation in America* (New York: Penguin Books, 1967).

25. See Keisha N. Blain, *Set the World on Fire: Black Nationalist Women and the Global Struggle for Freedom* (Philadelphia: University of Pennsylvania Press, 2018).

26. For more on the Illinois Chapter of the Black Panther Party and its alliance with Black Catholics in Chicago see Jakobi Williams, *From the Bullet to the Ballot: The Illinois Chapter of the Black Panther Party and Racial Coalition Politics in Chicago* (Chapel Hill: University of North Carolina Press, 2013) and Matthew J. Cressler, *Authentically Black and Truly Catholic: The Rise of Black Catholicism in the Great Migration* (New York: New York University Press, 2017).

27. Jeffrey Haas, *Assassination of Fred Hampton: How the FBI and the Chicago Police Murdered a Black Panther* (Chicago: Chicago Review Press, 2009).

28. Haas, *Assassination of Fred Hampton*, 96–97.

29. Michael D. Wamble, "Black Priests, Black Panthers: Breaking Barriers at Every Turn," *New World*, October 1, 2000. See also Interview with George Clements, conducted by Blackside, Inc., on October 19, 1989, for *Eyes on the Prize II: America at the Racial Crossroads 1965 to 1985*. Washington University Libraries, Film and Media Archive, Henry Hampton Collection; Interview with Bobby Rush, conducted on October 20, 1988.

30. Haas, *Assassination of Fred Hampton*, 98.

31. This narrative of Father George Clements and Afro-American Patrolmen's League is drawn from the Afro-American Patrolmen's League Records (hereafter AAPL) housed in the Chicago History Museum (hereafter CHM).

32. "Afro American Patrolmen's League," untitled pledge or mission statement, Box 37, Folder 8, AAPL, CHM.

33. "Black Priest Lists the Dreams of Black Catholics," *Religious News Service*, August 10, 1970, National Federation of Priests Council Papers, University of Notre Dame Archives.

34. Barbara Dianne Savage, *Your Spirits Walk beside Us: The Politics of Black Religion* (Cambridge, MA: Belknap Press of Harvard University Press, 2008).

35. Curtis J. Evans, *The Burden of Black Religion* (Oxford, UK: Oxford University Press, 2008).

36. This challenge is not limited to the Black Power era, of course. Shannen Dee Williams has reflected on the possibilities for racial justice presented by twenty-first century Black Catholics across the world; Williams, "The Global Catholic Church and the Radical Possibilities of #BlackLivesMatter," *Journal of Africana Religions* 3, no. 4 (2015): 503–15. Olga Segura has also recently written about the lessons the Movement for Black Lives holds for Catholic racial justice efforts: Olga Segura, *Birth of a Movement: Black Lives Matter and the Catholic Church* (Maryknoll, NY: Orbis Books, 2021).

37. Osagyefo Uhuru Sekou, "The Clergy's Place Is with the Protestors in Ferguson," *Aljazeera America*, November 23, 2014, http://america.aljazeera.com/opinions/2014/11/ferguson-protestmovementreligious.html.

38. Sarah van Gelder, "Rev. Sekou on Today's Civil Rights Leaders: I Take My Orders From 23-Year-Old Queer Women," *Yes Magazine*, July 22, 2015, https://www.yesmagazine.org/social-justice/2015/07/22/black-lives-matter-s-favorite-minister-reverend-sekou-young-queer.

39. Carmichael and Hamilton, *Black Power* (1967), 21.

40. My reading of Black Power and its anticolonial challenges to the US racial state is deeply indebted to Sylvester A. Johnson, *African American Religions, 1500–2000: Colonialism, Democracy, and Freedom* (Cambridge, UK: Cambridge University Press, 2015).

41. Sekou, "The Clergy's Place."

CHAPTER 2

Beyond *De-Christianization*

Rethinking the Religious Landscapes and Legacies of Black Power in the Age of #BlackLivesMatter

Kerry Pimblott

Since Black Lives Matter burst onto the scene in 2013, scholars and popular commentators have wrestled with the question of the movement's relationship to earlier black freedom struggles.[1] The Sixties, historian Clarence Lang argues, cast a particularly "long shadow," serving as an "existential yardstick" by which all subsequent movements are measured.[2] Iconic civil rights battles waged on buses and at lunch counters have become, in Eddie Glaude's words, "the standard model of political engagement for black America"; a template for "proper" protest that each new generation of activists is expected to follow.[3] A key element of this standard civil rights story is an understanding of the black church's centrality to the movement's efficacy during the heroic "classical" period from 1955 to 1965. Sacred edifices are often portrayed as the movement's natural staging grounds, clergy its charismatic leaders, congregants willing "foot soldiers," and gospel music the soundtrack of a coming revolution. Black Power, by contrast, is cast as the movement's irreverent offspring; its participants stridently anticlerical, if not wholly secular. This interpretation of the Black Freedom Movement's "de-Christianization" posits that the rise of Black Power after 1965 contributed to the de-centering of the black church within organizing traditions, the growth of alternative religious or secular philosophies, and—by some negative accounts—fragmentation and decline.[4] It is on this dichotomous premise that some commentators distinguish Black Lives Matter from earlier civil rights campaigns. In describing Black Lives Matter as not "your grandmother's civil rights movement" they allude—at least in part—to a departure from an organizing tradition focused on the black church that is imagined to have begun in the Black Power era.[5]

Perceptions of this shift differ, with detractors appealing to the historic pedigree of black churches as vehicles for racial justice activism, while others contend that a more pluralistic approach has created space for an inclusive and democratic movement to flourish. However, it is important to note that the "de-Christianization" thesis remains speculative and largely untested on the ground. With the subfield of "Black Power Studies" still in its infancy, a new generation of scholars are engaged in the vital work of recovering previously overlooked local actors, organizations, and sites of struggle.[6] Few among them have critically examined the religious dynamics of grassroots Black Power movements, and those that have break sharply with the dominant narrative.[7] Such accounts, at the very least, complicate interpretations of the movement's "de-Christianization," and with it any assumed teleological relationship to Black Lives Matter.

Taking this emergent scholarship as a starting point, this chapter advances what might appear to be a rather commonsensical claim: that the involvement of black churches in local protest traditions has never been inevitable—not even at the zenith of the civil rights movement—but is instead contingent on the skill of grassroots organizers in responding to distinctive and regionally specific religious cultures.[8] It seeks to move beyond the old dichotomies of what Jeanne Theoharis has called our "national fable," in favor of an approach that is attentive to the agency of activists building movements within very different structures of religious opportunities, based on their particular spatial (and temporal) locations.[9] In so doing, it contributes to a growing conversation among scholars about the significance of place in the Black Freedom Movement. Over the past two decades, scholars who have documented a series of parallel northern campaigns that coincided with the movement's "heroic" phase have upended the conventional account of a distinctly southern civil rights struggle.[10] Such studies have played an important role in "nationalizing" the civil rights story, but they also—as Clarence Lang admonishes—carry "the risk of flattening meaningful differences of historical place." As Lang asserts, white racism and black protest certainly existed on both sides of the Mason-Dixon Line, but regional variances in racial regimes and the movements that mobilized to topple them were both fundamental and decisive.[11] This chapter lends support to this supposition by highlighting significant regional variations in religiosity and their import to black freedom struggles.

A view from the grassroots suggests that place matters as much, if not more, than ideology in determining the black church's centrality to local protest traditions. Studies show that black churches and the theologies they harbored were "multidimensional" and sufficiently malleable to be recruited into a wide range of twentieth-century social movements,[12] from Garveyite nationalism to the radical ethos of the Socialist and Communist parties. Though examples of this malleability can be found nationwide, it was most apparent and necessary in southern communities, where African Americans exhibited higher rates of religious participation and greater homogeneity in their religious affiliations, and where black churches maintained an unrivalled position in what political scientist Michael Dawson has referred to as the "black counterpublic."[13] In contrast, several decades of migration rendered black northern metropolises a more complex religious terrain, where activists had to negotiate heterogeneous, often competing, religious traditions or else abandon the use of sacred discourses as a foundation for collective action altogether. These vastly different religious geographies provided the backdrop for postwar black freedom struggles of all ideological stripes. However, the tendency of traditional histories to conflate civil rights with the South and Black Power with the urban North or West has contributed to the assumption that it was the ideological shift to Black Nationalism that was the driving force behind the movement's supposed "de-Christianization."[14] In reality, grassroots Black Power activists with the requisite interest and skill to recruit black religious institutions and discourses into the movement proved just as adept as their liberal civil rights counterparts. As this chapter will illustrate, these regional variances in religious cultures have persisted, and, when combined with the more recent growth of the religiously unaffiliated, or "Nones," continue to inform the approaches activists employ.[15]

But what does this revised portrayal of the religious dynamics of Black Power mean for activists in the age of Black Lives Matter? If Black Power's religious legacy cannot be flatly characterized as one of "de-Christianization," how might it be better understood? Notwithstanding the limits of the extant scholarship, this chapter points to growing evidence of the use of religion by Black Power activists as both a "macro" and "micro" resource for political mobilization, with discernible consequences. "Macro" resources, political scientist Frederick Harris explains, are "tangible, material sources of mobilization," such as funding, communication networks, and meeting spaces.[16] Additional case studies will offer scholars a way to more comprehensively assess the extent to which local black churches, temples, and mosques provided these types of "macro" resources to grassroots Black Power formations in different parts of the country. But what is clear is that Black Power activists—in tandem with prominent black clergy—played a pivotal role in extracting substantial "macro" resources from some of the nation's largest predominantly white denominations, among them the Episcopal, Presbyterian, and Methodist churches. However, this fragile alliance would not last. It fell victim to state interference and a backlash from white congregants, who increasingly abandoned mainline churches in favor of more conservative alternatives. This exodus has continued in the decades since, further eroding the potential and significance of mainline denominations as coalitional partners to Black Lives Matter. Yet not all of Black Power's religious legacies left a deficit. While the recipients of these faith-based resources were not expected to display any particular religious orientation, some Black Power groupings— especially, though not exclusively, in southern communities—continued to mobilize what Harris calls the "less tangible" cultural and discursive "micro" resources of the black church to frame the movement's aims and facilitate collective political action.[17] In the transition from civil rights liberalism to Black Power nationalism, this involved drawing upon the black church's ritualistic culture of music, testimony, and charismatic sermonizing, but it also meant engaging innovations in Black Theology. These traditions have been extended in the decades since, and have given rise to distinctive Womanist and Humanist paradigms that offer important resources to many contemporary struggles for black liberation.[18]

Postwar Religious Landscapes

At the height of the postwar Black Freedom Movement, activists confronted a distinctive religious landscape. In contrast to many other industrialized democracies, the United States remained a highly religious culture. A 1957 Gallup poll revealed that 97 percent of all Americans held some kind of religious preference, with the vast majority identifying with Christian traditions.[19] Throughout the decade, fully seven in ten Americans said that religion was a "very important" aspect of their life, and nearly half reported attending a church or synagogue on a weekly basis, constituting a significant increase from the pre-war low of 37 percent in 1940.[20] This extraordinary growth in the ranks of the churched was especially apparent in mainline Protestantism, where denominational membership rolls reached an all-time high.[21] Christianity's pervasive effect on American public life reflected these statistical indices of postwar religious belief and belonging. During the Fifties, Billy Graham's revival crusades were televised live to a national audience, religious books topped the bestsellers list, and biblical dramas such as *The Ten Commandments* (1956) and *Ben-Hur* (1959) were box office blockbusters. From the

White House, President Dwight Eisenhower delivered a Cold War rhetoric that fused religion with a sense of patriotic duty, encouraging citizens to attend church and overseeing the passage of legislation that added the phrase "under God" to the nation's pledge and "In God We Trust" to its currency.[22]

Notwithstanding these general trends, the postwar religious landscape was far from static, and it exhibited important divergences along axes of region and race. A 1956 study performed by the National Council of Churches (NCC) showed that southerners had comparably high rates of church membership but greater homogeneity in affiliation than their northern and western counterparts. More than three-quarters (78.9 percent) of church members in the South identified as Protestant, compared to just 30.1 percent in northeastern states and 47.9 percent in the West. In the heart of the "Bible Belt," the percentage of Protestants was even higher, with the majority joining Baptist congregations that preached an evangelical gospel by emphasizing personal salvation, biblical inerrancy, and a direct and emotional relationship with God.[23] By contrast, northern and western states exhibited considerable religious diversity. Catholics predominated in northern metropolises, but shared the urban scene with significant Jewish and Protestant populations. In the West, church membership rates lagged behind the rest of the nation, with the exception of robust pockets of Catholicism in the Southwest and Mormonism in the Rocky Mountain West.[24]

These regional polarities were also apparent among African Americans though statistical evidence is more limited. Census data from 1957 indicates that 96 percent of "non-whites" (about 90 percent of whom were black) held some religious preference, a figure that closely resembled the national average. However, non-whites were even more likely to identify as Protestant (87.5 percent) and, of them, nearly half (46.6 percent) reported attending church on a weekly basis, mainly in Baptist and Methodist congregations.[25] This statistical composite best captures black religious traditions in the South, where the ranks of the churched outstripped all other regions, and where African Americans exhibited relative homogeneity in their denominational affiliations. Gallup surveys conducted in 1971 and

1972 specify that the majority of African Americans in the rural South (85.3 percent) and exactly half of those in cities were not only members of a church but had attended services at least once in the last six months.[26] Most black southerners joined black Baptist and Methodist congregations that, despite important differences in history and structure, demonstrated considerable ecumenism rooted in the regular practice of church visitations and a shared religious culture of charismatic sermonizing, hymn singing, collective prayer, testimony, and revivals.[27] Across the region, black churches stood at the forefront of the black counterpublic providing, in sociologist Aldon Morris's words, "an institutional alternative to, and an escape from, the racism and hostility of the larger society."[28] In small towns and rural areas, churches were often the only independent black institutions, and thus served as the principal locus of black sociability, cultural expression, mutual aid, and leadership. In southern cities, black churches were larger and better financed, permitting the development of a professional ministerial class as well as a wider range of programming and activities.[29] The exclusion of blacks from electoral politics in the South also ensured that black churches would become the default site for a black political discourse that fused the sacred and the secular.[30] Given the primacy of the church in the lives of southern blacks, some have described it as a "semi-involuntary" institution, in which participation was expected and served as a marker of good social standing.[31]

Outside the South, levels of black church membership and attendance remained high in rural communities (60 percent), but were substantially lower in suburban (36.8 percent) and metropolitan areas (28.4 percent) where decades of migration had wrought significant transformations.[32] In northern cities, African Americans experienced what C. Eric Lincoln and Lawrence Mamiya describe as a "process of differentiation," manifest in heightened class stratification, the establishment of secular institutions, and religious diversification.[33] Postwar metropolises were filled with recent migrants, many of whom abandoned the established black Baptist and Methodist congregations in favor of storefront churches that propagated Pentecostalism, spiritualism, and other religious expressions, such as the Nation of Islam (NOI) and the Moorish Science Temple of America.[34] Outside in the streets were also a growing number of black folk agnostic to questions of faith and, among them, some sceptics who actively embraced humanist alternatives.[35] Meeting the spiritual and material needs of these various city dwellers was no longer the sole preserve of churches, as the black counterpublic expanded to include a plethora of secular institutions. African American clergy— who approximated nearly 50 percent of all black professionals in the South—now shared their role with the burgeoning ranks of black social workers, lawyers, doctors, journalists, and educators. Moreover, the absence of formal barriers to political participation allowed for the rise of black elected officials.[36]

Religious Geographies of Postwar Black Freedom Struggles

This postwar religious landscape provided a distinctive structure of opportunities and resources that informed black freedom struggles in important ways. High levels of church membership and attendance among African Americans in the South necessitated that activists engage with black faith traditions as part of grassroots mobilization efforts. The fact that churches were often the only "free spaces" where southern blacks could assemble independently of whites made their recruitment all the more important. This fact was not lost on civil rights worker Stokely Carmichael:

> I instinctively understood that if my struggle was to be among my people, then any talk of atheism and the rejection of God just wasn't gonna cut it. I just knew that. My early political work in the rural South would confirm this. All our meetings were held in churches. They all began with prayer. When they approved, people would say, "'Son, you doing the Lord's work.'" If they were ambivalent, it'd be a question: "'Son, you sure that's the Lord's work?'" And the preacher, fearing for the church insurance or his standing with the white folk, would say in denying us the use of his church, "'Son, you know, that ain't the Lord's work now.'"

Recruits would usually tell you, "'If the Lord ain't in this movement, it ain't going nowhere,'" or, "'. . . then I ain't in it.'"[37]

Securing the blessing of black clergy, as Carmichael suggested, was not always straightforward. Studies show that only a small percentage of black ministers participated in civil rights activities, and some joined Reverend Joseph H. Jackson, head of the largest black denomination, the National Baptist Convention, U.S.A., Inc., in opposing church involvement in the movement.[38] Nonetheless, there is a general consensus among scholars that black churches, clergy, and congregants played an indispensable role in the region's iconic civil rights battles. In southern cities, large urban congregations served as the base of operations for coordinated mass direct action campaigns, and provided the "Big Four" civil rights organizations with access to indigenous "macro" resources, including charismatic leadership, meeting space, funding, and communication networks.[39] Of particular importance was the role of black churchwomen, who constituted the majority of congregants and often held key positions in church missionary and mutual aid societies. Through their voluntary activities, black churchwomen solidified their positions as respected community members and invaluable recruiters for local movements. In rural areas, where Baptist churches were unlikely to have a stable and educated clergy and could be financially beholden to white patrons, securing church support could be even more challenging. However, churchwomen filled the vacuum, often playing critical "nontraditional" leadership roles.[40] As a result, civil rights workers made significant headway, with many churches opening their doors for mass meetings and voter registration trainings.[41] In the process, the shared religious ethos of the region's black Baptist and Methodist congregations infused local movement cultures, providing activists with the discursive and emotional "micro" resources capable of transforming grievances into concerted mass action. Church people looked to the scriptures and a rich culture of congregational song, prayer, and testimony to assuage their fears and sustain their struggle.[42] Moreover, a new generation of southern ministers, typified by Martin Luther King Jr. and James Lawson, raised their voices in opposition to the sin of Jim Crow and delivered a social gospel of Christian nonviolence in service of the "Beloved Community" to frame the movement's dominant ideology and strategy.[43]

However, the aforementioned regional differences in black faith traditions ensured that this could not and would not be true everywhere. The sheer diversity of African American religious cultures in the North often worked to undercut the unifying potential of black churches and Christian discourses for political mobilization. Building a movement in this context required bridging potent intra-racial differences, rooted not only in class, generation, and origin, but also in religion. This is not to say that African American activists in northern cities were less religious, or that the contributions of black churches were insignificant; far from it. The nascent literature on civil rights in the North reveals a growing cast of religiously inspired rebels, as well as the importance of large urban congregations, such as those of Reverend Adam Clayton Powell Jr. in New York, Reverend Leon Sullivan in Philadelphia, and Reverend C. L. Franklin in Detroit, to local struggles.[44] However, it is important to note that movement organizations in the North were not as singularly reliant upon black churches for "macro" resources, due to the existence of a more expansive black counterpublic. As a result, northern activists had a much wider institutional base to draw upon; one that included churches, but also secular organizations such as labor unions, fraternal orders, schools, neighborhood block clubs, newspapers, political parties, and civil rights groups.

Furthermore, even the most pious activists had to confront the North's dynamic religious landscape that often militated against the use of the discursive "micro" resources of black churches as a vehicle for mass mobilization. It was this challenge—of building a movement that encompassed the masses of religiously diverse black northerners—that contributed, at least in part, to Christian pacifist James Farmer's decision to establish the Congress of Racial Equality in Chicago in 1942, on a foundation that historian Nishani Frazier describes as "strategically secular versus spiritually motivated."[45] A similar pragmatism appeared in the rhetoric and organizational approaches of Malcolm X following his departure from the NOI in

March 1964. In "The Ballot or the Bullet," a speech he would deliver in cities across the North in March and April of that year, Malcolm confronted the issue of sectarianism, calling on his audiences to "submerge" their religious differences and focus instead on the "common problem" of white supremacy. "Whether we are Christians or Muslims or nationalists or agnostics or atheists, we must first learn to forget our differences," Malcolm implored. "If we have differences, let us differ in the closet; when we come out in front, let us not have anything to argue about until we get finished arguing with the man." Malcolm's statements are revealing both of the plurality of black religious life in the North and his own pursuit of a united front strategy. "For Malcolm," historian Manning Marable argues, "a precondition for unity was finding a secular basis for common ground, which is why he also strove to decouple his identity as a Muslim cleric from his political engagements."[46]

This was a route that other religiously inspired activists had travelled before Malcolm. In fact, Eddie Glaude Jr. contends that, since the interwar period, increased religious diversity had contributed to the secularization of black public discourse in the North and spurred the development of new "moral languages" capable of sustaining a more inclusive dialogue about the conditions of black life.[47] During his final year, Malcolm developed his own moral languages, drawn from the wellsprings of Black Nationalist and Pan-African thought and operationalized through the strict separation of his religious organization, the Muslim Mosque Incorporated, and the secular Organization of African American Unity. While Malcolm appealed to notions of racial unity and human rights, many of his liberal civil rights contemporaries found different discursive weapons in what historian Felicia Kornbluh describes as the "secular language of political and constitutional rights."[48]

Religious Resources for Black Power

Given the South's unique structure of religious opportunities and resources, it seems implausible that Black Power activists would abandon their usage. Nonetheless, conventional interpretations of Black Power as a primarily northern phenomenon have served to obscure understanding of the movement's distinctive character and development in the region. Although a comprehensive account is still lacking, local studies suggest that Black Power in many southern communities "flowed seamlessly out of earlier organizing traditions," meaning that there were often religious continuities.[49] This is most obvious with respect to "macro" resources whereby churches that had provided organizations with meeting space, leadership, and membership continued to serve in that capacity even after Black Power supplanted civil rights liberalism as the movement's dominant ideological framework. This appears to have been particularly true of Black Power formations in the small towns and rural communities of Alabama and Mississippi, where the Student Nonviolent Coordinating Committee (SNCC) was active and churches were unrivalled within the black counterpublic. Hasan Kwame Jeffries's study of black freedom struggles in Lowndes County, Alabama, for example, shows that many of the same churches and congregants that had resourced SNCC's earlier civil rights projects subsequently supported the Lowndes County Freedom Organization's fight for black political empowerment.[50] Correspondingly, Akinyele Umoja's account of the activities of the United League in northern Mississippi reveals similar continuities, including "significant participation from Black clergy and laity." In fact, Umoja suggests that the League's members went further, drawing on "biblical characters and scriptures in their oratory" and dubbing the organization itself a "church on wheels." The contours of the League's theology are less clear, but Umoja offers compelling examples of League members repurposing theological discourses within Black Power politics.[51]

During the late 1960s, the efforts of these grassroots activists corresponded with a broader movement among black clergy and seminarians to render Christian discourses relevant to Black Power. Many of the participants were northern ministers serving in cities beset by urban rebellions, in which frustrated residents lashed out against poverty and discriminatory practices largely unchanged by the passage of civil rights legislation. Churches did not escape reproach; many viewed them as having failed to meet the needs of their constituents. Adherents of the NOI and other secular black power groups who joined in were among the loudest critics who condemned opportunistic and self-serving ministers for peddling an otherworldly "white man's religion." According to the late theologian James Cone, it was the urgency of this moment that spurred black clergy to "search for a radically new theological starting point that would clearly distinguish its perspective from the alternatives provided by whites and adopted by conservative blacks."[52] By the end of the decade, black ministers had formed separate caucuses in at least ten of the nation's largest predominantly white religious institutions and denominations, including the Black Unitarian Universalist Caucus and the Black Catholic Clergy Caucus documented by Christopher Cameron and Matthew Cressler in this collection. In 1966, black clergy also formed the ecumenical National Conference of Black Churchmen (NCBC). NCBC's first act was to take out a full-page ad in the *New York Times* on July 31, 1966, expressing its support for Black Power and its commitment to "make more meaningful in the life of our institution our conviction that Jesus Christ reigns in the 'here' and 'now.'"[53] The following year at the organization's founding convention in Dallas delegates called for the creation of a theological commission, whose members—among them Cone, Gayraud Wilmore, and Albert Cleage Jr.—would be charged with developing a systematic black theology rooted in the African American experience and responsive to demands for liberation.

Beginning with the publication of Cone's groundbreaking *Black Theology and Black Power* in 1969, black clergy took up this call, contributing to an outpouring of literary works and, in some cases, radical praxis. At the forefront was Cleage, pastor of the Shrine of the Black Madonna in Detroit and founder of the Black Christian Nationalist movement, who, historian Angela Dillard argues, championed a vision of the black church as "the cornerstone of the new Black nation."[54] In *Black Theology and Black Power*, Cone described the Detroit clergyman as "one of the few black ministers who has embraced Black Power as a religious concept and has sought to reorient the church-community on the basis of it."[55] However, in the years following the publication of Cone's book, there is evidence to suggest that these new theological discourses had captured the interest of other activist ministers involved in Black Power struggles further south. During the 1970s, Cleage's Black Christian Nationalist movement would expand beyond its base in Michigan, opening Shrines in Atlanta, Georgia, and Houston, Texas.[56] Among Cleage's devotees was the United Church of Christ minister Benjamin Chavis, who founded the First African Congregation of the Black Messiah in Wilmington, North Carolina, and embarked on a novel experiment to bring local youth into a movement that he styled both "revolutionary and holy." According to historian Kenneth Janken, Chavis asked his congregants to "read a book a week concerning some aspect of black history or culture," and to participate in "a prayer service [that] included a 'Pledge to the Black Flag,' the 'Black Christian Pan-Africanist Creed,' the 'Black National Anthem,' an antiphonal 'Nation Building' prayer, and various civil rights movement–era freedom songs, some of which were revised to include Black Power lyrics."[57]

This experiment appears to have been short-lived, stymied by Chavis' wrongful conviction during the Wilmington Ten trial in 1971. However, in Cairo, Illinois, Baptist minister Charles Koen led a more prolonged effort to unite black activists "under a banner of redefined, relevant Christianity." Cairo's religious culture more closely resembled that of southern communities, with the majority of black Cairoites attending a small number of Baptist and Methodist congregations that constituted the core of the declining river city's narrow black counterpublic. Under Koen's direction, the United Front—Cairo's leading Black Power organization—engaged with black theological texts, invited NCBC members to speak at "spiritual rallies," and sent local activists to receive training at seminaries. The Bible, correctly used, Koen argued, was a "handbook for the revolution."[58]

In addition to providing local Black Power struggles with new religious discourses, NCBC members also took the lead in leveraging significant financial resources from the nation's religious establishment. Exemplified by the *Black Manifesto*—James Forman's iconoclastic April 1969 appeal for $500 million from "the White Christian Churches and the Jewish Synagogues" of America[59]—these efforts succeeded in compelling church executives to create a plethora of new funding bodies responsible for disbursing millions of dollars directly to grassroots Black Power organizations. During the late 1960s, nearly all of the mainline denominations created black-led taskforces and grant-awarding bodies charged with channeling resources to local community development initiatives. The largest were the Episcopal Church's General Convention Special Program and the Presbyterian Church's National Committee for the Self-Development of People, formed in 1967 and 1970 respectively. Joining them was the Interreligious Foundation for Community Organizations, an ecumenical agency responsible for disbursing more than $4 million in grants to hundreds of domestic and international projects between 1967 and 1975. These activities constituted the apex of the "coalition of conscience" forged during the battle for the passage of the Civil Rights Act of 1964, and situated mainline denominations as vital coalitional partners to Black Power.[60]

Conclusion: Legacies in the Age of Black Lives Matter

This revised portrayal of Black Power, though nascent in its development, rubs uneasily against conventional accounts of the Black Freedom Movement's "de-Christianization." By shifting the lens to focus on the dynamics of local black freedom struggles, recent scholarship infers that place was often more important than ideology in shaping the role of religious institutions and discourses within protest traditions. Still, geography alone could not determine that role. It was up to human actors to respond to regionally specific and timebound structures of religious opportunities in their efforts to build effective mass movements. In the process, Black Power's religious innovators left behind their own legacies, including new religious "macro" and "micro" resources. Unfortunately, the "coalition of conscience" did not last; its new funding architecture was dismantled under the combined threat of governmental scrutiny and lay opposition.[61] The extraordinary growth of mainline Christianity that had underwritten these coalitional activities also stalled during the 1970s, as denominations experienced the opening salvo of what would become an uninterrupted decline in both numbers and confidence. Not all churches were shrinking, however; in 1967 the conservative Southern Baptist Convention surpassed the Methodists to become the nation's largest denomination, a development symptomatic of a broader rightward shift in faith and politics.[62]

These transformations have left contemporary activists with fewer coalition opportunities and set the stage for new forms of religious opposition. When asked in a 2015 survey whether they thought the recent killings of black men by police in Ferguson, Missouri, New York City, and Baltimore were "isolated incidents" or "part of a broader pattern of how police treat African Americans," nearly three-quarters (74 percent) of African Americans said that these incidents were part of a broader pattern, compared to 47 percent of white mainline Protestants and 29 percent of white evangelicals.[63] Black Lives Matter founder Alicia Garza captured this disparity in her comments following the 2015 massacre at the Emanuel AME Church in Charleston. "White denominations of faith," Garza asserted, "have been largely silent about the deliberate and racist targeting of black churches, and yet, these denominations are often the first to proclaim that 'All Lives Matter.'"[64] Following Black Lives Matter's first national convention in Cleveland in 2015, religious groups sympathetic to the movement's activities had an opportunity to express support. At the conference, hundreds of delegates from grassroots, black-led organizations joined to develop a platform and a united front structure called the Movement 4 Black Lives. Leaders also invited other political, labor, and religious groups to formally endorse the platform, a call hundreds of organizations responded to nationwide. However, fewer than thirty religiously affiliated groups offered their endorsement, most of which were faith-based peace organizations or local and predominantly black in their constituencies.[65] Despite this reluctance, a number of mainline denominations have passed resolutions in support of the wider Black Lives Matter movement and local congregations have engaged in solidarity activities at the grassroots level.[66] In a vital chapter on Unitarian Universalism in this book, Christopher Cameron traces the contributions of the Black Lives UU movement and their roots in Black Power–era caucus activities. However, the type of nationally coordinated ecumenical coalition-building effort that characterized the postwar period is noticeably absent.

The role of black churches in the Black Lives Matter movement is equally contested with evidence of active support *and* opposition, not to mention widespread criticism of congregational inactivity levied by activists. "I've been trying to get the church to step up more, hoping the theology of protest will catch up. . . . [But,] the church [has been] more cautious than Christ would have been," DeRay Mckesson informed an audience at Yale Divinity School in October 2015.[67] At the same time, activists confront an even more dynamic religious landscape than their predecessors, largely as a result of the rise of the "Nones." Back in 1966, Gallup polls indicated that only 2 percent of Americans had no religious preference. Fifty years later, that number had increased to 18 percent, or nearly one in five Americans.[68] The Pew Research Center's 2014 study puts that figure even higher, finding that nearly one-quarter (22.8 percent) of all Americans identified as either atheist, agnostic, or nothing in particular.[69] Although white Americans are more likely to identify as religiously unaffiliated, the share of African American "Nones" has undergone rapid growth, up from 12 percent in 2007 to nearly 19 percent in 2014. That same year, nearly three in ten (29 percent) African Americans between the ages of eighteen and twenty-nine identified as religiously unaffiliated.[70] Men are more likely to identify as religiously unaffiliated than women, though the latter group is growing; and, nearly half (46 percent) of all LGBTQ Americans say they are religiously unaffiliated, a figure that is close to double the national average.[71]

This exponential growth of the "Nones" carries particular significance for Black Lives Matter, which draws its core membership from among black women and LGBTQ millennials. However, geography still matters. The South remains the most religious region in the nation, with all but two of the top ten most religious states located within its boundaries. The "Nones" are on the rise there too—up from 13 percent in 2007 to 19 percent in 2014—but they constitute a much smaller constituency than in other parts of the country.[72] In many parts of the South and its contiguous areas, black communities continue to exhibit considerable religious homogeneity, and churches function as important staging grounds for movement mobilization. In the border state battles of Ferguson, for example, strategy meetings and rallies were held in local churches and ministers such as Reverend Traci Blackmon and black liberation theologian Osagyefo Sekou played prominent roles in support of youthful leaders.[73] According to historian Phillip Luke Sinitiere, "Christianity-based activism in Ferguson inspired similar actions in Waller County [Texas] a year later," following the death of Sandra Bland in police custody. Local activists converged at the Waller County Jail for a prayer vigil, a move that "sparked a political movement both steeped in and deeply inspired by Protestant Christianity."[74] In North Carolina, Reverend William Barber and the Moral Mondays movement have, once again, channeled religious discourses to create a potent coalition between southern white progressives, organized labor, and racial justice advocates. It was out of this movement that the Christian activist and Black Lives Matter adherent Brittany Ann "Bree" Newsome emerged in June 2015, climbing the flagpole and cutting down the Confederate flag at the South Carolina state capitol. "You come up against me with hatred, oppression, and violence," Newsome shouted from the top of the flagpole. "I come against you in the name of God. This flag comes down today."[75] Elsewhere, outgrowths of Black Theology, particularly of the Womanist and Humanist varieties, continue to inform the participation of activists who seek to build a movement capable of advancing an intersectional critique of racism, capitalism, and heteropatriarchy.[76] Still others, like movement co-founder Patrisse Cullors, have followed in the footsteps of an earlier generation of Black Power activists by reinterpreting African spiritual practices and beliefs.[77] Such examples push back against simplistic characterizations of Black Lives Matter as a secular movement that has broken radically with earlier phases of the black freedom struggle, but they also encourage scholars to consider the continued significance of regionally specific religious cultures to movements for racial change.

Birthed in the wake of George Zimmerman's 2013 acquittal in the shooting death of Trayvon Martin, Black Lives Matter has grown from its origins as a viral hashtag and online platform into what, arguably, constitutes a new stage of the Black Freedom Movement. Scholarly and popular commentary has focused considerable attention on the movement's relationship with earlier campaigns, positing that Black Lives Matter is not "your grandmother's civil rights movement." This slogan, I have argued, refers—at least in part—to the assumption that Black Lives Matter has jettisoned an older organizing tradition that placed primacy on the black church. In this formulation, Black Lives Matter is framed as extending a secularizing impulse that began in the Black Power era. Building on the nascent literature on religion in the Black Power and Black Lives Matter movements, this chapter has complicated the "de-Christianization" narrative by spotlighting the continued relevance of black churches and theological traditions to the freedom struggles of the post-civil rights era, particularly in the South and its contiguous areas. The black church's role in each stage of the Black Freedom Movement has hinged on the interest and skill of grassroots activists working within regionally specific religious cultures and shifting structures of religious opportunities. The relative homogeneity of Black faith traditions in the South, combined with high rates of church attendance and a lack of competing institutions, ensured that the region's black congregations would continue to operate as vital movement hubs in the transition from civil rights to Black Power. In contrast, the religious diversity of northern metropolises spurred even religiously inspired activists to adopt secular discourses in their efforts to build a mass movement. These important regional distinctions in black religious cultures persist and constitute an important, albeit overlooked, variable in contemporary grassroots struggles. At the same time, a re-examination of Black Power reveals new and important religious legacies including valuable discursive resources rooted in Black Theology and its Womanist and Humanist strains.

NOTES

The author would like to thank the History Department at Sussex University and the Race, Roots & Resistance Collective for providing constructive feedback on this chapter. An early draft was also presented at the Scholar Activism in the Twenty-First Century Conference hosted at the British Library in June 2018. Special thanks are owed to the editors of this volume, Phillip Luke Sinitiere and Christopher Cameron, as well as to Anne-Marie Angelo, Robert Beckford, Natalia Cecire, Denise James, Althea Legal-Miller, Meghan Tinsley, and Natalie Zacek.

1. The scholarship on Black Lives Matter is at a formative stage with important early works including Keeanga-Yamahtta Taylor, *From #BlackLives-Matter to Black Liberation* (Chicago: Haymarket, 2016) and Barbara Ransby, *Making All Black Lives Matter: Reimagining Freedom in the Twenty-First Century* (Berkeley: University of California Press, 2018). On the relationship between Black Lives Matter and earlier black freedom struggles, see Frederick C. Harris, "The Next Civil Rights Movement?" *Dissent*, Summer 2015, https://www.dissentmagazine.org/article/black-lives-matter-new-civil-rights-movement-fredrick-harris; Francis Schor, "'Black Lives Matter' Constructing a New Civil Rights and Black Freedom Movement," *New Politics* 15, no. 3, Summer 2015, https://newpol.org/issue_post/black-lives-matter-constructing-new-civil-rights-and-black-freedom-movement; Stefan M. Bradley, "The Rise of #blacklivesmatter," *American Book Review* 37, no. 3 (2016): 5; Russell Rickford, "Black Lives Matter: Toward a Modern Practice of Mass Struggle," *New Labor Forum* 25, no. 1 (2016): 34–42; Taylor, *From #BlackLivesMatter to Black Liberation*, esp. 1–20; Titilayo Rasaki, "From SNCC to BLM: Lessons in Radicalism, Structure, and Respectability Politics," *Harvard Journal of African American Public Policy*, vol. 2015-16: 31–38; Jane Rhodes, "Preface to the New Edition," in *Framing the Black Panthers: The Spectacular Rise of a Black Power Icon* (Urbana: University of Illinois Press, 2017), ix–xxxii; Dewey M. Clayton, "Black Lives Matter and the Civil Rights Movement: A Comparative Analysis of Two Social Movements in the United States," *Journal of Black Studies* 49, no. 5 (2018): 448–80.

2. Clarence Lang, *Black America in the Shadow of the Sixties: Notes on the Civil Rights Movement, Neoliberalism, and Politics* (Ann Arbor: University of Michigan Press, 2015), x, 1.

3. Eddie S. Glaude Jr., *In a Shade of Blue: Pragmatism and the Politics of Black America* (Chicago: University of Chicago Press, 2007), 149. The quote on "proper" protest is taken from Matthew J. Cressler, *Authentically Black and Truly Catholic: The Rise of Black Catholicism in the Great Migration* (New York: New York University Press, 2017), 14.

4. The term *"de-Christianization"* was coined by religious studies scholar Gayraud Wilmore in *Black Religion and Black Radicalism: An Interpretation of the Religious History of Afro-American People*, 2nd ed. (Maryknoll, NY: Orbis Books, 1983). For accounts that characterize the shift from civil rights to Black Power as the de-Christianization of the movement, see Charles Marsh's *God's Long Summer: Stories of Faith and Civil Rights* (Princeton, NJ:

Princeton University Press, 1997) and *The Beloved Community: How Faith Shapes Social Justice, from the Civil Rights Movement to Today* (New York: Basic Books, 2005).

5. Sharon Gary-Smith, "Not Your Grandmother's Movement," *Social Change in Oregon* (blog), MRG Foundation, September 18, 2015, https://www.mrgfoundation.org/not-your-grandmothers-movement.

6. Historian Peniel Joseph dubbed the subfield "Black Power Studies" in "Black Liberation Without Apology: Reconceptualizing the Black Power Movement," *Black Scholar* 31, no. 3-4 (2001): 2–19. Studies of local Black Power struggles include Matthew J. Countryman, *Up South: Civil Rights and Black Power in Philadelphia* (Philadelphia: University of Pennsylvania Press, 2006); Donna Jean Murch, *Living for the City: Migration, Education, and the Rise of the Black Panther Party in Oakland, California* (Chapel Hill: University of North Carolina Press, 2010); Peniel E. Joseph, ed., *Neighborhood Rebels: Black Power at the Local Level* (New York: Palgrave Macmillan, 2010); Hasan Kwame Jeffries, *Bloody Lowndes: Civil Rights and Black Power in Alabama's Black Belt* (New York: New York University Press, 2010); Clarence Lang, *Grassroots at the Gateway: Class Politics and Black Freedom Struggle in St. Louis, 1936–75* (Ann Arbor: University of Michigan Press, 2010); Kerry Pimblott, *Faith in Black Power: Religion, Race, and Resistance in Cairo, Illinois* (Lexington: University Press of Kentucky, 2017); Nishani Frazier, *Harambee City: The Congress of Racial Equality in Cleveland and the Rise of Black Power Populism* (Fayetteville: University of Arkansas Press, 2017).

7. Angela D. Dillard, *Faith in the City: Preaching Radical Social Change in Detroit* (Ann Arbor: University of Michigan Press, 2007); Angela D. Dillard, "Black Power/ Black Faith: Rethinking the "De-Christianization" of the Black Freedom Struggle," in *The Religious Left in Modern America*, ed., L. Danielson, M. Mollin, and D. Rossinow (London: Palgrave Macmillan, 2018); Pimblott, *Faith in Black Power*.

8. Here, I expand upon claims initially developed in *Faith in Black Power* about the relationship between the black church, politics, and region. I also build upon the work of Barbara Dianne Savage who has similarly challenged the idea of a natural or inevitable link between African American politics and religion. Savage asserts that this false *perception* emerged during the civil rights movement and "eclipsed the history and memory of intraracial conflicts about the place of religion in political struggle." Savage, *Your Spirits Walk beside Us: The Politics of Black Religion* (Cambridge, MA: Belknap Press, 2008), 270.

9. Jeanne Theoharis, *A More Beautiful and Terrible History: The Uses and Misuses of Civil Rights History* (Boston: Beacon Press, 2018), xiv.

10. Jeanne F. Theoharis and Komozi Woodard, eds., *Freedom North: Black Freedom Struggles outside the South, 1940–1980* (New York: Palgrave Macmil-

lan, 2003); Thomas J. Sugrue, *Sweet Land of Liberty: The Forgotten Struggle for Civil Rights in the North* (New York: Random House, 2008); Brian Purnell and Jeanne Theoharis with Komozi Woodard, eds., *The Strange Careers of the Jim Crow North: Segregation and Struggle Outside of the South* (New York: New York University Press, 2019).

11. Clarence Lang, "Locating the Civil Rights Movement: An Essay on the Deep South, Midwest, and Border South in Black Freedom Studies," *Journal of Social History* 47, no. 2 (December 2013), 371, 373.

12. Frederick C. Harris, *Something Within: Religion in African-American Political Activism* (New York: Oxford University Press, 1999), 7.

13. Michael C. Dawson, "A Black Counterpublic? Economic Earthquakes, Racial Agenda(s), and Black Politics," *Public Culture* 7 (1994): 195–223. On the religious dimensions of interwar black radical and nationalist formations in the US South, see Robin D. G. Kelley, "'Comrades, Praise Gawd for Lenin and Them!': Ideology and Culture among Black Communists in Alabama, 1930–1935," *Science and Society* 52, no.1 (Spring 1988), 59–82; Kelley, *Hammer and Hoe: Alabama Communists during the Great Depression* (Chapel Hill: University of North Carolina Press, 1990); Jarod Roll, *Spirit of Rebellion: Labor and Religion in the New Cotton South* (Urbana: University of Illinois Press, 2010); Mark Fannin, *Labor's Promised Land: Radical Visions of Gender, Race, and Religion in the South* (Knoxville: University of Tennessee Press, 2003).

14. Historian Matthew Cressler also points to this scholarly tendency to associate the movement's secularization with its shift to "militancy" and "radicalism." See Cressler, *Authentically Black and Truly Catholic*, 14.

15. The nascent literature on Black Lives Matter and religion offers support for this regional hypothesis with religious institutions and discourses featuring prominently in several southern and border state struggles. For example, see Leah Gunning Francis, *Ferguson and Faith: Sparking Leadership and Awakening* (St. Louis, MO: Chalice Press, 2015); Phillip Luke Sinitiere, "Religion and the Black Freedom Struggle for Sandra Bland," in *The Seedtime, the Work, and the Harvest: New Perspectives on the Black Freedom Struggle in America*, ed. Jeffrey L. Littlejohn, Reginald K. Ellis, and Peter B. Levy (Gainesville: University Press of Florida, 2018): 197–226; Vincent Lloyd, "How Religious Is #BlackLivesMatter," in *Humanism and the Challenge of Difference*, ed. Anthony B. Pinn (Cham, Switzerland: Palgrave Macmillan, 2018): 215–37.

16. Harris, *Something Within*, 27–28.

17. Harris, *Something Within*, 27–28.

18. On the continued relevance of Black Theology and it's Womanist and Humanist variants to the Black Lives Matter movement, see Kelly Brown Douglas, *Stand Your Ground: Black Bodies and the Justice of God* (New York: Orbis, 2015); Vincent Lloyd, Wes Alcenat, Ahmad Greene-Hayes, Su'ad Abdul Khabeer, Pamela R. Lightsey, Jennifer C. Nash, Jeremy Posadas et al., "Religion,

Secularism, and Black Lives Matter," *The Immanent Frame*, September 22, 2016, https://tif.ssrc.org/2016/09/22/religion-secularism-and-black-lives-matter; Terrence L. Johnson, "Black Lives Matter and the Black Church," *Berkley Forum*, October 19, 2016, https://berkleycenter.georgetown.edu/ responses/black-lives-matter-and-the-black-church; Juan Floyd-Thomas, "'A Relatively New Discovery in the Modern West': #BlackLivesMatter and the Evolution of Black Humanism, *Kalfou* 4, no. 1 (2017): 30–39.

19. According to 1957 Gallup polls, Protestants constituted 70 percent of all Americans, followed by Catholics at 24 percent and Jews at 3 percent. Notably, adherents of other faiths constituted just 1 percent of the American public, as did individuals who indicated no religious preference at all, a group we now refer to as the "nones." The annual Gallup surveys on religious preference are available online at http://news.gallup.com/poll/1690/religion.aspx.

20. Frank Newport, "In U.S., Four in 10 Report Attending Church in Last Week," Gallup News, December 24, 2013, http://news.gallup.com/poll/166613/four-report-attending-church-last-week.aspx.

21. Leading the way was the Methodist Church, which grew from eight million before the war to nearly eleven million in the 1950s. Other denominations witnessed comparable growth: the Episcopal Church grew from 1.4 million in 1945 to 2.2 million in 1965, and the Presbyterians from 2.2 million just after the war to 3.2 million by the early 1960s. See Dean R. Hoge, Benton Johnson, and Donald A. Luidens, *Vanishing Boundaries: The Religion of Mainline Protestant Baby Boomers* (Louisville, KY: Westminster/John Knox Press, 1994), 1–2.

22. On religion in postwar America, see Robert Wuthnow, *Restructuring of American Religion: Society and Faith since World War II* (Princeton, NJ: Princeton University Press, 1988); Robert S. Ellwood, *The Fifties Spiritual Marketplace: American Religion in a Decade of Conflict* (New Brunswick, NJ: Rutgers University Press, 1997); Patrick Allitt, *Religion in America since 1945: A History* (New York: Columbia, 2003); Kevin Michael Schultz, *Tri-Faith America: How Catholics and Jews Held Postwar America to Its Protestant Promise* (New York: Oxford University Press, 2011).

23. National Council of Churches, *Churches and Church Membership in the United States: An Enumeration and Analysis by Counties, States, and Regions* (1956). On southern religious traditions, see Samuel S. Hill Jr., *Southern Churches in Crisis* (Boston: Beacon Press, 1968); Charles Reagan Wilson, ed., *Religion in the South* (Jackson: University of Mississippi Press, 1985); Edward L. Queen II, *In the South the Baptists Are the Center of Gravity: Southern Baptists and Social Change, 1930–1980* (Brooklyn, NY: Carlson, 1991); Paul Harvey, *Redeeming the South: Religious Cultures and Racial Identities among Southern Baptists, 1865–1925* (Chapel Hill: University of North Carolina, 1997); Harvey, *Freedom's Coming: Religious Culture and the Shaping of the South from the Civil War*

through the Civil Rights Era (Chapel Hill: University of North Carolina, 2005); Kevin M. Kruse, *One Nation under God: How Corporate America Invented Christian America* (New York: Basic Books, 2015).

24. On the religious geography of postwar America, see Wilbur Zelinsky, "An Approach to the Religious Geography of the United States: Patterns of Church Membership in 1952," *Annals of the Association of American Geographers* 51 (June 1961): 139–93.

25. Norval D. Glenn and Erin Gotard, "The Religion of Blacks in the United States: Some Recent Trends and Current Characteristics," *American Journal of Sociology* 83, no. 2 (September 1977): 444–45. See also Robert D. Putnam and David E. Campbell, *American Grace: How Religion Divides and Unites Us* (New York: Simon and Schuster, 2010), 614.

26. Statistical data taken from Hart M. Nelsen, "Unchurched Black Americans: Patterns of Religiosity and Affiliation," *Review of Religious Research* 29, no. 4 (June 1988): 402.

27. Hans A. Baer and Merrill Singer, *African-American Religion in the Twentieth Century: Varieties of Protest and Accommodation* (Knoxville: University of Tennessee Press, 1992), 30–44. For an account of black southern Baptist traditions and culture, see Harvey, *Redeeming the South.*

28. Aldon D. Morris, *The Origins of the Civil Rights Movement: Black Communities Organizing for Change* (New York: Free Press, 1984), 6.

29. Morris, *The Origins of the Civil Rights Movement,* 6; Doug McAdam, *Political Process and the Development of Black Insurgency, 1930–1970* (Chicago: University of Chicago Press, 1982), 90–92, 98–100.

30. E. Franklin Frazier and C. Eric Lincoln, *The Negro Church in America* (New York: Schocken Books, 1974), 48–49. On the political activities of southern black churches in the decades preceding the civil rights movement, see Harvey, *Redeeming the South,* especially chapter 8, and *Freedom's Coming,* especially chapter 2.

31. Christopher G. Ellison and Darren E. Sherkat, "The 'Semi-involuntary Institution' Revisited: Regional Variations in Church Participation among Black Americans," *Social Forces* 73, no. 4 (June 1995): 1417–18. Also, on the 'semi-involuntary' character of the southern black church, see Hart M. Nelsen, Raytha L. Yokley, and Anne K. Nelsen, eds., *The Black Church in America* (New York: Basic Books, 1971).

32. Statistical data taken from Nelsen, "Unchurched Black Americans," 402.

33. C. Eric Lincoln and Lawrence H. Mamiya, *The Black Church in the African American Experience* (Durham, NC: Duke University Press, 1990), 8–10.

34. On the Great Migration, urbanization, and religious diversification, see Hans A. Baer and Merrill Singer, "Religious Diversification during the Era of Advanced Industrial Capitalism," in *African American Religious Thought: An Anthology,* ed. Cornel West and Eddie S. Glaude Jr. (Louisville, KY: Westminster/John Knox

Press, 2003), 495–533; Arthur H. Fauset, *Black Gods of the Metropolis* (Phila-delphia: University of Pennsylvania Press, 1971); Milton C. Sernett, *Bound for the Promised Land: African American Religion and the Great Migration* (Durham, NC: Duke University Press, 1997); Jacob S. Dorman, *Chosen People: The Rise of American Black Israelite Religions* (Oxford, UK: Oxford University Press, 2013); Judith Weisenfeld, *New World A-Coming: Black Religion and Racial Identity during the Great Migration* (New York: New York University Press, 2016).

35. On African American humanism, see Anthony B. Pinn, *African American Humanism: A Documentary History* (New York: New York University Press, 2003); Pinn, *The End of God-Talk: African American Humanist Theology* (New York: Oxford University Press, 2012); Juan M. Floyd-Thomas, *The Origins of Black Humanism in America: Reverend Ethelred Brown and the Unitarian Church* (New York: Palgrave Macmillan, 2008).

36. Adolph Reed, *The Jesse Jackson Phenomenon* (New Haven: Yale University Press, 1986), 43–46; Frazier and Lincoln, *The Negro Church in America*, 55.

37. Stokely Carmichael, *Ready for the Revolution: The Life and Struggles of Stokely Carmichael (Kwame Ture)* (New York: Scribner, 2003), 94.

38. William Brink and Louis Harris, *The Negro Revolution in America* (New York: Simon and Schuster, 1964), 108; Adam Fairclough, "The Southern Christian Leadership Conference and the Second Reconstruction, 1957–1973," *Southern Atlantic Quarterly* 80 (1981): 183; Charles M. Payne, *I've Got the Light of Freedom: The Organizing Tradition and the Mississippi Freedom Struggle* (Berkeley: University of California Press, 1995), 191. On Reverend Joseph H. Jackson, see Wallace Best, "'The Right Achieved and the Wrong Way Conquered': J. H. Jackson, Martin Luther King, Jr., and the Conflict over Civil Rights," *Religion and American Culture: A Journal of Interpretation* 16, no. 2 (Summer 2006), 195–226.

39. Morris, *The Origins of the Civil Rights Movement*.

40. Quote from Jeffries, *Bloody Lowndes*, 73. See also Payne, *I've Got the Light of Freedom*, 188–92, 272; Mark Newman, *Divine Agitators: The Delta Ministry and Civil Rights in Mississippi* (Athens: University of Georgia Press, 2004), 22, 52, 70; Wesley C. Hogan, *Many Minds, One Heart: SNCC's Dream for a New America* (Chapel Hill: University of North Carolina Press, 2007), 66.

41. For example, see Carmichael, *Ready for the Revolution*, 289–91; John Lewis, *Walking with the Wind: A Memoir of the Movement* (New York: Simon and Schuster, 1998), 400, 262.

42. On the role of black church culture and "micro" resources in the civil rights movement, see Johnny E. Williams, *African American Religion and the Civil Rights Movement in Arkansas* (Jackson: University Press of Mississippi, 2003).

43. On the role of ministers in crafting this message of nonviolence, see Allison Calhoun-Brown, "Upon This Rock: The Black Church, Nonviolence, and the Civil Rights Movement," *PS: Political Science and Politics* 33, no. 2 (June 2000): 168–74.

44. On the role of black churches and ministers in northern civil rights campaigns, see Dillard, *Faith in the City*; Randal Maurice Jelks, *African Americans in the Furniture City: The Struggle for Civil Rights in Grand Rapids* (Urbana: University of Illinois Press, 2006); Countryman, *Up South*; Brian Purnell, *Fighting Jim Crow in the County of Kings: The Congress of Racial Equality in Brooklyn* (Lexington: University Press of Kentucky, 2013).

45. Frazier, *Harambee City*, 21.

46. Malcolm X, "The Ballot or the Bullet," in *Imprisoned Intellectuals: America's Political Prisoners Write on Life, Liberation, and Rebellion*, ed. Joy James (Lanham, MD: Rowman and Littlefield, 2003), 51; Manning Marable, *Malcolm X: A Life of Reinvention* (New York: Penguin, 2012), 302–3.

47. Eddie S. Glaude Jr., "Babel in the North: Black Migration, Moral Community, and the Ethics of Racial Authenticity," in *A Companion to African-American Studies*, ed. Lewis R. Gordon and Jane Anna Gordon, 494–511 (New York: Blackwell Publishing, 2006): 504.

48. Felicia Kornbluh, "Black Buying Power: Welfare Rights, Consumerism, and Northern Protest," in *Freedom North*, Theoharis and Woodard, 199–223, (New York: Palgrave Macmillan, 2003), 200.

49. Tracy E. K'Meyer, "Empowerment, Consciousness, Defense: The Diverse Meanings of the Black Power Movement in Louisville, Kentucky," in *Neighborhood Rebels: Black Power at the Local Level*, ed. Peniel E. Joseph, 149–71 (New York: Palgrave Macmillan, 2010), 150.

50. See Jeffries, *Bloody Lowndes*.

51. Akinyele Omowale Umoja, *We Will Shoot Back: Armed Resistance in the Mississippi Freedom Movement* (New York: New York University Press, 2013), 243.

52. James H. Cone, *For My People: Black Theology and the Black Church* (Maryknoll, NY; Orbis Books, 1984), 24.

53. The full statement of the National Committee of Black Churchmen is reproduced in Gayraud S. Wilmore and James H. Cone, *Black Theology: A Documentary History, 1966–1979* (Maryknoll, NY: Orbis Books, 1979). 23–30.

54. Dillard, *Faith in the City*, 237.

55. James H. Cone, *Black Theology and Black Power* (New York: Seabury Press, 1969), 117.

56. Aswad Walker contends that the expansion of the Shrine into the South corresponded with the involvement of Cleage's Black Slate, Inc., in black electoral politics. See Walker, "Politics Is Sacred: The Activism of Albert B. Cleage Jr." in *Albert Cleage Jr. and the Black Madonna and Child*, ed. Jawanza Eric Clark (New York: Palgrave Macmillan, 2016), 97–114.

57. Kenneth Robert Janken, *The Wilmington Ten: Violence, Justice and the Rise of Black Politics in the 1970s* (Chapel Hill: University of North Carolina Press, 2015), 45–46.

58. Pimblott, *Faith in Black Power*, 106, 128, 147–48.

59. "The Black Manifesto," in *Black Manifesto: Religion, Racism and Reparations*, ed. Robert S. Lecky and H. Elliott Wright (New York: Sheed and Ward, 1969), 114.

60. Pimblott, *Faith in Black Power*, 7, 163, 179–80.

61. Pimblott, *Faith in Black Power*, esp., 193–209.

62. Dean M. Kelley, *Why Conservative Churches Are Growing: A Study in Sociology of Religion* (New York: Harper and Row, 1972).

63. Robert P. Jones, *The End of White Christian America* (New York: Simon and Schuster, 2016), 151–54

64. Alicia Garza, "What I Meant when I Said That #BlackLivesMatter: A Birthday Card for a Movement," *Those People*, July 13, 2015, https://medium.com/thsppl/what-i-meant-when-i-said-blacklivesmatter-9add3419091d.

65. List of Endorsing Organizations provided on the Movement 4 Black Lives website, https://policy.m4bl.org/about (accessed July 29, 2018).

66. "Support the Black Lives Matter Movement: 2015 Action of Immediate Witness," Unitarian Universalist Association, July 1, 2015, https://www.uua.org/action/statements/support-black-lives-matter-movement; Bob Allen, "Statement Applauds American Baptists' Contributions to Civil Rights," *Baptist News*, March 17, 2015, https://baptistnews.com/article/statement-applauds-american-baptists-contributions-to-civil-rights; General Assembly of the Christian Church (Disciples of Christ) "Resolution 1518—Black Lives Matter: A Movement for All," Christian Church (Disciples of Christ) in the United States and Canada, April 27, 2015, https://ga.disciples.org/resolutions/2015/1518-black-lives-matter-a-movement-for-all; "The Power of the Black Lives Matter Banner," Side with Love, accessed July 29, 2018, https://sidewithlove.org/the-power-of-the-black-lives-matter-banner; Kenny Wiley, "Black Lives Matter Banner 'Brings Out Conversation,'" *UU World*, Summer 2015, https://www.uuworld.org/articles/blm-banner-brings-out-conversation; Kenny Wiley, "Five Ways to Support Black Lives Matter," *UU World*, Winter 2015, https://www.uuworld.org/articles/5-ways-support-black-lives-matter.

67. Quote taken from "#BlackLivesMatter Leader DeRay McKesson Brings Race Justice Conversation to YDS," Yale Divinity School News, October 7, 2015, https://divinity.yale.edu/news/blacklivesmatter-leader-deray-mckesson-brings-race-justice-conversation-yds. On the contested relationship between black churches and clergy and the Black Lives Matter movement, see Angel Jennings, "Why the Bedrocks of L.A.'s Civil Rights Movement Won't Embrace Black Lives Matter," *Los Angeles Times*, August 29, 2016; Adelle M. Banks, "A Movement with a Theology: Churches Take Many Paths to Address Black Lives Matter," *Harvard Divinity Bulletin*, 45, no. 1-2 (Spring/Summer 2017); Brown, "The Movement for Black Lives vs. the Black Church"; Kevin C. Winstead, "Black Catholicism and Black Lives Matter: The Process towards Joining a Movement," *Ethnic and Racial Studies* 40, no. 11 (2017): 1855–

63; John Eligon, "Where Today's Black Church Leaders Stand on Activism," *New York Times*, April 3, 2018.

68. The annual Gallup surveys on religious preference are available online on the Gallup, Trends A-Z website, http://news.gallup.com/poll/1690/religion.aspx.

69. "America's Changing Religious Landscape," Pew Research Center, Religion and Public Life, May 12, 2015, http://www.pewforum.org/2015/05/12/americas-changing-religious-landscape.

70. David Masci, "5 Facts about the Religious Lives of African Americans," Pew Research Center, Fact Tank, February 7, 2018, http://www.pewresearch.org/fact-tank/2018/02/07/5-facts-about-the-religious-lives-of-african-americans.

71. Daniel Cox and Robert P. Jones, "America's Changing Religious Identity," Public Religion Research Institute (PRRI), June 9, 2017, https://www.prri.org/research/american-religious-landscape-christian-religiously-unaffiliated.

72. "America's Changing Religious Landscape," Pew Research Center, Religion and Public Life, May 12, 2015, http://www.pewforum.org/2015/05/12/americas-changing-religious-landscape.

73. On the role of clergy and churches in the Ferguson movement, see Ransby, *Making All Black Lives Matter*, 60–61, 64, 72; Gunning Francis, *Ferguson and Faith*.

74. Sinitiere, "Religion and the Black Freedom Struggle for Sandra Bland," 210.

75. Lottie Joiner, "Bree Newsome Reflects on Taking down South Carolina's Confederate Flag 2 Years Ago," *Vox*, June 27, 2017, https://www.vox.com/identities/2017/6/27/15880052/bree-newsome-south-carolinas-confederate-flag. On Newsome's faith, see Wesley Lowery, *They Can't Kill Us All: Ferguson, Baltimore, and a New Era in America's Racial Justice Movement* (New York: Little, Brown and Company, 2016), 168–84; Lloyd, "How Religious Is #BlackLivesMatter?," 227–29.

76. Douglas, *Stand Your Ground*; Lloyd et al., "Religion, Secularism, and Black Lives Matter"; Johnson, "Black Lives Matter and the Black Church"; Floyd-Thomas, "'A Relatively New Discovery in the Modern West'"; Lloyd, "How Religious Is #BlackLivesMatter?," 225–27.

77. Hebah Farrag, "The Spirit in Black Lives Matter: New Spiritual Community in Black Radical Organizing," *Transition* 125 (2017): 76–88; Lloyd, "How Religious Is #BlackLivesMatter?," 224.

CHAPTER 3

MOVE, Mourning, and Memory

Richard Kent Evans

"The condition of black life," wrote Claudia Rankine in a widely read and influential 2015 essay in the *New York Times Magazine*, "is one of mourning." A few months before Rankine's essay appeared, Sandra Bland was found dead in her jail cell. In June, Dylan Roof, a twenty-one-year-old white supremacist, murdered nine members of Emanuel African Methodist Episcopal Church as they worshipped. The previous year witnessed the deaths of Eric Garner, Tamir Rice, Michael Brown, Laquan McDonald, and many others. As a movement of historical proportions gathered steam in the streets of Ferguson, New Orleans, and the Bronx, Rankine called for "a sustained state of national mourning for black lives"—one that includes reckoning with painful histories. She challenged us to read the chants of "black lives matter," and "I can't breathe" as dirges, as songs of collective suffering, and as invitations to mourn.[1]

Collective mourning—what Black Lives Matter challenges us to do—is an exercise in historical memory. Assigning agency and victimhood is crucial to the performance of the production of history. In that moment when what happened becomes what is said to have happened, those with the power to form historical narratives often determine whose lives should be mourned, and whose should not. If the state is essentially a relationship of domination made possible by violence-deemed-legitimate, then determining who is the agent and who is the victim is essential to the legitimation of that founding violence. Black Lives Matter is an exhortation to artists, activists, and historians to revisit the racial violence of our nation's past and revive the humanity so often obscured by that violence—to show that, as Rankine noted, "history's authority over us is not broken by maintaining a silence about its continued effects."[2]

How should historians approach our work in the wake of Black Lives Matter? How are we to approach these matrixes of mourning, history, and memory—of lives destroyed, forgotten, and buried? Saidiya Hartman, in her work on the legacies of the Atlantic slave trade, offers us a meditation on the paradoxes historians face when we do our work. For those of us who work on the history of racial violence, the archives are often a "death sentence, a tomb, a display of the violated body . . . an asterisk in the grand narrative of history."[3] It can be difficult to sift through the detritus of the archives, the sometimes brutal, most often numbing, banal, and bureaucratic records generated by those with power to shape our understanding of the past, to find the humanity buried therein, to find the stories of lives, of religion, of belief and practice, faith and family beneath mountains of ballistics reports, depositions, and investigation summaries. Even if we succeed—even if we recover the lives buried in the archives—how do we tell their stories? How do we faithfully recreate lives from archives built to erase them? How, as Joseph Winters explores in this volume, do we affirm the lives that might otherwise go unmourned and ungrieved?[4] How do we use the past to "describe obliquely the forms of violence licensed in the present" without subjecting the "dead to new dangers and to a second order of violence?"[5] It was with these questions in mind that I entered the archive of the MOVE bombing during that turbulent summer of 2015.

MOVE is a small religious movement that emerged in 1972 around the prophetic writings and embodied teachings of John Africa.[6] John Africa was born Vincent Leaphart in 1931. He grew up in West Philadelphia in a large, working-class, African American family, the fourth

of ten children. Leaphart had a learning disorder and was function-
ally illiterate. He dropped out of school at sixteen, having completed
only through the third grade. He never held a steady career but made
ends meet with a variety of odd jobs. In 1952, when he was twenty,
Leaphart was drafted into the Army and served a tour of duty in
Korea. After the war, he spent a decade bouncing between Philadelphia, New York, and Atlantic City, finding work wherever he could.
In 1961, he married Dorothy Clark. The marriage was unhappy and,
at times, violent. The two could not have children, which was a great
disappointment to them both. In the late 1960s, Vincent Leaphart
began to retreat from the world. He ended most of his relationships,
including his marriage, disposed of most of his possessions, and
holed up in a second floor apartment in Powelton Village. When he
came down from that apartment, he emerged as John Africa, a figure MOVE people describe as "a supreme being." Soon, he attracted
a small band of converts, mostly African Americans in their twenties. A good number of those initial converts were blood relatives of
Vincent Leaphart. They adopted the surname "Africa" to mark their
new religious commitments.

John Africa taught that the natural world is perfect in essence
but has been corrupted by humankind. Human invention produced
what John Africa called the system—a supernatural, evil force that
includes but supersedes human institutions like government, law,
and economics. The system holds humankind, and all the natural
world, in captivity. Only by following the teachings of John Africa
can one escape the system and live in true harmony with God in
nature. That is what John Africa offered his followers, and that is
what MOVE people were, and are, trying to do.[7]

MOVE has never been a particularly large organization. At its
first peak in the mid-1970s, there were around fifty MOVE people—
a category that includes both devoted, exclusive MOVE members
and more casual supporters. Around twenty of them shared a house
in Powelton. From its earliest days, MOVE operated under the sus-
picion of law enforcement. The city's Civil Disobedience Squad
(later renamed the Civil Affairs Unit) began surveilling the group
as early as 1972.[8] MOVE's relationship with the police worsened as

MOVE people considered the surveillance to be oppressive and an unconstitutional infringement upon their freedom to practice their religion. In the summer of 1974, the city of Philadelphia granted its police department an injunction barring MOVE from gathering to protest near any government buildings. Because of the injunction, over the next two years, law enforcement arrested MOVE people over four hundred times.[9] From MOVE's founding to the summer of 1976, MOVE was not unusual; similar groups sprang up in droves in the tumult of the late 1960s and early 1970s.

MOVE's story is untellable without addressing the MOVE bombing. On May 13, 1985, local, state, and federal law enforcement collaborated to drop a bomb on a house that MOVE people shared. The bomb caused a fire, which officials chose to let burn in order to force out those who were inside. When the survivors tried to escape the flames, they were met with police gunfire, forcing some of them back inside. Thirteen people were in the house, many of them children. Eleven died, five of them children.

Like many historical episodes of racial violence, the MOVE bombing is notable for how thoroughly it has been forgotten. It is not a part of our national narrative. Indeed, many news articles written to mark another anniversary of the MOVE bombing allude incredulously to the fact that so few people, especially outside the city of Philadelphia, seem to know about it.[10] Why has the MOVE bombing been forgotten? Claudia Rankine's article provides a clue: I suspect the reason the MOVE bombing was largely forgotten was because it was unclear to many who deserved to be mourned. In the immediate aftermath of the MOVE bombing, government officials and the media went to work teaching Americans how they should understand the trauma they witnessed on their televisions, whom they should hold responsible, and whose lives they ought to mourn. Americans were taught not to mourn MOVE people. They were taught that MOVE people were responsible for their own deaths, that they had sacrificed their children to a self-evidently false theology. Americans were taught that the MOVE bombing was unavoidable—a tragedy, yes, but one devoid of agency.

The MOVE bombing was not unavoidable. It was the end of a long chain of events that began on March 28, 1976. That morning, a physical altercation between MOVE and several police officers occurred in the front of the MOVE house. When the smoke cleared, MOVE people discovered that six-week-old Life Africa was dead—crushed beneath his mother, who had been knocked down by a police officer. The death of Life Africa changed MOVE. It transformed their theology, repositioned their movement within a cosmic drama, and set them on a trajectory that culminated in the MOVE bombing. Persecution has a way of galvanizing a religious movement. In MOVE's case, what they viewed as a sustained campaign of police harassment, followed by the murder of a MOVE infant, convinced them that the system was out to exterminate MOVE in order to destroy the teachings of John Africa and the threat they posed to systems of domination.[11]

After the death of Life Africa, MOVE holed up in their Powelton Village home, refusing to surrender to police. The standoff went on for months, and the Philadelphia Police Department [PPD] erected a blockade of the MOVE house, preventing food and water from going through in order to "starve them out."[12] The standoff ended on August 8, 1978, when the PPD launched an assault on the house. MOVE people began shooting (though MOVE people claim, to this day, that the police shot first), and a violent confrontation began. When the dust settled, hours later, the MOVE people in the house had been arrested, and a police officer—James Ramp—had been killed by a bullet to the head.[13] Incensed at the death of their colleague, police were caught on news cameras beating Conrad Africa with their metal helmets and batons. Ballistics evidence shows the four men were the only ones in the MOVE house who had fired weapons that day.[14] Still, all nine MOVE people in the house were sent to prison for the murder of Officer James Ramp.[15] MOVE people contend that the MOVE Nine were convicted unjustly.[16]

The remaining members of MOVE, including the founder, prophet, and spiritual leader, John Africa, went into hiding in Philadelphia, Pennsylvania, Rochester, New York, and Richmond, Virginia. Federal law enforcement, especially the FBI and the ATF, located the MOVE contingent in Rochester and arrested all the members there, including John Africa.[17] In 1981, federal prosecutors took John Africa to trial on charges of conspiring to manufacture and possess explosives in a plot to blow up federal government buildings.[18] John Africa represented himself and was acquitted of all charges, returning to Philadelphia to rebuild his religion. However, it was not to be.

On May 30, 1984—nearly a year before the MOVE bombing—FBI field office head in Philadelphia John Hogan, Secret Service head Kevin Tucker, and representatives from the Justice Department met with mayor Wilson Goode, district attorney Ed Rendell, city manager Leo Brooks, state police commissioner Robert Armstrong, and city solicitor Barbara Mather to discuss legal grounds for raiding the house. They found none. The Secret Service had investigated MOVE's threats against President Reagan and found them to be too vague to prosecute. Neither the FBI nor the Justice Department could think of a justifiable reason to storm the house or to remove the children. There were no outstanding federal or state warrants.[19] Despite having no legal reason to raid the house, after that meeting police commissioner Gregor Sambor began drawing up plans for an offensive against the occupants of the MOVE house on Osage Avenue. The plan they created involved the use of explosives, delivered either by construction crane or helicopter, to force MOVE to surrender.[20] On August 8, 1984, the Philadelphia Police Department, still without legal pretense, gathered outside the MOVE house to put the plan into effect. All they needed to begin the assault was one gunshot from MOVE. MOVE did not take the bait. After waiting for several hours, the police packed up and went home.[21]

Nine months later, the police tried again. On May 13, 1985, around three hundred police officers and firefighters gathered outside of a house that MOVE people shared on Osage Avenue in West Philadelphia. There were thirteen MOVE people inside: John Africa, six other adult MOVE people, and six children ranging in age from nine to fourteen. When the police force outside was ready, Police Commissioner Gregor Sambor announced over a bullhorn, "Attention, MOVE. This is America. You have to follow the laws of the United States." Sambor listed the outstanding warrants and told the MOVE people inside that they had fifteen minutes to evacuate the house before the police would move in. The adults, who had slept in the same room as the children that night in anticipation of the attack, hurried the children down two stories to the basement. Ramona Africa, the only MOVE adult to survive the day, took to the bullhorn and told Sambor to go fuck himself.[22]

From an upstairs window, Raymond Africa, Frank Africa, and John Africa took up arms against the police outside, waging a futile defensive in a conflict they believed to be of cosmic proportions.[23] The police responded by firing more than ten thousand rounds into the MOVE house over the course of ninety minutes, using Uzi submachine guns, shotguns, Thompson submachine guns, sniper rifles, and M-16s—weapons that they had acquired from the FBI and the ATF for the purposes of the raid.[24] At around 8:30 in the morning, police officers outside began throwing bundles of C-4 (a powerful and highly flammable explosive that the PPD had acquired from the FBI for the purposes of the raid) and Tovex at the MOVE house. The first bomb destroyed the front porch. A second bomb, thrown around 10:40 in the morning, blew the front wall off the house, killing John Africa and destroying the stairs leading to the basement. There was no shooting from the MOVE house after that. Hours later, at 5:20 p.m., a member of the PPD's Bomb Disposal Unit dropped a third bomb from a state police helicopter onto the roof of the MOVE house. The bomb created a fireball that reached over seven thousand degrees Fahrenheit and caused a concussion felt blocks away. What was left of the roof burst into flames immediately. The fire department, on site to support the police action, turned off the large water cannons that had been running all day. Within minutes, the fire began to spread throughout the MOVE house and across the roof to the adjacent houses. As the fire grew, Sambor and fire commissioner William Richmond discussed what to do about it. Sambor decided to let the fire burn. He could use the fire as a tactical weapon. If the water, tear gas, bombs, and gunfire could not drive MOVE out of the house, perhaps fire could.[25]

As the fire spread above them, the MOVE people inside the house decided to surrender. According to Birdie Africa's testimony, the water in the basement that MOVE people had been wading in all day began to grow hot. Conrad Africa lit a match to try to find out what was going on. They realized that the haze in the air wasn't tear gas anymore, but smoke. The house was on fire. The heat grew more and more intense. Conrad used a monkey wrench to unlatch the door to the rear of the house and announced that the children were coming out. His announcement was answered with a volley of gunfire. He waited for the shooting to die down and tried again. Conrad, Ramona, and Rhonda Africa repeatedly tried to tell the police that they were sending the children out, but each time they tried to step out of the garage, the police opened fire.[26] Eventually, one adult, Ramona Africa, and one child, Birdie Africa, managed to escape. Everyone else died in the house. Remains from one of the children—examiners were unable to determine who, though it was likely nine-year-old Tomaso Africa—contained buckshot pellets from a police shotgun.[27] Birdie did not remember anything after he bolted through the flames out of the house, but a press photographer captured a picture of him sitting in the back of the police van. He was naked, gasping for air, and burned over much of his body. Ramona was arrested in the back alley on charges of inciting a riot. She was taken to the hospital for her burns but refused treatment. Fire fighters lost control of the fire, which eventually burned the entire city block, destroying sixty-four houses.[28]

The day after the bombing, the nation awoke to confusing and bewildering reports coming out of Philadelphia, mostly based on Goode's initial press conference. The morning *Chicago Tribune* reported that MOVE and the police had been involved in a protracted gun battle which lasted all day and into the night, and that the battle culminated in police dropping a bomb onto the MOVE house, causing a fire. The *Tribune* reported that "at least four members of the radical group, which calls itself MOVE, emerged from the inferno" and continued firing upon police officers. The shootout, combined with "a severe lack of water pressure," prevented the fire department from extinguishing the fire before it was too late.[29] The report in the *Chicago Tribune* was typical of one line of storytelling to emerge from the MOVE bombing: MOVE had been heavily armed and shooting at the police nearly all day. The police used an explosive device to dislodge a bunker on the roof, causing an unexpected fire. The fire forced at least some of the MOVE people outside where they continued their gun battle with police, preventing firefighters from extinguishing the flames. However, as early as the morning of the fourteenth, a second account of events began to emerge—one based on at-the-scene interviews rather than Goode's press conference. The *New York Times*, for example, reported that the police responded to shooting at around six in the morning, and that MOVE and the police traded gunfire for ninety minutes. Most of the day, they reported, there was no activity at the MOVE house at all—at least nothing that the bystanders and press members observed from several blocks away.[30]

While reporters struggled to determine the series of events, city officials offered a narrative for framing the MOVE bombing that positioned MOVE as the perpetrators and their neighbors as the victims. On May 14, 1985, mayor Wilson Goode, police commissioner Gregor Sambor, and fire commissioner William Richmond gave a joint press conference. This time, Goode read a prepared statement meant to "put the tragic events of the past two days in perspective." Goode told his citizens that MOVE was "a group dedicated to the destruction of our way of life." He reminded them that MOVE killed a police officer in 1978. Goode's message to the press was that the neighbors whose homes burned were the victims of the MOVE bombing—not MOVE, not even the MOVE children. The police commissioner explained that the bomb dropped from the helicopter was a two-pound bundle of Tovex explosive and alleged that "there would never have been any fire unless it was assisted by some inflammatory material." He was insinuating that Ramona Africa had poured gasoline onto the roof of the house in anticipation of the bomb—something she had threatened to do over the bullhorn. Sambor insisted that the "plan was a good one." He explained that MOVE had heavily fortified their row home. Aside from the "bunker" on the roof, they had brought in large tree trunks to reinforce the walls. He also speculated that MOVE people had dug a system of tunnels beneath the house, which they could have used to escape into the neighborhood. Perhaps most importantly, the officials reiterated their belief that MOVE people "were prepared to die, to go on a suicide mission." Even so, Sambor insisted, "as far as we're concerned" the planned raid presented "no possible danger to the children."[31]

Goode's reframing of the MOVE bombing as an unavoidable tragedy, with the neighbors as the victims, proved influential. In the days after the bombing, a few newspapers ran the photograph of Birdie Africa in the police van. Others ran photographs of Ramona Africa surrendering to police. But the majority of news accounts of the MOVE bombing ran several photographs taken by news helicopters that showed the entire 6200 block of Osage Avenue—sixty-four houses in all—decimated by fire. Both the *New York Times* and *Time* magazine ran photos of the burned-out block on their covers. For the time being, the neighbors whose homes had been destroyed provided sympathetic victims. If the public could not mourn for MOVE people, they could sympathize with the neighbors whose houses burned.[32]

Within a few days, news trickled out that bodies had been discovered in the rubble. City officials used cranes to knock down the remaining walls so that they would not collapse on investigators. But this piled yet another layer of rubble onto the bodies they were trying to recover. Investigators brought in large claw machines to clear the debris, which only further destroyed the bodies—many of which were already charred beyond recognition. Once the wreckage cooled, federal and local forensics teams sifted through the rubble, separated human bones from dog bones, and pieced together fragments of burned bodies. The process took weeks, but they eventually found the remains of eleven people. John Africa had died early in the day, probably from the second bomb blast. Examiners were unable to provide a positive identification, as only a burned torso remained. Frank Africa and Raymond Africa had died either from the same bomb or from police gunfire shortly thereafter. There was no smoke or ash in the remains of their lungs, indicating that they were dead before the fire. Conrad Africa, Rhonda Africa, and Theresa Africa died sometime after the final bomb, either from gunshot wounds, smoke inhalation, or the flames. The children—Sue Africa's nine-year-old son, Tomaso; Consuella Africa's two daughters, Zanetta and Tree, thirteen and fourteen; Jeanine and Phil Africa's ten-year-old son, Phil; and Delbert and Janet Africa's twelve-year-old daughter, Delisha—died in the basement.[33]

Once it became clear that several of the victims of the MOVE bombing had been children, journalists, activists, and religious leaders began to construct a new narrative of the MOVE bombing—one that contrasted the culpability of the MOVE adults with the innocence of the children. On May 15, several national newspapers reported that six bodies had been recovered from the rubble, at least two of them children. Within a week, the body count was up to eleven, four of them children. It took nearly six months for investigators to determine that five children and six adults had died. Responding to the news, Gregory Williams, a child psychiatrist, wrote an essay in which he pondered a broader lack of empathy toward children within American culture. He wrote about how he was raised "a Baptist Protestant Christian" but had lost his faith as he "wondered, with great philosophical concern and anxiety," whether God would have damned him to hell merely for being born into the wrong religion— something that he had no control over. Williams, like the MOVE children, had been "indoctrinated with views" that he never chose. Like the children of MOVE, he and the countless other children that were taught God had damned them to hell were "innocent victims" to their parents' ideologies. Who could believe in a God, Williams wondered, who would "wantonly cause the death and suffering of what [he] considered innocent children?" But, to Williams, society was as cruel as this false God. Clearly, he reasoned, "we do not unambivalently love children." If we did, the state would have removed the MOVE children years ago. According to Williams, "the adult members of MOVE have been labeled by us as being pathologically dangerous or emotionally ill," and "to shackle one's children with an archaic system of magical beliefs of superiority and omnipotence hardly prepares them for a future world." For those reasons, it was "our responsibilities as citizens in a democracy" to remove the MOVE children from MOVE long before their lives were ever put at risk.[34]

Many people in Philadelphia and around the country echoed Williams's sentiment. In the weeks that followed the bombing, the American Friends Service Committee (AFSC) devised a series of projects that shaped the way the broader public understood the MOVE bombing. Their first major undertaking, begun four months after the bombing, was the Philadelphia Perspectives Project, in which AFSC staffers conducted in-depth one-on-one interviews with people living in and around Philadelphia to gauge their reactions to the MOVE bombing. To find their respondents, staff members at the AFSC cold-called Philadelphians and asked them a series of questions ranking their knowledge of MOVE and the MOVE bombing, the strength of their opinions, and their willingness to participate in an interview. AFSC staffers conducted interviews with those who ranked highly on the phone questionnaire, either at the AFSC offices downtown or at the respondents' homes. The Philadelphia Perspectives Project gathered audiotapes and produced transcripts from interviews with forty-five people. Though the Philadelphia Perspectives Project made no pretensions of being a scientific poll, the respondents were a relatively close sampling of the Philadelphia community. They interviewed twenty-four African Americans and thirteen whites. Five respondents identified as Hispanic, and three as Asian. Twenty-six of the respondents were female. Many of the respondents requested anonymity, and some asked to review the transcripts to make sure there was no identifying information. The interviews were generalized into a report called "Voices from the Community," which the AFSC made available to the press.[35]

Almost all of the respondents believed that the MOVE adults in the house were culpable for—and even welcomed—their own deaths. A forty-eight-year-old African American man who worked as a mail carrier placed "ninety-nine and nine tenths of the blame on MOVE." He believed it was "disgraceful how they carried on" and suggested that he "might have punched a few of them" if he'd had the chance. He told the interviewer that he was not surprised when he learned of the MOVE bombing, "for the simple reason, anyone who would go to any length to force their ideas and their way of living on someone else" invites violent conflict. "This is what they wanted. Total destruction . . . they were just a form of a cult, a form of terror." A Black man in his late sixties was reluctant to say conclusively that MOVE intended to die on May thirteenth, but did say that suicidal behavior was not out of character for groups like MOVE who were "willing to die for their cause. People, more recently in Jonestown come to my mind."[36]

A second point on which most of the respondents agreed was that the children were not MOVE people, but innocent victims held captive to MOVE. A middle-aged white man, who worked as a chef and lived in West Philadelphia, told his interviewer that "one thing I could never conceive of is . . . adults keeping their children, you know, forcing them into staying and living that type of life." Another respondent agreed that the MOVE children should not be thought of in the same category as the adults. "As an adult you have options. You choose how you want to live. You choose what your beliefs and your creeds are. The children don't." Another respondent lamented that the MOVE children "didn't have the say whether they should stay with these people." A couple of respondents dissented from the view that the children were not authentically religious people. A white housewife in her late thirties rejected her interviewer's suggestion that the children were "hostages" to MOVE. "That's totally alien to me," she said. "Whatever I am, my children are. I'm of a different religious persuasion. My children were reared in this religious persuasion also. I was questioned very often about this by the community. 'Why do your children do so and so?' And then I would say, 'Well, don't your children follow your ways? Why is it that my children shouldn't follow mine?' To this respondent, MOVE was "their own little community. The children need the parents and the parents need the children."[37]

A third point on which most of the respondents agreed was that the MOVE adults martyred their children and that they, not the government, were ultimately responsible for their deaths. A white schoolteacher in her early thirties said that she "felt the city's hopelessness." MOVE, she thought "were willing to sacrifice children, they weren't going to even let the children out of the house. And that, to me—I'm a child advocate, and that was the very horrendous, not even pathetic—it was just a horrendous thing to do." She agreed with many of the respondents that MOVE adults wanted "to be a martyr," but that, as a decent human being, you "don't take the children with you." The forty-eight-year-old mail carrier voiced a common

theme. "Who would board their wives and children inside a building
. . . would have open warfare with police?" he asked. "They have no
respect for children. So as far as their children getting killed or their
way of life to be a martyr, it didn't surprise me." Another respondent
believed that the children "were a sacrificial lamb," that "they just
happened to be caught in the middle," and that "they were victims.
Victims of a cause."[38]

The construction of this narrative of the MOVE bombing, in
which the MOVE children were hostages caught in the crossfire of an
unavoidable conflict, shifted some of the blame for their deaths away
from political leaders, but city leaders were not altogether spared
from criticism. New York City mayor Ed Koch made national news
when he trashed Philadelphia's handling of the situation, saying that
he would fire a police commissioner on the spot if he presented such
a "stupid" idea.[39] City politicians and community leaders began calling for resignations. City manager Leo Brooks announced his resig-
nation on June 3, effective at the end of the month. He attempted
to distance himself from the decision to drop the bomb by telling
reporters that he was out of town visiting his parents in Virginia the
week before the raid.[40] Police Commissioner Gregor Sambor resigned
on November 13 in a tearful speech at the police academy. He com-
plained to reporters on his way out of office that Mayor Goode had
forced him to resign, a claim that Goode denied. Fire commissioner
William Richmond had been considering leaving the fire department
prior to the MOVE bombing. At the urging of his family and the
mayor, he chose to stay on until his retirement in 1988.[41]

Wilson Goode received much less criticism than either Sambor
or Brooks. *Time* magazine polled Philadelphians weeks after the
bombing and found that 71 percent thought the mayor "had done a
good or excellent job handling the MOVE confrontation."[42] Partly,
Goode's initial support was due to the loyalty of Philadelphia's African Americans, who supported the city's first Black mayor at levels
approaching one hundred percent. Though the MOVE Commission
report placed the blame for the MOVE bombing squarely on the
mayor's shoulders as the city's chief executive, Goode was reelected
to a second term as mayor in 1987, fighting off district attorney Ed

Rendell in the primary and defeating Frank Rizzo in the general election. James Berghaier, the police officer who rescued Birdie after he collapsed in the rear alleyway, left the police department after he was subjected to harassment for what he had done. In one instance, his colleagues wrote "nigger lover" on his locker.[43]

The only person to be charged with a crime relating to the MOVE bombing was Ramona Africa. She faced trial on three counts of aggravated assault, three counts of recklessly endangering another person, and one count of criminal conspiracy to riot. Ramona represented herself in court. A jury acquitted her on the assault and reckless endangerment charges, but found her guilty of conspiracy to riot. A juror told reporters that the jury was "trying to make a statement in the decision that both parties were wrong, MOVE and the city." The prosecutor announced after the trial that the verdict was a "compromise." Ramona Africa was sentenced to a minimum of five months and a maximum of seven years in prison. She was eligible for parole for most of her sentence, under the condition that she sever all ties to MOVE. She refused, served all seven years of her sentence, and returned to MOVE upon her release.[44]

The story that government officials crafted in the wake of the MOVE bombing—that MOVE themselves and no one else were culpable for their own deaths—has proven influential. In 2017, the Pennsylvania Historical and Museum Commission, after years of avoiding the issue, erected a historical marker at the location of the MOVE bombing. The marker read:

> On May 13, 1985, at 6221 Osage Avenue, an armed conflict occurred between the Phila. Police Dept. and MOVE members. A Pa. State Police helicopter dropped a bomb on MOVE's house. An uncontrolled fire killed eleven MOVE members, including five children, and destroyed 61 homes.

The marker does not speak the truth, except to say that something happened here that people aren't quite ready to deal with. The vague wording deflects attention away from the actions of those responsible. "An armed conflict occurred. . . ." A "helicopter dropped a bomb. . . ." "An uncontrolled fire killed. . . ." One could read that sign and believe that what happened on Osage Avenue on May 13, 1985, was an act of nature. And that is precisely the point. The history of the MOVE bombing was carefully crafted so that we would not know who to mourn. Those with the power to shape the process of historical narration ensured that there would be no mourning, no remembering, no victims of the MOVE bombing except, perhaps, the neighbors whose homes burned down.[45]

Despite the influence this story has had, it is beginning to change. Since 2015, a new generation of activists, artists, and scholars—many of whom were not yet born in 1985—have found in the MOVE bombing a powerful simulacrum for how racism functions through state violence. They see in the MOVE bombing an eerily familiar pattern: the state kills Black people, then blames them for their own destruction. The MOVE bombing, once a forgotten footnote in American history, is becoming a powerful symbol in the Black Lives Matter movement.

The MOVE bombing serves as a powerful symbol in a new opera titled "*We Shall Not Be Moved*," which opened in Philadelphia in September of 2017 before moving to the Apollo Theater in New York and the Hackney Empire in London. Created by composer Daniel Bernard Roumain and librettist Marc Bamuthi Joseph, and directed and choreographed by Bill T. Jones, "*We Shall Not Be Moved*" follows a group of five teenagers from North Philadelphia who, orphaned with nowhere else to go, find refuge in an abandoned house that sits on the site of the MOVE house on Osage that burned in 1985. The teens—four of them are named John, an allusion to John Africa—form a family unit together in that house and escape their lives of broken families, underfunded and closed schools, and street violence. But they are not alone. The house is haunted by the children who died in the MOVE bombing, who see the teens' taking up residence in the home "as a matter of destiny and resistance." However, a police officer named Glenda, who, like the teens in the house, grew up in North Philadelphia, discovers their hideout and threatens to arrest the makeshift family. Act one closes with Glenda accidentally firing her sidearm, injuring one of the teens, John Henry. The rest of the teens overpower Glenda and handcuff her to a chair.[46]

In act two, the teens try to decide what to do with Glenda and with John Henry, who lies bleeding on the floor. They worry that if they let Glenda go, she will have them arrested before they can get John Henry to a doctor. It is at this moment of indecision that the ghosts "infuse the home with a spirituality that is palpably felt by the young people in particular." Inspired by the spirits of the MOVE children, the teens tell Glenda their backstories in hopes that she will understand their plight and her own. However, in the process of telling their stories, Glenda learns that it was one of the teens, John Blue, who killed her brother. In act three, the teens decide that the only way to solve their problem is to "disappear" Glenda. One of the teens, named Un/Sung, attacks Glenda, though the audience is left to decide for themselves whether Glenda is dead. In the closing scene, the teens use candles to set fire to the house they shared. "The image is not of arson, but of ritual." The teens have turned the home "into an altar, perhaps an instrument of forgiving, of letting go, of release, and of renewal." As the opera ends, "the last remaining image on stage is of the skeleton of a house, lit up like a shrine, while the [ghosts] move around it in holy rites."[47]

"We Shall Not Be Moved" is a meditation on Black Lives Matter, about religion's role in that movement, and about the ways the past continues to haunt the present. But the opera also performs the historical mourning that Black Lives Matter demands. When the characters build a family in that home, they enter an archive of racial violence. The presence of the ghosts of the MOVE children erases the boundaries between past and present. The problems the teens face—police brutality, street violence, broken homes—are the same problems that drew people to MOVE in the 1970s. Like historians of racial violence, the characters are unsure how best to tell the stories of the lives lost in that archive. The opera is not an attempt to revive the past to inform the present. It is not a celebration of progress. It is not a happy story; it is, rather, deeply ambivalent. Violence begets violence, mourning begets mourning. A house, once burned, burns again.

We must not confuse this ambivalence with defeat. Black Lives Matter is an invitation to mourn, and mourning lives destroyed by the state is profoundly radical. It is a fundamental critique of the state—of the violence that underpins it, of the violence that defines it. That is important, because as the history of MOVE shows, the inability to mourn lives is an invitation to forget that they existed, that they were destroyed. It is to be complicit in erasure. When we ask whose lives should be mourned, we are making a historical claim. This is why people fight so hard to deny victimhood to those killed by police. It is why reactionary voices strain to remind us that the dead were "no angels." They are begging us not to grieve, to avoid the humanity lying on the street. They are begging us not to see those who died as lives that should be mourned.

It is not the historian's job to make moral claims, and I won't. But it is the historian's job to tell the truth about the past—to assign agency where it belongs, even when it hurts; to uncover the humanity buried beneath the archive; to "[redress] the violence that produced numbers, ciphers, and fragments of discourse."[48] It is the historian's job—now more than ever—to show that "history's authority over us is not broken by maintaining a silence about its continued effects."[49]

NOTES

1. Claudia Rankine, "The Condition of Black Life Is One of Mourning," *New York Times Magazine*, June 22, 2015, https://www.nytimes.com/2015/06/22/magazine/the-condition-of-black-life-is-one-of-mourning.html.

2. Rankine, "The Condition of Black Life."

3. Saidiya Hartman, "Venus in Two Acts," *Small Axe* 26 (June 2008): 2.

4. Joseph Winters, "Death, Spirituality, and the Matter of Blackness."

5. Hartman, "Venus in Two Acts," 5.

6. The best record of John Africa's life comes from his sister. See Louise Leaphart James, *John Africa . . . Childhood Untold until Today* (self-pub., Xlibris, 2016).

7. Richard Kent Evans, *MOVE: An American Religion* (New York: Oxford University Press, 2020).

8. Philadelphia Special Investigation Commission, Examination of Officers Cresse and Draper of Civil Affairs, October 8, 1985, Box 19, Records of the Philadelphia Special Investigation (MOVE) Commission, Urban Archives and Special Collections, Temple University, Philadelphia, PA.

9. MOVE, untitled document, undated [calculated between June 25 and July 24, 1974] Box 91a, Folder 1, Philadelphia Yearly Meeting of the Religious Society of Friends, Friends Peace Committee, Friendly Presence Papers, Friends Historical Library, Swarthmore College, Swarthmore, PA.

10. Gene Demby, "Why Have So Many People Never Heard of the MOVE Bombing?" *Code Switch*, NPR, May 18, 2015, https://www.npr.org/sections/codeswitch/2015/05/18/407665820/why-did-we-forget-the-move-bombing.

11. MOVE published their version of what happened on March 28, 1978, in a series of newspaper articles. See Louise Africa, "On the MOVE," *Philadelphia Tribune*, April 9, 1976; Louise Africa, "On the MOVE," *Philadelphia Tribune*, April 10, 1976; and Linn Washington, "MOVE Says Mth.-Old Baby Killed in Clash With Police," *Philadelphia Tribune*, March 30, 1976.

12. "City Agrees to Starve MOVE Out," *Philadelphia Daily News*, July 11, 1977; Powelton Emergency Human Rights Committee, "Open Letter to Mayor Frank L. Rizzo," Box General Admin., Folder 3423, Philadelphia Police Abuse Project, Philadelphia Surveillance Program, American Friends Research Center, Philadelphia, PA.

13. Perhaps the most detailed retelling of the events of August 8, 1978, and of those leading up to it, can be found in an unpublished memoir written by a Catholic priest who was in the MOVE house negotiating minutes before the shooting began. See Msgr. Charles Devlin, *I Am Ready and Willing . . . with the Help of God: A Portrait of the Priesthood as Seen through Icons of Ministry and Service by a Priest—One among Many*, unpublished manuscript, Cardinal's Commission on Human Relations Files, Philadelphia Archdiocesan Research Center, Wynnewood, PA.

14. Federal Bureau of Investigation, Lab Report, September 8, 1978, Box 8, Folder 5, Records of the Philadelphia Special Investigation (MOVE) Commission, Urban Archives and Special Collections, Temple University, Philadelphia, PA.

15. Joyce Gemperlein, "9 in MOVE Get 30 Years for Killing," *Philadelphia Inquirer*, August 5, 1981.

16. John Africa to Conrad Africa, Box 5, Folder "MOVE Writings," Philadelphia Special Investigation (MOVE) Commission Records, Urban Archives and Special Collections, Temple University, Philadelphia, PA.

17. Sue Africa, transcript of an oral history conducted 2017 by Richard Kent Evans, MOVE Oral History Project, Special Collections and Urban Archives, Temple University, Philadelphia, PA; Ashley Halsey, "Tracing the Movements of MOVE Group in Hiding," *Philadelphia Inquirer*, May 17, 1981; Mumia Abu-Jamal, "MOVE Hid in Plain Sight," *Philadelphia Tribune*, June 19, 1981; Ashley Halsey, "Tracing the Movements of MOVE Group in Hiding," *Philadelphia Inquirer*, May 17, 1981; Ashley Halsey, "Founder of MOVE and 8 others, sought since '77, arrested in N.Y." *Philadelphia Inquirer*, May 14, 1981.

18. Transcripts of the trial, *United States v. Leaphart and Robbins* (1981), can be found in Boxes 66 and 67, Records of the Philadelphia Special Investigation (MOVE) Commission, Urban Archives and Special Collections, Temple University, Philadelphia, PA.

19. United States Attorney Edward S. G. Dennis to William H. Brown III, January 3, 1986, Box 7, Folder 2, PSIC; Emerson Moran to Bill Brown, January 9, 1986, Box 7, Folder 2, PSIC; Philadelphia Police Department Chronology of Meetings Attended by Major Investigation Division Intelligence Regarding MOVE, May 23, 1985, Box 51, Philadelphia Special Investigation (MOVE) Commission, Urban Archives and Special Collections, Temple University, Philadelphia, PA.

20. Philadelphia Special Investigation Commission, Interview with Police Officer Herbert Kirk, September 11, 1985, Philadelphia Special Investigation (MOVE) Commission, Urban Archives and Special Collections, Temple University, Philadelphia, PA.

21. "MOVE Staked out on 6th Anniversary: Police, Firefighters Respond to Threats on Goode's Life. Siege Ends with No Violence," *Philadelphia Tribune*, August 10, 1984.

22. My recreation of events in the house relies on witnesses who were in the house at the time. Ward Testimony, PSIC; Philadelphia Police Department Homicide Division, Investigation Interview Record, May 14, 1985, Box 63, Folder 9, PSIC; Philadelphia Police Department Homicide Division, Investigation Review Record, May 18, 1985, Box 63, Folder 9, PSIC; Ralph Teti to William Lyton, July 9, 1985, Box 63, Folder 7, PSIC [enclosure]; Philadelphia Police Department Civil Affairs Unit, Confidential Police Report, May 15, 1985, Box 63, Folder 9, PSIC; Philadelphia Police Department Juvenile Aid Division, Interview of Birdie Africa, undated, Box 63, Folder 9, PSIC.

23. There is some evidence to suggest that the police shot first; William Lyton to Emerson D. Moran, September 9, 1985, Box 8, Folder 1, PSIC.

24. Philadelphia Special Investigation Commission, The Findings, Conclusions, and Recommendations of the Philadelphia Special Investigation Commission, PSIC.

25. Testimony of Leo Brooks, PSIC; Testimony of William Richmond, PSIC; Testimony of Gregor Sambor, PSIC; Philadelphia Special Investigation Commission, The Findings, Conclusions, and Recommendations of the Philadelphia Special Investigation Commission, PSIC

26. Michael Ward Testimony, PSIC; Philadelphia Police Department Homicide Division, Investigation Interview Record, May 14, 1985, Box 63, Folder 9, PSIC; Philadelphia Police Department Homicide Division, Investigation Review Record, May 18, 1985, Box 63, Folder 9, PSIC; Ralph Teti to William Lyton, July 9, 1985, Box 63, Folder 7, PSIC [enclosure]; Philadelphia Police Department Civil Affairs Unit, Confidential Police Report, May 15, 1985, Box 63, Folder 9, PSIC; Philadelphia Police Department Juvenile Aid Division, Interview of Birdie Africa, undated, Box 63, Folder 9, PSIC.

27. According to police records, five hundred rounds of buckshot were brought to the scene, and zero were used. Autopsy records, however, show that the

remains of one child contained buckshot pellets. See Autopsy Reports, Box 50, Folder 19, PSIC.

28. Testimony of James Berghaier, PSIC; Vernon Loeb and Russell Cooke, "Goode Says He's 'Fully Accountable' for Siege," *Philadelphia Inquirer*, May 14, 1985; "The Move Siege: Chronology of Events," *Philadelphia Inquirer*, May 14, 1985.

29. "Philadelphia Inferno: Cop Attack on Radicals Backfires," *Chicago Tribune*, May 14, 1985.

30. William K. Stevens, "Police Drop Bomb on Radicals' Home in Philadelphia," *New York Times*, May 14, 1985.

31. May Lee and John J. Goldman, "6 Bodies in Rubble of Bombed House Goode Vows to Rebuild Neighborhood as He Defends Raid on Radical Cult," *Los Angeles Times*, May 15, 1985; "Goode: The Right Decision, Despite the Consequences," *Philadelphia Inquirer*, May 15, 1985.

32. Frank Trippett, Kenneth W. Banta, and Joseph N. Boyce, "It Looks Just Like a War Zone": A Police Raid in Philadelphia Turns to Tragedy," *Time* 125, no. 21 (May 27, 1985): 16; Lindsey Gruson, "Search for Bodies, and for Reason, in Smoky Ruins," *New York Times*, May 15, 1985.

33. Associated Press, "Pathologist: 5 MOVE Children Homicide Victims, Fire Could Have Been Extinguished, Expert Says," *Morning Call*, November 6, 1985.

34. Gregory Williams, "And What of the Children?," Father Paul Washington Papers, Box 26, Folder 4, Charles L. Blockson Afro-American Collection, Philadelphia, PA.

35. I have chosen to honor these original requests for anonymity. This is why I am not using respondents' names and am using general references to the collection as a whole. However, I have included some information about the respondents including race, gender, and age. American Friends Service Committee, "Voices from the Community," 1986, American Friends Service Committee Archives, Philadelphia, PA; Philadelphia Perspectives Project, American Friends Service Committee Archive, Philadelphia, PA.

36. Philadelphia Perspectives Project, AFSC.

37. Ibid.

38. Ibid.

39. Frank Trippett, Kenneth W. Banta, and Joseph N. Boyce, "'It Looks Just Like a War Zone': A Police Raid in Philadelphia Turns to Tragedy," *Time* 125, no. 21 (May 27, 1985): 16.

40. Russell Cooke, "Brooks Discloses Plan to Resign: Notified the Mayor Weeks Ago," *Philadelphia Inquirer*, May 22, 1985; Tommie Hill, "Brooks Resigns," *Philadelphia Tribune*, June 4, 1985.

41. Lee Linder, "Sambor Resigns in Phila.: Police Chief Steps Down 6 Months after MOVE," *Morning Call*, November 14, 1985; Ann Moore, "Sambor Says

Goode Forced Him to Quit," *Philadelphia Inquirer*, February 9, 1986; Howard Schneider, "Goode: Did Not Coerce Sambor," *Philadelphia Daily News*, February 11, 1986; Robin Clark, Robert J. Terry, and William K. Marimow, "Sambor Expected to Quit Today: Deputy Seen as Successor," *Philadelphia Inquirer*, November 13, 1985; Joseph R. Daughen, Joe O'Dowd, and Kit Konolige, "Sambor Resigns as City's Top Cop," *Philadelphia Daily News*, November 13, 1985

42. Trippett, Banta, and Boyce, "'It Looks Just Like a War Zone,'" 22.

43. Craig R. McCoy, "Ex-Officer Bares His Torment to Move Jury," *Philadelphia Inquirer*, May 31, 1996.

44. Ramona Africa Trial; "The Ramona Africa Verdict," *Philadelphia Inquirer*, February 11, 1986; "The Ramona Africa Sentence," *Philadelphia Inquirer*, April 16, 1986; Jim Quinn, "Move v. the City of Philadelphia," *Nation* 242, no. 12 (March 29, 1986): 441–58.

45. Bobbi Booker, "Historic Marker for '85 MOVE Bomb Site", *Philadelphia Tribune*, March 31, 2017.

46. "We Shall Not Be Moved Synopsis." Opera Philadelphia, accessed February 3, 2018, https://www.operaphila.org/whats-on/on-stage-2017-2018/we-shall-not-be-moved/full-synopsis.

47. Ibid.

48. Hartman, "Venus in Two Acts," 3.

49. Rankine, "The Condition of Black Life Is One of Mourning."

CHAPTER 4

Black Lives Matter and the New Materialism

Past Truths, Present Struggles, and Future Promises

Carol Wayne White

As a contemporary social movement that began in response to state-sanctioned violence against unarmed Blacks in the United States, Black Lives Matter (BLM) is arguably one of the most visible forms of Black protest against the legacy of white supremacy. In this chapter, I explore the richness and significance of BLM by situating it within a wider intellectual trajectory of the "New Materialism" that has emerged in the past thirty years. New Materialism encompasses a variety of theoretical frameworks intent on rethinking reality and assessing the complex materiality of life. These perspectives challenge older, static ontologies that have upheld impoverished binary views of alterity: white/black, divine/human, male/female, human/nonhuman, normal/abnormal, able-bodied/disabled, normal/queer, so on.[1]

The specific new materialist discourse that I align with BLM in this chapter is religious naturalism, which is a radical departure from traditional religiosity.[2] Religious naturalism offers a variety of perspectives and ideas that often depart from traditional forms of Western religion, specifically in rejecting, reinterpreting, or reconceptualizing traditional concepts of God (or supernatural theism), and in using current developments in science to primarily conceptualize humanity and our ethical orientations, aesthetic appreciations, and religious values. Reframing humans as material processes in relationship with other forms of material nature, religious naturalism encourages humans' processes of transformative engagement with each other and with the more-than-human worlds that constitute our existence. Accordingly, religious naturalism functions as a fundamental orientation in life, and its practice is inspired by an aesthetic-ethical vision that acknowledges the inherent worth of all entities. In my reading, BLM's uncompromising demand that Black lives be viewed and treated as intrinsically valuable life forms reflects religious naturalism's relational ontology. As well, the movement's resistance to isolationist rhetoric and politics (Black lives versus all lives, racialized bodies versus gendered bodies, secular versus religious, queer versus heterosexual, etc.) underscores one of religious naturalism's basic tenets that all materiality is interconnected in endless forms of relationality. When set within this theoretical framework, BLM's recent attention to the violations against Black lives and its resistance to the forces of anti-blackness become important points of departure—indeed evocations of a moral imagination—for comprehending and championing the value of all materiality.

In grounding my assessment of BLM in the tenets of religious naturalism, I advance a naturalistic conception of our shared humanity that reframes older "religious" articulations that have been steeped in problematic epistemic frameworks. Within Africana religious culture, this materialist conception of humanity sheds new light on older liberationist motifs; it also celebrates an enduring intellectual legacy that has consistently promoted expansive views of our humanity. Moreover, this naturalist approach raises important ethical and theoretical questions that I believe the BLM movement is forcing us to ask: What does it mean to be human and to affirm the essential value of Blacks? How do we continue to advance political and religious justifications that indeed all humans share in the same ontological reality? Why do racialized conceptions of Blacks' humanity remain woefully impoverished and inadequate in light of current scientific views that show a deep interrelatedness among all biotic life forms?

In raising these questions in this chapter, I attend to one of the key themes of this volume, namely, that BLM is part of an expansive Black intellectual tradition and specific cultural-historical expressions that have persistently used religion as a viable and existential response to the material conditions of life. As such, my chapter underscores the broad and inclusive model of religiosity found in Anthony Pinn's scholarship on Black religiosity, which views Black agents affirming life and naming their own lived reality as they counter myriad anti-life tendencies emanating from the institutionalization of anti-black rhetoric. This approach is not unlike the earlier account of Black religiosity described aptly by W. E. B. Du Bois in *The Souls of Black Folk* as Blacks' demanding rights to fullness of life as agents valuing and embracing their own humanity—this is a point I return to later in the chapter.

This chapter is divided into three sections. In the first part, I introduce some key themes of the BLM movement, as found in its mission, political platforms, and rhetoric. I then interpret the historical value of these themes, connecting them to an Africana intellectual trajectory that has dignified and valued the humanity of Blacks in response to modernist processes of racialization. In the second section, I introduce a materialist view of humanity grounded in religious naturalism, aligning it with BLM's key aspirational goals and principles. I also reflect on BLM's creative usage of religious language, exploring its significance through the notion of religious functionalism. In this context, BLM's rallying cry provides a linchpin to actualizing past convictions more fully. In the third section, I address the promises of the BLM movement. I envision the movement as one effective vector, among others, aimed at creating future societal formations that refuse strict separations among humans, and between humans and other-than-human nature. While addressing current, rampant anti-black ideologies, the BLM movement also conjoins with other materialist discourses that demand justice for myriad nature.

Part 1. Black Lives Matter and Modern Processes of the Diseased Imagination

In 1853 while addressing the National Colored Convention, Frederick Douglass offered an astute observation about the lived experiences of Black people in America: "Our white fellow-country men do not know us. They are strangers to our character, ignorant of our capacity, oblivious of our history and progress, and are misinformed as to the principles and ideas that control and guide us as a people. The great mass of American citizens estimate us as an characterless and pur-poseless people."[3] In this passage, Douglass confronts the perceived Black degradation rooted in the minds of white individuals held cap-tive by the ideology of white supremacy—what he elsewhere labels the "diseased imagination."[4] A century later, at the height of the civil rights era, James Baldwin poignantly addressed the effects of this diseased imagination with his creative use of the bastard epithet. For Baldwin, the bastard metaphor revealed the pathology inherent in many whites' refusal to embrace their familial kinship with Blacks, based on the false notion of Black cultural and biological inferiority.[5] Since Douglass's era, countless other visionaries, artists, and think-ers of African descent have expressed the conundrum of affirming life and embracing one's humanity in a world (or culture of values) where blackness—its symbolic resonance and its tactile materiality—has been the target of dehumanization processes. In recent years, the formation of the BLM movement, and the controversies surrounding its title, have resuscitated important questions and cultural debates that stretch back to Douglass's era: When will Blacks' full humanity cease being questioned and devalued in the United States? How best to counter violent cultural forces and regimes of power that sanc-tion and perpetuate this ongoing diseased imagination?

In 2014, Alicia Garza, one of BLM's founders, confirmed the signifi-cance of raising these questions in the twenty-first century. Amid the escalating force of police brutality, particularly numerous police kill-ings of unarmed African Americans across the nation, Garza described BLM as "an ideological and political intervention in a world where Black lives are systematically and intentionally targeted for demise.

It is an affirmation of Black folks' contributions to this society, our humanity, and our resilience in the face of deadly oppression."[6] In creative collaboration with Opal Tometi and Patrisse Cullors, Garza created #BlackLivesMatter. This twitter hashtag symbolizes a critical Black consciousness aimed at embracing and promoting the inherent value of blackness (historically, materially, symbiotically, existentially) in a country mesmerized by the dangerous construction of whiteness.

In the years since it has been conceived, the BLM moniker has expanded to become an umbrella term for diverse groups, each of which has its own local character and aim. These organizations are of varying sizes and take different approaches. Altogether, they form a spectrum of gender identity, sexuality, region, age, class, and political belief. Conflict does arise, as some members expressed in a 2017 article: "We are not always in full agreement, as we have competing ideas and we will undoubtedly upset each other in the process of making difficult decisions. We are here because we believe that our victories in service of black people are bigger and better when we win together."[7] All of the groups are united in bringing forceful attention to the unresolved problem first identified by Douglass in the nineteenth century. While BLM is often viewed by most casual observers as "in the trenches" resistance to anti-black police brutality, those actively involved in the movement often describe their efforts as rebuilding a global Black liberation movement. On its webpage, BLM's call to action identifies the aspiration of connecting "Black people from all over the world who have a shared desire for justice to act together in their communities."[8] This aspirational rhetoric includes a moral imagination driven by the willingness to participate in movements of cultural transformation that seek to honor the value of all humans and challenge ill-conceived racial distinctions that white supremacy seeks to insert among humans around the globe. This moral aspiration also entails a commitment to working with others in helping marginalized folk secure the means to live humanely and with dignity.

In confronting the persistent and layered processes of white supremacy through active protest, BLM is often compared with the paradigmatic civil rights movement (1954–1965) associated with Martin Luther King. Scholarly appraisals, however, suggest that the BLM movement departs from the earlier one in significant ways. Among the major differences are BLM's rejection of respectability politics, its explicit focus on gender and sexuality, and its use of social media—particularly Twitter—that can reach individuals throughout the nation and across the world in milliseconds, drastically shortening the time it takes to organize protests.[9] In particular, scholars have focused on the chosen leadership style of BLM. They note its grassroots style of organizing and intentional move away from the charismatic leadership model that has dominated Black politics for the past half century, epitomized by Martin Luther King and the clergy-based, male-centered hierarchal structure of the organization he led.[10]

According to political scientist Frederick Harris, BLM activists view the many achievements of the 1960s civil rights movement with a critical eye. From their vantage point, a major failing of the earlier movement was its facile response to the racialized degradation Black people endured at the hands of the police. Harris further suggests that "BLM protests have not only put police reform on the policy agenda but demanded that American society reconsider how it values black lives."[11] Harris' assessment that BLM emphasizes *valuing* Black lives is noteworthy, as it underscores the creative reach and theoretical import of the movement that I explore in this chapter. In my estimation, the BLM movement is distinctive in prioritizing a referendum that unabashedly declares the sacrality of Black humanity. Addressing a rally in October 2014, Ashley Yates, a Ferguson activist and co-founder of Millennial Activists United, stated why the focus on Black humanity has been used as a catalyst for political action:

> And at the very core of this is humanity—Black Lives Matter. We matter. We matter. Black lives matter because they are lives. Because we are human. Because we eat. Because we breathe. Because he [Michael Brown] had a dream, because he made rap songs, they may have had cuss words in them. Yeah. He was human. And when we neglect to see that we end up where we are today.[12]

Yates' words are instructive. She describes the very materiality of Black lives and the intrinsic value that must be afforded them, which I believe the overall movement is advancing in its various ways. Specifically, I am suggesting that BLM is much more than another important protest movement against myriad social injustices; its platform and principles help generate a conceptual space for further exploration of humanistic values related to how we come to terms with life itself. With this claim, I share Alexandra Hartmann's sense in Chapter 10 that complex humanistic concepts of agency, identity, and subjectivity are also at the center of BLM. As Hartmann suggests, "As agentic beings, humans can take up the struggle for complex subjectivity and reject the reduction of identity by external powers. This endeavor rests at the heart of Black religion in general and of Black humanism in particular."[13] The BLM movement emphasizes the agency of Black subjects affirming life itself. Note co-organizer Opal Tometi's description of the movement: "We wanted to affirm to our people that we love one another, and that no matter how many times we hear about the extrajudicial killing of a community member, we would mourn, and affirm the value of their life."[14] Tometi's rendering of BLM focuses on Blacks as agents of history, not mere objects of circumstance, who have a profound sense of love for each other, for life, and for blackness.

BLM has unabashedly embraced these values while declaring its continuity with the aspirations of past Black movements that have resisted the dehumanizing forces of whiteness. One key tenet asserts, "Our continued commitment to liberation for all Black people means we are continuing the work of our ancestors and fighting for our collective freedom because it is our duty."[15] This principle conveys the depth and magnitude of Black liberation that the BLM movement seeks. To better comprehend the holistic nature and theoretical force of this aspiration, I present a brief overview of influential modernist processes of racialization that provide an important historical backdrop for BLM. The moral outrage and existential distress of the BLM platform cannot be fully appreciated without such historical contextualization.

The Racialization of Nature and the Rise of White Supremacy

One crucial factor contributing to the rise of white supremacy that the BLM movement confronts is an early modern binary construct that originated in Western Europe. This construct divided human culture from nature into spheres of greater-lesser value. This ideology of dualism was an integral component of Western European cultural imperialism, where the purported "civilized" races of Europe distinguished their own normative humanity against other groups they encountered in the Americas, Asia, and Africa. When measured against the idealized Western bourgeois human, African-descended peoples, in particular, were found to be deficient in requisite cognitive, aesthetic, physical, and moral attributes.[16] Later, nineteenth-century scientific studies sanctioned this epistemological framework where notions of racial differences often presented the social inequalities between various cultural groups as reflecting the prescripts of Nature. Around this time, emerging views of Black animality also appeared in influential studies on both sides of the Atlantic. For example, in his very popular text *The Races of Men* (1851), Robert Knox included images of the slant of the brow to draw connections between the "Negro" and the "Oran Outan" and differences between those two and the "European."[17] Knox's work expressed the dominant view of the time in the West that race was a major determinant of culture, behavior, and character. Such views were later used to support both slavery and anti-Semitism.

Not to be outdone by the Europeans, in 1854, two prominent American scientists, Josiah C. Nott and George R. Gliddon, documented in an influential ethnological study (*Types of Mankind*) their perception of objective racial hierarchies with illustrations comparing Blacks to chimpanzees, gorillas, and orangutans.[18] They also included images comparing the skulls of the Greek, the Negro, and the chimpanzee, seeking to show a hierarchy of development linking Blacks to primates. Anticipating the generative power of the diseased imagination reflected in this publication, Frederick Douglass specifically targeted it during a commencement speech he gave at the Western Reserve College in July 1854. Toward the end of the speech, Douglass stated, "of all the efforts to disprove the unity of the human family, and to brand the Negro with natural inferiority, the most compendious and barefaced is the book, entitled 'Types of Mankind,' by Nott and Gliddon."[19]

Several years later in Europe in 1868, Ernst Haeckel, a respected German zoologist, promoted his theory of polygenesis, countering Darwin's theory of evolution that proposed a common ancestry for humanity. The significance of including Haeckel's ideas in this discussion is that he represented the human species in a hierarchy from lowest to highest, ranking negroes among the lowest races and depicting them as savages related to apes.[20] Haeckel also believed people of African descent were psychologically nearer to other mammals— apes and dogs—than to the civilized Europeans, and he consequently assigned a totally different value to their lives. Haeckel's scientific theories help show the wide range of white supremacy at this time. His evolutionary ideas were embedded within his notion of racial purity for Germans, supporting the view that the inexorable laws of evolution conferred on favored races the right to dominate others.[21]

Some of these earlier scientific studies contributed uniquely to the idea of whiteness as a normative category for establishing a group's humanity as well as declaring the superiority of the human species over other organic life and animals, as found in this passage by the French thinker Arthur de Gobineau:

> I have shown the unique place in the organic world occupied by the human species, the profound physical, as well as moral differences separating it from all other kinds of living creatures. Considering it by itself, I have been able to distinguish, on physiological grounds alone, three great and clearly marked types, the black, the yellow, and the white. . . . The negroid variety is the lowest, and stands at the foot of the ladder. The animal character, that appears in the shape of the pelvis, is stamped on the negro from birth, and foreshadows his destiny. His intellect will always move within a very narrow circle.[22]

This particular racist construction of Black animality cannot be underestimated. It was a key ingredient in the scientific perspectives that proposed a gradation from civilization to barbarism, reinforcing the singular role of the Europeans as a civilizing force—a colonizing belief that is transferred to American shores.[23] As a toxic component of the construct of whiteness, Black animality is rooted in Western colonization, chattel slavery, and capitalism.

In the American context, the notion of Black animality played a vital role in perpetuating the inferiority of Blacks; projected images of people of African descent as apes, monkeys, or gorillas helped justify the institution of slavery and informed miscegenation laws. The animalization of Blacks also contributed to the still-widespread stereotypes of Black men as beasts with unmanageable sexuality. These past biases, depicted as commonsense, empirically driven truths, underscore the materialist spin of white supremacy. As scientific theories, they also help us make sense of the materialist implications of BLM's rhetoric and themes, which emphasize the "natural" goodness of Black bodies and lives. I will develop this theme further when conjoining the aims of BLM with tenets of religious naturalism. For now, I address the lingering adverse effects of the Black animality trope in describing some of the spurious representations of BLM as a destructive, wild force in American life.

The affirmation of blackness that Garza and other BLM leaders celebrate has caused alarm and anxiety for many conservative critics, who often describe the protestors as unruly, wild teenagers bent on destructive aims. In 2016 during a CNN interview, Carol Swain, a Black political science and law professor at Vanderbilt, denounced BLM as "misleading black people," and a "very destructive force in America" after five police officers died in Dallas during a protest sponsored by the local BLM.[24] The Dallas protest was among many taking place nationwide in response to the deaths of Alton Sterling in Baton Rouge, Louisiana, and Philando Castile in Falcon Heights, Minnesota. Swain's critiques are representative of many conservative responses to the perceived violence associated with BLM protests, reinforcing some critics' characterization of the movement as mobbish, dangerous, and antithetical to American values. Some early civil rights activists, exemplifying a politics of respectability, have also distanced themselves from BLM protestors. Comparing earlier civil rights protestors like herself to BLM activists in 2015, Barbara Reynolds, an ordained minister, observes, . . . "at protests today, it is difficult to distinguish legitimate activists from the mob actors who burn and loot. The demonstrations are peppered with hate speech, profanity, and guys with sagging pants that show their underwear. Even if the Black Lives Matter activists are not the ones participating in the boorish language and dress, neither are they condemning it."[25] While sympathizing with the overall aims of BLM, Reynolds nonetheless considers its approach the very antithesis of what a respectable movement should be: "Unfortunately, church and spirituality are not high priorities for Black Lives Matter, and the ethics of love, forgiveness and reconciliation that empowered Black leaders such as King and Nelson Mandela in their successful quests to win over their oppressors are missing from this movement."[26]

Perhaps one of the most interesting criticisms of BLM came in the form of a 2017 petition sent to the White House during Obama's presidency, which requested that the movement be listed as a "terror" group. As reported in the media, the petition said BLM "earned this title due to its actions in Ferguson, Baltimore, and even at a Bernie Sanders rally, as well as all over the United States and Canada."[27] The petition asked the Pentagon to recognize the group as terrorist on the grounds of principle, integrity, morality, and safety. In these various examples, a determining factor in denouncing BLM is the representation of the movement (or its protestors) as an unprincipled, immoral, and dangerous presence or force in the United States. The rhetorical power of this language reinforces the Black animality trope, in which BLM becomes the quintessential display of unwarranted, uncivilized behavior that needs to be monitored, curtailed, and contained. Underlying this sentiment, too, is the older culture-nature binary: as a movement that appears to insert blackness over the dominant white culture, BLM appears, to many, as lacking the requisite cognitive, aesthetic, and moral attributes associated with normative movements of reform.

BLM, Values Discourse, and Religious Functionalism

These perceptions fail to recognize the ingenuity and significance of BLM as a type of critical humanistic discourse. Careful study of BLM's principles, literature, and rhetorical phrases demonstrate that the movement consistently uses ethical, values-based language aimed at transformative processes of self and other. According to Vincent Lloyd, "a generally spiritual language . . . pervades Black Lives Matter and the broader social movement to which this hashtag has come to refer."[28] Lloyd further notes the creative use of religious symbolism and ethical language in both the civil rights movement and BLM—an important observation given that the majority of religious institutions (Black, white, and other) have remained silent and indifferent since BLM's inception. Other thinkers share Lloyd's insights. Wes Alcenat, for example, has drawn attention to the BLM activists' rhetorical genius in using the spiritual language of Black Liberation Theology: "Talk of 'Black love,' 'beloved community,' and a 'belief that everybody's life is sacred,' is a common refrain."[29] These phrases are included in the umbrella organization's guiding principles found in its webpages, which often read as an ethical manifesto of community building around the concept of loving blackness and embracing all things Black.[30]

What Lloyd and Alcenat describe as the general spiritual language of BLM I consider to be an essential type of values discourse. As humans experience existence, the meaningfulness of that experience is mediated through values discourse. In other words, humans do more than just exist—we actualize ourselves or engage in processes of becoming through subjectivizing the world around us, using specific principles, standards, or ideals that both inform and guide that actualization.[31] Among the various value systems are ethical ones concerned with basic questions of how humans ought to live, what we ought to hope for, and what we aspire to in our actions. Insofar as BLM has vigilantly affirmed Blacks' full humanity amid the movement's emancipatory aims, it has persisted in associating Black agents with a fundamental propensity toward life, paradigmatically demonstrating the central political force of BLM's social and ethical values. For example, one of BLM's guiding principles focuses on intentional community building in which self-determining agents create and maintain forms of relationality that help to expand rather than diminish their humanity: "We intentionally build and nurture a beloved community that is bonded together through a beautiful struggle that is restorative, not depleting."[32] Another interesting feature of their community formation is daily commitment or faithfulness to health, wholeness, and cultural intactness: "Every day, we recommit to healing ourselves and each other, and to co-creating alongside comrades, allies, and family a culture where each person feels seen, heard, and supported."[33]

These principles help illustrate the expansive sense of Black religion in this volume, defined as an ongoing existential quest of making meaning in response to life's material realities. They echo the ancient Hebrews' prophetic vision of justice that entailed preserving the dignity and value of all vital constituents. BLM's usage of these religious expressions is also semiotic, reminiscent of W. E. B. Du Bois's rhetorical genius in *The Souls of Black Folk*. In that text, Du Bois sketched the complex unfolding of nineteenth-century African American religiosity, revealing the institutionalization of a people's hopes, fears, core values, and ethical convictions. In doing so, he offered a compelling view of Black religiosity as an evolving, humanistic enterprise with monumental social and communal implications.[34] Many of BLM's principles resonate with, and further advance, this Du Boisian approach to Black religiosity, namely, emphasizing the ingenuity of a people constantly striving to inhabit their humanity and eke out a meaningful existence for themselves against the backdrop of culturally coded white supremacist notions and practices. Giving an overview of its collective work since Ferguson, the BLM website highlights some of its achievements in culture building:

> We've accomplished a lot in four short years. Ferguson helped to catalyze a movement to which we've all helped give life. Organizers who call this network home have ousted anti-Black politicians, won critical legislation to benefit Black life, and changed the terms of the debate on Blackness around the world. Through movement and relationship building, we have also helped catalyze other movements and shifted culture with an eye toward the dangerous impacts of anti-Blackness.[35]

Du Bois's humanistic views on Black religion have remained on the margins of Black culture. Moreover, his functionalist approach has been overshadowed by a theological view associated with the dominant Christian tradition in the US. In this tradition, specific images, symbols, and rituals that function to address fundamental issues of life or death to Black agents intent on living fully and with dignity are primarily associated with the God referent.[36] Consequently, in African American religious culture, the symbol God has functioned to affirm the value of Black humanity as well as the fact that all humans share in the same ontological reality as other humans.[37] Historically, it has been posited as an ultimate value—indeed, an *a priori* notion—in Black religious expression, symbolizing the means by which particular limitations on human potentiality could be dissolved or at least addressed. With Anthony Pinn and other scholars, I am not persuaded by this appeal to the God symbolism (or to any form of supernaturalism) in my reading of Black religiosity. What is crucial here, I suggest, is recognizing the creative energies of Blacks who rejected the impoverished conceptions of their humanity used to justify slavery, Jim Crow laws, segregation, and other unjust social practices and cultural norms through the last several hundred years. Today, BLM is a current manifestation of this creative Black energy.

In making these claims, I view traditional Black religiosity primarily through the lens of religious functionalism, which, as Loyal Rue has suggested, places the proper focus on who actually creates and uses religion: humans.[38] Religious functionalism in this context is a method of analyzing and interpreting religious experiences and expressions as natural events having natural causes. In advancing this theoretical orientation, I do not presume that religious phenomena can be completely explained; rather, I suggest that the extent of our understanding is contingent on efforts to grasp these phenomena in terms of underlying natural processes. In the Western history of ideas, this general approach is not all that new, having been advanced many times in the past. As Loyal Rue asserts, notable thinkers such as Kant, Feuerbach, Marx, Durkheim, and Freud have argued that "regardless of what religion *says* it is about, it has to *do* fundamentally with meeting the challenges to a full life."[39] I share the conviction that religion both originates in human experience and is properly understood in natural terms, as opposed to those theories that see it emerging from some transcendent order or given by divine revelation.

Du Bois's example is instructive here, again, given his anti-metaphysical leanings when describing Blacks' rights to fullness of life vis-à-vis their accountability of their own humanity.[40] Du Bois held a complex and wide range of perspectives on religion that could support any number of interpretations regarding his own religiosity; however, with a growing number of scholars, I focus on Du Bois's general agnostic orientation throughout his life. This agnosticism was often evident in public speeches and personal correspondence, where Du Bois often emphasized human ingenuity and avoided metaphysical speculation. In a 1956 letter to Herbert Aptheker, he writes:

> I assumed that human beings could alter and re-direct the course of events as to better human conditions. I knew that this power was limited by environment, inheritance and natural law, and that from the point of view of science these occurrences must be a matter of Chance and not of Law. I did not rule out the possibility of some God also influencing and directing human action and natural law. However, I saw no evidence of such divine guidance. I did see evidence of the decisive action of human beings.[41]

BLM also offers a fresh iteration of this general humanistic orientation, setting it within the layered context of racialized living in the twenty-first century—both in the US and around the world. Given their emergence from the historical realities of slavery, Black cultural and religious expressions in the US bring into relief an important point that other white humanists have failed to grasp: Black slaves and their descendants have never had the luxury of asking these questions in abstraction. In surviving and making a distinctive claim about the value of life, American Blacks have lived these questions into the future. When seen through the lens of functionalism, BLM's semiotic use of Black religious expression underscores this truth. Moreover, BLM's presence in the twenty-first century extends the wide range of affirmations of Blacks' valuable humanity that have been reiterated in past centuries. My point here is that BLM's declarations that "Black lives matter" are more than necessary emancipatory claims; they are also important affirmations constituting an important shift in humanistic thinking, challenging us to raise an important, more fundamental question: How do we understand the complex, material human being that has been affirmed in Africana liberationist discourses, in response to the distortions perpetuated by racialization processes?

In the next section, I further explore this question. I introduce a materialist, relational conception of all humans as distinct movements of nature itself where deep relationality and interconnectedness become key metaphors for honoring all life forms. This naturalistic view of humanity, I contend, has the potential to invigorate materialist discourses, and it offers a fuller sense of the rich, layered texture of BLM's rallying cry to honor Black lives. With this naturalist orientation, I contribute to the capacious conception of religiosity structuring this volume, showing how BLM makes inextricable connections between past historical truths and current values and aspirations associated with Black religious thought and expression. I also consider how advocates and allies of the BLM movement might situate themselves between past convictions and future social, ethical, and ecological concerns in honoring the fullness of life for all.

Part 2. BLM and Religious Naturalism

As one model of new materialism, religious naturalism champions a communal ontology grounded in the observational conviction that nature is ultimate.[42] Additionally, the qualifier "religious" in religious naturalism affirms the natural world as the center of humans' most significant experiences and understandings. Religious naturalism does not posit any ontologically distinct and superior realm (God, soul, heaven) to ground, explain, or give meaning to this world. Rather, attention is focused on the events and processes of this world to provide what degree of explanation and meaning are possible to this life. As suggested by Wesley Wildman, a shared conviction among religious naturalists is the ceaseless, explicit focus on myriad nature in "its beauty, terror, scale, stochasticity, emergent complexity, and evolutionary development."[43]

For my purposes, religious naturalism's theoretical appeal is its fundamental conception of humans as natural processes intrinsically connected to other natural processes. The advances of the sciences, through both physics and biology, have served to demonstrate not only how closely linked human animals are with nature, but that we are simply one branch of a seemingly endless natural cosmos. Understanding the deep history of the cosmos is thus profoundly important for any basic understanding of the materiality of being human, of being alive in the manner we currently find ourselves. Big Bang cosmology, for example, shows the world evolving naturally, based on the interconnection and interaction of all of its fundamental components. Bearing in mind these insights, I share Loyal Rue's contention that humans are "ultimately the manifestations of many interlocking systems—atomic, molecular, biochemical, anatomical, ecological—apart from which human existence is incomprehensible."[44] Human life is also part of an evolutionary history showing a trend toward greater complexity and consciousness. As Stephen Jay Gould and other scientists have noted, there has been an increase in the genetic information in DNA and a steady increase in the ability of organisms to gather and process information about the environment and respond to it.[45]

As by-products of other natural processes and intimate participants with them, humans are material beings through and through. Consider, for example, Michael W. Fox's compelling account that "our bodies contain the mineral elements of primordial rocks; our very cells share the same historically evolved components as those of grasses and trees; our brains contain the basic neural core of reptile, bird, and fellow mammal."[46] We are also structured by relationality. In *The Sacred Depths of Nature*, Ursula Goodenough offers a lucid account of humans as relational natural organisms, providing sound scientific data that supports our fundamental interconnectedness with other living beings. As she puts it: "And now we realize that we are connected to all creatures. Not just in food chains or ecological equilibria. We share a common ancestor. We share genes for receptors and cell cycles and signal-transduction cascades. We share evolutionary constraints and possibilities. We are connected all the way down."[47] Goodenough's observations support my view that humans are, by our very constitution, relational beings, and our wholeness occurs within a matrix of complex interconnectedness— in ways of conjoining with others that transform us. In this context, I offer a naturalistic view of humans as complex social organisms capable of loving, connecting deeply with others, and symbolizing their environment (or engaging in world formation) through values and language. We are, in short, multilevel psychosomatic unities— both biological organisms and responsible selves.

Appreciating human life as one distinct biotic form emerging from, and participating in, a series of evolutionary processes that constitute the diversity of life has monumental implications for African American culture. Here, the scientific epic becomes the starting point for positing a religious humanism constituted by a central tenet: humans are relational processes of nature; in short, we are nature made aware of itself. In declaring such, I contend that our humanity is not a given, but rather an achievement. Consider that from a strictly biological perspective, humans are organisms that have slowly evolved by a process of natural selection from earlier primates. From one generation to another, the species that is alive now has gradually adapted to changing environments so that it could continue to survive. Our animality, from this perspective, is living under the influence of genes, instincts, and emotions, with the prime directive to survive and procreate. Yet, this minimalist approach fails to consider what a few cognitive scientists and most philosophers, humanists, and religionists tend to accentuate: our own personal experience of what it is like to be an experiencing human being. As I have argued elsewhere, becoming human, or actualizing ourselves as human beings, in this sense, emerges out of an awareness and desire to be more than a conglomeration of pulsating cells. It is suggesting that our humanity is not reducible to organizational patterns or processes dominated by brain structures; nor do DNA, diet, behavior, and the environment solely structure it. Human

animals become human destinies when we posit fundamental questions of value, meaning, and purpose to our existence. Our coming
to be human destinies is structured by a crucial question: How do
we come to terms with life?[48]

Within the specifics of African American historical and cultural
realities, the materialist conception of humanity I have described
above accentuates the key aspirations of BLM. The movement demonstrates the uncontestable recognition of Blacks' longing to take
our highest ideals or values seriously: the irrefutable, essential value
of our humanity. On a more general level, BLM also illustrates why
a tradition of "Black love" is grounded in an appreciable, expanded
view of our shared human nature. As an experience of religiosity (both
individually and culturally), the act of embracing and valuing blackness is inextricably connected to how African Americans *become* our
humanity—how we literally transform our material animality from
the abjection that the dominant culture has prescribed as our destiny.
As BLM demonstrates, the very presence of this longing in Africana
cultures attests to an awareness or sense of distance between what
we are (beautiful, value-laden organisms) and what white supremacist racial views suggest we are. In short, BLM reminds us that
African-descended peoples have been compelled to seek realms of
possibility. Positing and celebrating African-descended peoples as
humans—and as having the right to become our humanity—has been
one way, among many, for Africana visionaries to contest impoverished and oppressive models of Black animality conceived by cultural spin doctors bogged down by distorted ontological gravitas.

BLM and Binary Configurations

A major tenet of religious naturalism is its emphasis on humans as
relational beings—we are part of the evolving universe, and those values that we confer upon events are more or less the universe appreciating dimensions of itself. Granted, this process is not merely nar-
cissistic introspection, isolating any one of us from the contexts in
which we live our destinies. All action, all reality, is for the concrete,
material individual: I am right now where I am. It is akin to discov-
ering worlds of possibility beyond the sterile fear of non-existence,

beyond enforced solitariness founded on illusions of separateness and universal abstractions. These ideals are echoed in the BLM assertion that "we embody and practice justice, liberation, and peace in our engagements with one another."[49] Part of embodying justice in a materialist framework requires approaching materiality differently— we become daringly positive about our materiality and embrace materiality in its diverse manifestations. For religious naturalists, this means consciously resisting binary thinking that demarcates certain spheres of life as superior and others as inferior, justifying the exploitative practices of the former.[50] This important insight is creatively expressed in BLM's efforts, protest marches, and aspirations.

In her 2018 memoir, *When They Call you a Terrorist: A Black Lives Matter Memoir*, co-founder Patrisse Khan-Cullors reflects on these truths in a personal style that is moving and inspiring. Khan-Cullors begins her memoir with a stunning narrative of listening to a talk delivered by astrophysicist Neil deGrasse Tyson a few days after the 2016 elections. Khan-Cullors' friend (and co-author), Asha Bandele, had sent the link to deGrasse Tyson's talk as a symbol of hope, and together they listened to the scientist expand upon a truth that I have outlined here as a maxim of religious naturalism: humans are relational, material beings inextricably connected to other natural processes in the universe. In Khan-Cullors' personal rendering, these scientific truths reinforce the power and majesty of why Black lives matter, and why her activism is an act of love for her ancestors and for all African-descended peoples whose humanity has been stripped of its essential material value by white supremacy. She states:

> We listen together . . . the very atoms and molecules in our bodies are traceable to the crucibles in the centers of stars that once upon a time exploded into gas clouds. And those gas clouds formed other stars and those stars possessed the divine-right mix of properties needed to create not only planets, including our own, but also people, including us, me and her. He is saying that not only are we in the planet, but that the universe is in us. He is saying that we, human beings, are literally made out of star dust.

And I know when I hear Dr. deGrasse Tyson say this that he is telling the truth because I have seen it since I was a child, the magic, the stardust that we are, in the lives of the people I come from.[51]

As Khan-Cullors suggests in her memoir, advocating for Black lives and why they matter is a fight not just for Black humanity, but for all humanity, and, by default, a fight for the future of our planet.

The BLM movement unequivocally asserts that full liberation for all Blacks (indeed for all humans) requires a rejection of the dualistic, binary structures that support problematic racialized views of our shared humanity. Alicia Garza reiterated this theme in 2014 when describing the holistic vision of the movement in its focus on the proliferation of anti-black tactics viewed on a daily basis:

> When we are able to end hyper-criminalization and sexualization of Black people and end the poverty, control, and surveillance of Black people, every single person in this world has a better shot at getting and staying free. When Black people get free, everybody gets free. This is why we call on Black people and our allies to take up the call that Black lives matter. We're not saying Black lives are more important than other lives, or that other lives are not criminalized and oppressed in various ways. We remain in active solidarity with all oppressed people who are fighting for their liberation and we know that our destinies are intertwined.[52]

Garza's words emphatically state that a relational politics of the "one and all" is central to BLM's mission. This sentiment is found in another key principle: "We are unapologetically Black in our positioning. In affirming that Black Lives Matter, we need not qualify our position. To love and desire freedom and justice for ourselves is a prerequisite for wanting the same for others."[53] When declaring that it works "vigorously for freedom and justice for Black people and, by extension, all people," BLM is unabashedly asserting that embracing blackness is essential to human flourishing—personally, nationally, and globally.[54] In doing so, BLM advances new humanistic goals, validating and dignifying new images of ourselves, creatively inscribed onto the tissues, bones, and liquids that constitute human animals.

The communal ontology that undergirds BLM's mission inspires its leaders and members to respect and celebrate differences and commonalities among all constituents. Rather than appeal to a normative expression of humanity in the abstract, BLM is "guided by the fact that all Black lives matter, regardless of actual or perceived sexual identity, gender identity, gender expression, economic status, ability, disability, religious beliefs or disbeliefs, immigration status, or location."[55] Intersectional at its core, the BLM movement continues to resist the lure of a generic, universal construction of "man" that has justified the devalued status of women and other subjects relegated to minority status: "we build a space that affirms Black women and is free from sexism, misogyny, and environments in which men are centered."[56] This principle contributes to ongoing feminist appraisals that have contested Enlightenment configurations of the normative human as white, propertied, male, and rational. Additionally, BLM seeks to target pervasive enactments of sexism and misogyny that ground "traditional family" values—a point that Black feminists have deplored for some years now. On their website, they affirm the disruption of "the Western-prescribed nuclear family structure requirements by supporting each other as extended families and 'villages' that collectively care for one another, especially our children, to the degree that mothers, parents, and children are comfortable."[57]

BLM's politics of the one and all is far-reaching in adopting a queer positionality—or what Michael Warner has described as resistance "to regimes of the normal."[58] Intentionally making space for transgender persons to participate and lead in their movement, BLM asserts, "we are self-reflexive and do the work required to dismantle cisgender privilege and uplift Black trans folk, especially Black trans women who continue to be disproportionately impacted by trans-antagonistic violence."[59] As queer enactment, BLM calls for a radical relationality in which experiences of love overcome arbitrary boundaries held in place by normalizing cultural markers. It seeks a modality of existence based in transformation; in such a vision, our expanded humanity as sentient beings is porous—we suffuse each other with care and a sense of belonging together.

Some critics have noted that with such a purposeful focus on queer lives, BLM disrupts the usual binary of the "sacred-secular" valuation that has gripped much of traditional Black religiosity. In her brief essay "Why Are Queer Black Lives 'Secular'?" Ahmad Greene-Hayes astutely homes in on this important insight. She writes, "Scholars and activists have long wrestled with the binaristic construction of sacred versus secular. Debates have recently emerged about the characterization of Black Lives Matter (BLM) as more secular than the civil rights movement. The conversation alone, though, reveals our collective discomfort with messiness, life in the gray, and/or lived experiences that cannot be traditionally qualified."[60] Greene-Hayes sheds light on a forced and false dichotomy about material reality that has been influential in much Western thought. Paradigmatically exemplified in Aristotelian thought, this dualistic system of ordering and comprehending materiality has animated later troubling and toxic reformulations that have informed how people approach theological, racial, environmental, and sexual truths. Greene-Hayes elaborates on the fuller dualistic narrative and its lingering effects within Black culture:

> Our dominant discourses have shortchanged us, sold us a narrative of ourselves that is not true: a fallacy built on the erasure of women, LGBTQ lives, and those who were not respectable. Alas, as there is Patrisse Cullors, Alicia Garza, Opal Tometi, Darnell Moore, Elle Hearns, Larry Fellows, and Ashley Yates, there was Pauli Murray, Bayard Rustin, Audre Lorde, Marsha P. Johnson, and James Baldwin. The conflation of queerness (both as political project and sexual identity), then, with "secular" (which more-oft-than-not has a negative connotation within Christocentrism), or the constant coding of queerness as anti-sacred, is a byproduct of the heterosexualization of religion. It is homophobia guised as an intellectual project, and only serves as another means to border queer bodies from the Divine.[61]

With the materialist spin of religious naturalism I have offered, the various principles found in BLM undergird the theoretical assumption that gender, race, class, abled-bodiedness, and other socially derived markers do not provide the basis of our humanity; rather, they are highly complex categories constructed in contested discourses and other social practices. When these constructions are used to support racism, sexism, and other forms of cultural superiority, they become forced impositions on the wholeness of natural interrelatedness and deep homology that evolution has wrought.

Part 3. The Diseased Imagination and Future Visions for BLM

One of the main goals of materialist discourses is to think against the grain of ontological and epistemic exceptionalisms that have set humans over and against other forms of animal life, and human culture, society, and economy over and against the ecological systems upon which they depend.[62] Part of what religious naturalism brings to these efforts is sound reasoning for challenging persistent forms of anthropocentricism that lurk in many of our religious, ethical, and philosophical articulations. Specifically, religious naturalism confronts a colonizing legacy that also depends on the dominant cultural fantasy of human exceptionalism, which anchors humans on one side of the Great Divide, away from all other species. This premise assumes that the human alone is not a spatial and temporal web of interspecies dependencies. Religious naturalism emphatically rejects this phantasm, which has lent theoretical support to popular myths of the self-made individual in the United States. It also encourages us to join with Donna Haraway in appreciating our intricate entanglement with other material processes:

> I love the fact that human genomes can be found in only about 10 percent of all the cells that occupy the mundane space I call my body; the other 90 percent of the cells are filled with the genomes of bacteria, fungi, protists, and such, some of which play in a symphony necessary to my being alive at all, and some of which are hitching a ride and doing the rest of me, of us, no harm. I am vastly outnumbered by my tiny companions;

better put, I become an adult human being in company with these tiny messmates. To be one is always to *become with* many.[63]

Haraway's point underscores my conviction as a religious natural-ist that all human endeavors arise from the critical awareness that we are part of an inextricable network of natural processes that make the very category of the human itself intelligible. Our embeddedness with myriad nature invigorates a fuller sense of our expansive humanity as already, always entangled becoming. As I have argued elsewhere, any conceivable notion of our common humanity will be ontologically enmeshed and entangled with other forms of natural life.[64] In keep-ing with the tenets of religious naturalism, we consistently resist the aims of traditional humanism that have posited humans outside of myriad nature and eclipsed the interrelatedness of all natural processes.

To explain this point better, I bring to mind the naturalist frame-work outlined earlier of humans as emergent life forms amid spec-tacular natural diversity. As recent insights in ecological studies show, "organisms of various types, including human beings, are inextricably bound together in a web of mutual interdependence for their contin-ual flourishing and survival as they make common if varied use of the energy of the sun."[65] Within each web, each species of animal has a niche for which it is more or less adapted, and has attributes that others lack. This ecological orientation challenges those who would use evo-lutionary history as the basis for deciding who is better than whom. Equally important, these ecological perspectives lead us to interpret evolution in a much more expansive sense, shorn of the distortions of conventional anthropocentric orientations. Rather than construct evolution as the meta-narrative of an increasing capacity of human nature to manipulate other forms of nature, we now emphasize the successive emergence of new forms of opportunity, or the continual diversification of new modes of being. Within this ecological context, evolution is associated with new patterns of harmonious coexistence among bountiful nature rather than the progressive development of increased specialization. All members of an ecosystem are equally important, comprising it as a functional whole. Aldo Leopold, who was among the first influential naturalists to remind us of the distortions of deeply ingrained anthropocentricism, provided compelling articulations of these ideas. In his later writings, specifically *Sand County Almanac* (1949), Leopold emphasized the radical interdependence of plants and animals in their natural environments, including the observation that human organisms are intimate participants in ecological relations and belong to a wider biotic community.[66]

In a religious context, the notion of humans seeking, finding, and experiencing community with others—an essential aspect of our humanity—is important. (And this is a value that we have seen expressed creatively by BLM.) Thus, further exploring the tenets of religious naturalism in conjunction with values discourse, I consider humans' awareness and appreciation of our connection to "all that is," as an expression of the sacred, or of what we perceive and value as ultimately important. Value in this sense refers to an organism's facility to sense whether events in its environment are more or less desirable.[67] As Holmes Rolston suggests, minimally, this facility evokes the notion of adaptive value, which is the basic matrix of Darwinian theory. Within a larger ecological framework, however, this truth takes on fuller meaning: "An organism is the loci of values defended; life is otherwise unthinkable. Such organismic values are individually defended; but, as ecologists insist, organisms occupy niches and are networked into biotic communities."[68]

I bring these theoretical convictions to my vision of BLM as a critical materialist discourse in the twenty-first century. While celebrating its extraordinarily rich intersectional analysis, queer positionality, and expansive conceptions of Black humanity, I also think the movement has the potential to deepen its expansive humanistic vision. I am thinking of a capacious moral imagination that resists the logic of white supremacy on *all* forms of materiality.

What would BLM's important concept of the beloved community look like within this wider ecological context? I offer a few thoughts. First, while denouncing Black degradation and inferiority through the use of the animal other, BLM goes even further to analyze the speciesism that is evident in these formulations. What I am suggesting is that BLM's Black liberationist discourse is well positioned to evoke a moral imagination that compels us to question racist and antiracist discourses that are predicated on a repudiation of animality. One creative humanistic intervention is blurring the arbitrary ontological lines that human animals have erected between themselves and other species and natural processes. For example, as BLM continues resisting the wide-ranging violence embedded in European colonialism and its processes of racialization on Black bodies as natural, material bodies, the movement has the potential to consider fully the colonization of other animals. On this matter, Jeremy Bentham offered an important insight in the eighteenth century:

> The day has been . . . in which the greater part of the species, under the denomination of slaves, have been treated by the law exactly upon the same footing as, in England for example, the . . . animals are still. . . . The French have already discovered that the blackness of the skin is no reason why a human being should be abandoned without redress to the caprice of a tormentor. It may come one day to be recognized, that the number of the legs, the villosity of the skin, or the termination of the *os sacrum*, are reasons equally insufficient for abandoning a sensitive being to the same fate. . . . The question is not, Can they *reason*? nor, Can they *talk*? but, Can they *suffer*?[69] (italics in original)

Bentham's emphasis on sentience is crucial. White supremacy and species supremacy distort the wholeness of animal sentience. One step toward decolonizing myriad nature, toward making it less vulnerable, perhaps, is in honoring nature's sentience, which is an essential part of being alive, experiencing others, being affected by others, and experiencing well-being.

The insights of geographer Karen Morin are invaluable here. In *Carceral Space, Prisoners and Animals*, Morin demonstrates how the processes of "animalization" have subjugated both certain humans and certain nonhumans into hierarchies of worthiness and value. As she writes: "Fundamental to how and why certain prisoners and certain animals can be exploited, objectified, or made killable within the prison, the farm, the research lab, and the zoo are the social constructions of the human-nonhuman divide—the carceral logics and social meanings that attach to various bodies and populations."[70]

Morin further observes that the forms of violence spanning these various carceral spaces are all a part of ordinary, everyday, industrialized violence in the United States and elsewhere. Additionally, Morin notes that racial difference is foundational to much of the "criminal as animal" rhetoric, particularly via animalistic representations of Black and other minoritized men. With their life-affirming principles, I think BLM activists are uniquely positioned to address these disturbing, intimate linkages of white supremacy and speciesism. Second, I think BLM's desire to eradicate the many forms of Black degradation globally also strengthens the case for seeing the movement's capacity to address under-analyzed elements of ecological degradation, which are at the heart of the environmental justice movement. Part of the legacy of white supremacy in the United States includes perspectives that both justified slavery and the exploitation of the more-than-human natural worlds.[71] As summarized by Paul Outka, this colonizing legacy consisted of whites viewing dark-skinned peoples as part of the natural world, and then proceeding to treat them with the same mixture of contempt and real exploitation that also marks American environmental history.[72] In response, important political organizing has been done by Black (and other racialized) communities in the environmental justice movement. Often without any explicit theological anthropology, this movement appeals to a view of humanity that is inseparable from other natural processes. It has also produced generations of activists of color engaged in struggles to advance natural resource conservation, environmental protection, civil rights, and social equity.[73]

These workers assert the irrefutable interconnectedness of all life when they concurrently advocate against the depletion of natural resources; challenge the policies that both create land polluted by landfills, oil refineries, and nuclear-waste repositories and force poor racial and ethnic communities to live near these sites; and fight for referendums that preserve the delicate ecosystems supporting whales and dolphins. As these efforts suggest, BLM activists and environmental justice advocates share a general maxim: harm done to any one sector of natural processes, inclusive of human organisms, is harm done to all. With their intersectional analysis, sense of community building, and expansive notion of Black love, BLM members are also positioned well to share further in these efforts. The materialist view of the relational, material human that I formulated earlier, and one that I suggest BLM celebrates, underscores why human histories—not only the histories of the West—are intimately connected to the history of the Earth. Understanding this linkage compels us to make inseparable ethical connections between humanity's relationality with other natural processes on the planet and humans' activities with each other. It is not an either-or situation.

In this chapter, I have presented and assessed the unique value and significance of the BLM movement within the context of a new religious orientation (religious naturalism) that is associated with the New Materialism. As a materialist epistemology, religious naturalism reframes humans as material processes in relationship with other forms of material nature, and it supports an ethical vision that encourages humans' processes of transformative engagement with each other and with the more-than-human worlds that constitute our existence. With its resistance to white supremacy and the binary ordering of existence upon which it is built and advanced, the BLM movement's uncompromising demand that Black lives be viewed and treated as intrinsically valuable reflects religious naturalism's relational ontology. Thus, in aligning the BLM movement with religious naturalism, I show that this contemporary protest movement is theoretically rich in its aims, vision, and moral claims. Its key principles are grounded in ethical claims, humanistic values, and political aspirations that have always been a part of an expansive notion of Black religiosity enacted throughout African American culture and history.[74] My chapter has emphasized the relational human that embarks on an incessant quest for meaning and value-affirming life, associating it with the principles and platform of the BLM. In doing so, my chapter contributes to this volume's aim of displaying the richness of Black religious pluralism. I have also argued that the BLM movement's resistance to isolationist rhetoric and politics (Black lives versus all lives, racialized bodies versus gendered bodies, secular versus religious, queer versus heterosexual, etc.) is one of its most astute insights. In the final analysis, I affirm that BLM's recent attention to the violations against Black lives and its resistance to the forces of anti-blackness become important points of departure—indeed evocations of a moral imagination—for comprehending and championing the value of all materiality.

NOTES

1. Representative works of the New Materialism include Karen Barad, *Meeting the Universe Halfway: Quantum Physics and the Entanglement of Matter and Meaning* (Durham, NC: Duke University Press, 2007); Jane Bennett, *Vibrant Matter: A Political Ecology of Things* (Durham, NC: Duke University Press, 2010); Diana Code, *New Materialisms: Ontology, Agency, and Politics* (Durham, NC: Duke University Press, 2010); Rick Dolphijn and Iris van der Tuin, *New Materialism: Interviews and Cartographies* (Ann Arbor: MPublishing—University of Michigan Library, 2012); Rosi Braidotti, *Metamorphoses: Towards a Materialist Theory of Becoming* (Cambridge, UK: Polity Press 2002); Elizabeth Wilson, *Psychosomatic: Feminism and the Neurological Body* (Durham, NC: Duke University Press, 2004); Elizabeth Wilson, "Gut Feminism," in *Differences: A Journal of Feminist Cultural Studies* 15, no. 3 (2004): 66–94; Cary Wolf, ed., *Zoontologies: The Question of the Animal* (Minneapolis: University of Minnesota Press, 2003); Cary Wolf, *Animal Rites: American Culture, the Discourse of Species, and Posthumanist Theory* (Chicago: University of Chicago Press, 2003).

2. For a sampling of current works in religious naturalism, see Ursula Goodenough, *The Sacred Depths of Nature* (New York: Oxford University Press, 2000); Loyal Rue, *Religion Is Not about God* (New Brunswick, NJ: Rutgers University Press, 2006); Chet Raymo, *When God Is Gone, Everything Is Holy* (Notre Dame, IN: Sorin Books, 2008); Jerome Stone, *Religious Naturalism Today: The Rebirth of a Forgotten Alternative* (New York: State University of New York Press, 2008); Donald Crosby, *The Thou of Nature* (New York: State University of New York, 2013); Michael Hogue, *The Promises of Religious Naturalism* (Lanham, MD: Rowman and Littlefield, 2010); Carol Wayne White, *Black Lives and Sacred Humanity: Toward an African American Religious Naturalism* (New York: Fordham Press, 2016).

3. Frederick Douglass, *Frederick Douglass: Selected Speeches and Writings*, edited by P. S. Foner and Y. Taylor (Chicago: Chicago Review Press 2000), 269.

4. Frederick Douglass, "The Color Line" (1881) in John Stauffer, ed., *The Portable Frederick Douglass* (New York: Penguin Classics, 2016), 501–11.

5. James Baldwin, "No Name in the Street," in *Baldwin: Collected Essays*, edited by Toni Morrison (New York: Library of America, 1998), 468.

6. Alicia Garza, "A Herstory of the #BlackLivesMatter Movement," *Feminist Wire*, October 7, 2014, https://thefeministwire.com/2014/10/blacklivesmatter-2.

7. Monique Judges, "'What Happened to Black Lives Matter?' Movement for Black Lives Responds," *The Root*, June 23, 2017, https://www.theroot.com/what-happened-to-black-lives-matter-movement-for-b-1796383582.

8. "Guiding Principles," Black Lives Matter, accessed March 2019, https://blacklivesmatter.com/about/what-we-believe.

9. Dewey Clayton, "Black Lives Matter and the Civil Rights Movement: A Comparative Analysis of Two Social Movements in the United States," *Journal of Black Studies*, 49, no. 5 (2018): 457–61.

10. Clayton, "Black Lives Matter," 459–62. See also Frederick Harris, "The Next Civil Rights Movement?" *Dissent Magazine*, Summer 2015, https://www.dissentmagazine.org/article/black-lives-matter-new-civil-rights-movement-fredrick-harris.

11. Harris, "The Next Civil Rights Movement?" Harris suggests that BLM members share more of an affinity with the young activists of the sixties Civil Rights Movement associated with the Student Nonviolent Coordinating Committee (SNCC). SNCC's efforts were pivotal in Black Americans successfully securing civil and political rights historically denied to them, such as access to and use of public accommodations, fair employment, and housing opportunities.

12. Quoted in Harris, "The Next Civil Rights Movement?"

13. Alexandra Hartmann, "The Sounds of Hope: Black Humanism, Deep Democracy, and Black Lives Matter," 251.

14. Jamilah King, "#blacklivesmatter: How Three Friends Turned a Spontaneous Facebook Post into a Global Phenomenon," *California Sunday Magazine*, March 3, 2015, https://stories.californiasunday.com/2015-03-01/black-lives-matter.

15. "Guiding Principles," Black Lives Matter, accessed March 2019, https:///blacklivesmatter.com/about/what-we-believe.

16. Charles Mills, *The Racial Contract*, 1st ed. (Ithaca, NY: Cornell University Press, 1999), 15. See also Emmanuel Eze, *Race and Enlightenment* (Malden, MA: Blackwell Publishers, 1996), 5ff; Jean Stefancic and Richard Delgado, *Critical Race Theory: The Cutting Edge* (Philadelphia, PA: Temple University Press, 2013).

17. Robert Knox, *The Races of Men* (1851). Knox himself was an anatomist and physiologist, and used his studies of Black people in South Africa to build a theory of human history based on racial distinction.

18. Josiah Nott, George Gliddon, et al., *Types of Mankind* (Philadelphia, PA: Lippincott, Grambo and Co.), 1854.

19. Frederick Douglass, *The Claims of the Negro, Ethnologically Considered: An Address before the Literary Societies of Western Reserve College, at Commencement, July 12, 1854* (Rochester, NY: Press of Lee, Mann and Co., 1854), 10.

20. Ernst Haeckel, *The History of Creation; or, The Development of the Earth and Its Inhabitants by the Action of Natural Causes* (New York: Appleton, 1876), 10.

21. Haeckel, *The History of Creation*, 332. Harvard paleontologist Stephen Jay Gould writes, "[Haeckel's] evolutionary racism; his call to the German people for racial purity and unflinching devotion to a 'just' state; his belief that harsh, inexorable laws of evolution ruled human civilization and nature alike, conferring upon favored races the right to dominate others . . . all contributed to the rise of Nazism," Stephen Jay Gould, *Ontology and Phylogeny* (Cambridge, MA: Harvard University Press, 1977), 77–78.

22. Arthur de Gobineau, *An Essay on the Inequality of the Human Races*, trans. A. Collins (London: Heinemann, 1915), 205–12.

23. Sylvia Wynter, "Unsettling the Coloniality of Being/Power/Truth/Freedom: Towards the Human, after Man, Its Overrepresentation—An Argument," *CR: The New Centennial Review* 3, no. 3 (2003): 287–88.

24. Danielle Diaz, "African-American Professor Carol Swain Slams Black Lives Matter," CNN Politics, July 29, 2016, 3:21 PM, https://www.cnn.com/2016/07/09/politics/carol-swain-black-lives-matter-smerconish/index.html.

25. Barbara Reynolds, "I Was a Civil Rights Activist in the 1960s. But It's Hard for Me to Get Behind Black Lives Matter," *Washington Post*, August 24, 2015, https://www.washingtonpost.com/posteverything/wp/2015/08/24/i-was-a-civil-rights-activist-in-the-1960s-but-its-hard-for-me-to-get-behind-black-lives-matter.

26. Reynolds, "I Was a Civil Rights Activist in the 1960s."

27. Reena Flores, "White House Responds to Petition to Label Black Lives Matter a 'Terror' Group," July 17, 2016, CBS News, 7:36 pm, https://www.cbsnews.com/news/white-house-responds-to-petition-to-label-black-lives-matter-a-terror-group.

28. Vincent Lloyd, "Religion, Secularism, and Black Lives Matter: An Introduction," *The Immanent Frame*, September 22, 2016, https://tif.ssrc.org/2016/09/22/religion-secularism-and-black-lives-matter.

29. Wes Alcenat, "'Shall It Be a Woman?': Black Lives Matter and Leadership in the Face of Black Patriarchy," *The Immanent Frame*, September 2016, https://tif.ssrc.org/2016/09/22/religion-secularism-and-black-lives-matter.

30. "Guiding Principles," Black Lives Matter, accessed March 2019, https://blacklivesmatter.com/about/what-we-believe.

31. In its broadest sense, "value theory" is a catch-all label in philosophical thinking that encompasses some "evaluative" aspect. In values discourse, types of values include ethical/moral, doctrinal/ideological (religious/political), social, and aesthetic ones. Furthermore, its history includes debates on whether some values are innate. In some systems where there is a hierarchy of values, subordinate values derive all of their value from a relation to a supreme value, single value, or highest good that justifies the rest. One exemplary model is Platonism, which posits the form of the Good as beyond being

or transcendent. Accordingly, the Good is the source of the reality of other forms and also their copies in the visible realm. Later medieval philosophers appropriated this hierarchy of values, establishing in various metaphysical systems the concept of God as the Highest Good, or, in more familiar terms, as the most perfect being and the source of all other beings. For a sampling of works in values discourse, including ethical works, see Aristotle, "Nicomachean Ethics," in *The Complete Works of Aristotle: The Revised Oxford Translation*, vol. 2, ed. Jonathan Barnes (Princeton, NJ: Princeton University Press, 1984); Immanuel Kant, *Groundwork for the Metaphysics of Morals*, Mary Gregor, trans. (1785; Cambridge, UK: Cambridge University Press, 1997); Richard Kraut, *What Is Good and Why: The Ethics of Well-Being* (Cambridge, MA: Harvard University Press, 2007); Joseph Raz, *Engaging Reason: On the Theory of Value and Action* (Oxford, UK: Oxford University Press, 1999); Susan Wolf, *The Variety of Values: Essays on Morality, Meaning, and Love* (Oxford, UK: Oxford University Press, 2014); Susan Wolf, *Meaning in Life and Why It Matters* (Princeton, NJ: Princeton University Press, 2012); Michael Zimmerman, *The Nature of Intrinsic Value* (Lanham, MD: Rowman and Littlefield, 2001).

32. "Guiding Principles," Black Lives Matter.
33. "Guiding Principles," Black Lives Matter.
34. W. E. B. Du Bois, "The Souls of Black Folk" in *W. E. B. Du Bois: Writings*, ed. Nathan Huggins (New York: Library of Congress, 1986), 359–553.
35. "Guiding Principles," Black Lives Matter.
36. See Cornel West and Eddie S. Glaude's introductory essay "Towards New Visions and New Approaches" in *African American Religious Thought: An Anthology* (Louisville, KY: Westminster John Knox Press, 2003), xiii–xv.
37. David Evans, *We Have Been Believers: An African-American Systematic Theology* (Minneapolis, MN: Ausburg Fortress Press, 1992), 54; 67. See also Major J. Jones, *The Color of God: The Concept of God in Afro-American Thought* (Macon, GA: Mercer University Press, 1987); Kurt Buhring, *Conceptions of God, Freedom, and Ethics in African American and Jewish Theology* (New York: Palgrave Macmillan, 2008).
38. Loyal Rue, *Religion Is Not about God: How Spiritual Traditions Nurture Our Biological Nature and What to Do When They Fail* (New Brunswick, NJ: Rutgers University Press, 2005), 1.
39. Rue, *Religion Is Not about God*, 3.
40. For further reading, see W. E. B. Du Bois, *The Autobiography of W. E. B. Du Bois: A Soliloquy on Viewing My Life from the Last Decade of Its First Century* (New York: International Publishers, 1968), 285; Philip S. Foner, ed., *Du Bois Speaks: Speeches and Addresses, 1920–1963* (New York: Pathfinder, 1970), 111; Herbert Aptheker, ed., *The Correspondence of W. E. B. Du Bois*, vol. 3, *Selections, 1944–1963* (Amherst: University of Massachusetts Press, 1978); David Levering Lewis, ed., *W. E. B. Du Bois: A Reader* (New York: Holt, 1995), 134.

41. Du Bois to Herbert Aptheker, January 10, 1956, *The Correspondence of W. E. B. Du Bois*, 3: 395–96. For fuller accounts of Du Bois's agnostic orientation and his complex relationship with religion, see Phil Zuckerman, *Du Bois on Religion* (Lanham, MD: Altamira Press, 2000); Jonathon S. Kahn, *The Divine Discontent: The Religious Imagination of W. E. B. Du Bois* (New York: Oxford University Press, 2009); Edward J. Blum and Jason R. Young, ed., *The Souls of W. E. B. Du Bois: New Essays and Reflections* (Macon, GA: Macon University Press, 2009); Carol Wayne White, *Black Lives and Sacred Humanity: Toward an African American Religious Naturalism* (New York: Fordham Press, 2016), chapter 4.

42. In claiming this, I follow a general model of religious naturalism that is identified by Donald Crosby as materialist metaphysics, or a view of reality that regards all existence as diverse forms and functions of matter. In "Matter, Mind, and Meaning, in *The Routledge Handbook of Religious Naturalism* (New York: Routledge, 2018), Crosby writes, "It is meant to take into account all that we have learned (and much we still have to learn) in physics about the nature and capabilities of matter since Newton's time, but it does not restrict its conception of matter to what can be described or explained by the discipline of physics. Rather than being reductionist in this sense, it is emergentist or expansionist in its character. Approaches to a proper understanding of matter require the resources of all fields of thought, from physics, to chemistry, to biology, to psychology, to sociology, to philosophy, to art, to religion, and to the experiences of everyday life" (18).

43. Wesley Wildman, "Religious Naturalism: What It Can Be, and What It Need Not Be," *Philosophy, Theology and the Sciences* 1, no. 1 (2014): 41.

44. Rue, *Religion Is Not about God*, 25.

45. Stephen Jay Gould, *Wonderful Life: The Burgess Shale and the Nature of History* (New York: W. W. Norton, 1990); Terrence Deacon, "The Hierarchic Logic of Emergence: Untangling the Interdependence of Evolution and Self-Organization," in *Evolution and Learning: The Baldwin Effect Reconsidered*, ed. Bruce H. Weber and David J. Depew (Cambridge, MA: MIT Press, 2007), 273–307; Terrence Deacon, "Emergence: The Hole at the Wheel's Hub," in *The Re-Emergence of Emergence: The Emergentist Hypothesis from Science to Religion*, ed. Philip Clayton and Paul Davies (Oxford, UK: Oxford University Press, 2006), 111–50.

46. Michael W. Fox, "What Future for Man and Earth? Toward a Biospiritual Ethic," in *On the Fifth Day: Animal Rights and Human Ethics*, ed. Richard Knowles Morris and Michael W. Fox (Washington, DC: Acropolis Books, 1978), 227.

47. Ursula Goodenough, *The Sacred Depths of Nature* (New York: Oxford University Press, 2000), 73.

48. White, *Black Lives and Sacred Humanity*, 34ff.

49. "Guiding Principles," Black Lives Matter.

50. White, *Black Lives and Sacred Humanity*, 120.

51. Patrisse Khan-Cullors and Asha Bandele, *When They Call You a Terrorist: A Black Lives Matter Memoir*, with forward by Angela Davis (New York: St. Martin's Press, 2018), 3–4.

52. Alicia Garza, "A Herstory of the #BlackLivesMatter Movement."

53. "Guiding Principles," Black Lives Matter.

54. "Guiding Principles," Black Lives Matter.

55. "Guiding Principles," Black Lives Matter.

56. "Guiding Principles," Black Lives Matter.

57. "Guiding Principles," Black Lives Matter.

58. Michael Warner, introduction to *Fear of a Queer Planet: Queer Politics and Social Theory*, ed. Michael Warner (Minneapolis: University of Minnesota Press, 1993), xxvii.

59. "Guiding Principles," Black Lives Matter.

60. Ahmad Greene-Hayes, "Why Are Queer Black Lives 'Secular'?," *The Immanent Frame*, September 22, 2016, https://tif.ssrc.org/2016/09/22/religion-secularism-and-black-lives-matter.

61. Ahmad Greene-Hayes, "Why are queer black lives 'secular'?"

62. Michael Hogue, *American Immanence: Democracy for an Uncertain World* (New York: Columbia University Press, 2018), 8–13.

63. Donna Haraway, *When Species Meet* (Minneapolis: University of Minnesota Press, 2008), 3–4.

64. Carol Wayne White, "Stubborn Materiality: African-American Religious Naturalism and Becoming Our Humanity," in *Entangled Worlds: Science, Religion, and Materiality*, ed. Catherine Keller and Mary-Jane Rubenstein (Bronx, NY: Fordham University Press, 2017): 251.

65. Donald Crosby, *The Thou of Nature* (New York: State University Press of New York, 2013), 16.

66. Aldo Leopold, *Sand County Almanac: And Sketches Here and There* (New York: Oxford University Press, 1987), 204.

67. R. J. Dolan, "Emotion, Cognition, and Behavior," *Science* 298 (November 2002): 1191–94.

68. Holmes Rolston III, "Environmental Ethics and Religion/Science" in *The Oxford Handbook of Religion and Science*, ed. Philip Clayton and Zachary Simpson (New York: Oxford University Press, 2006), 911.

69. Jeremy Bentham, *An Introduction to the Principles of Morals and Legislation* (1798; Scotts Valley, CA: CreateSpace Independent Publishing Platform, 2018), 227.

70. Karen Morin, *Carceral Space, Prisoners and Animals* (New York: Routledge, 2018), 7.

71. For further reading, see Dianne Glave, *Rooted in the Earth: Reclaiming the African American Environmental Heritage* (Chicago: Chicago Review Press, 2010); Carolyn Finney, *Black Faces, White Spaces: Reimagining the Relationship of African Americans to the Great Outdoors* (Chapel Hill: University of North Carolina Press, 2014).

72. Paul Outka, *Race and Nature: From Transcendentalism to the Harlem Renaissance* (New York: Palgrave Macmillan, 2008), 3.

73. See Luke W. Cole and Sheila R. Foster, *From the Ground Up: Environmental Racism and the Rise of the Environmental Justice Movement* (New York: New York University Press, 2001).

74. See Christopher Cameron and Philip Sinitiere's definition in the introduction of this book.

CHAPTER 5

The Faith of the Future

Black Lives of Unitarian Universalism

Christopher Cameron

In July 2015, a group of Black Unitarian Universalists met at the Movement for Black Lives Convening in Cleveland, Ohio, and formed a new organization: the Black Lives of Unitarian Universalism Organizing Collective (Black Lives UU, or BLUU). While this group, which included Leslie Mac and Lena Gardner, both activists in the Movement for Black Lives, did not set out for Cleveland to create a new organization or faith community, that is exactly what they did. Drawing from the seven Principles of the broader Unitarian Universalist (UU) movement, as well as the ideology of the Black Lives Matter movement, Black Lives UU developed its own seven principles, including "All Black lives matter," "Love and self-love is practiced in every element of all we do," and "Spiritual growth is directly tied to our ability to embrace our whole selves." The group quickly grew and engaged in effective fundraising that allowed it to bring more than two hundred Black Unitarian Universalists to the Unitarian Universalist Association (UUA) General Assembly in 2017, a record for Black attendance at that annual meeting. It likewise boasts a vibrant social media presence that has made the organization the go-to space for

Black UUs around the country and around the world to share ideas, support one another, and build community.[1]

While the creation of Black Lives UU is certainly a novel development in the history of both Black and liberal religion, African Americans have engaged with and been key figures in American religious liberalism since the eighteenth century. Gloster Dalton, a freed slave, was a founding member of the first Universalist church in the United States in 1779. Amy Scott, a free Black woman, was likewise a founding member of the First Universalist Society in Philadelphia in 1790. Egbert Ethelred Brown founded a Unitarian congregation in Jamaica in 1908 and then moved to Harlem, where he assembled the Harlem Unitarian Church in 1920. In 1947, Lewis A. McGee founded the Free Religious Fellowship in Chicago, a Unitarian church that is still in existence. Along with these pioneers, Black members of the denomination founded the Black Unitarian Universalist Caucus (BUUC) in the late 1960s in an attempt to make the denomination more responsive to the demands of the Black Power Movement. While that organization lasted just six years, it provided a model for the contemporary Black Lives UU movement.

Just as BUUC aimed to wed the political principles of Black Power with the theology of Unitarian Universalism, so too has BLUU endeavored to bring together the politics of the broader Movement for Black Lives with the religious ideals of the denomination. Indeed, for the leaders of the BLUU Organizing Collective as of August 2020—including Lena Gardner, Takiyah Nur Amin, and Mykal Slack—there is no sharp distinction between their faith and politics. If Unitarian Universalists proclaim the "inherent worth and dignity of every person" as the first of their seven Principles, then leaders of BLUU would argue all members of the denomination should be advocates of Black Lives Matter (BLM), both as a movement and as a political ideology. Additionally, BLUU has become a spiritual resource and home for BLM activists who are wary of traditional Black churches. Rather than show up and pass out church flyers at activist gatherings and events, BLUU leaders instead show up, take part in, and help fund these events, activities that provide a powerful example of faith in action for activists suspicious of faith leaders. BLUU has thus built on the powerful historical legacy of its predecessors in the denomination while creating something entirely new—a community of Black religious liberals with the funding to control their own organization and the drive to improve the lives of those on the margins, especially Black women and LGBTQ identified individuals.

BLUU's existence and rapid growth between 2015 and 2021 demonstrates the way that the Movement for Black Lives has shifted the contours of African American religion, a dynamic to which multiple other essays in this volume speak. Iman AbdoulKarim demonstrates the varied ways that engagement with BLM has pushed female Muslims to interpret Islamic texts from a feminist lens (Chapter 8), while Alexandra Hartmann shows how participants in BLM have advanced a multifaceted humanist worldview that finds expression in the works of artists ranging from Beyoncé to Kendrick Lamar to Usher (Chapter 10). Like Hartmann, Carol Wayne White examines the rise of a nontraditional religious perspective, religious naturalism, and its relation to BLM (Chapter 4). Black Lives UU is in this same vein and represents yet another example of the religious pluralism that is both reflected in and has resulted from the diverse coalition making up the Movement for Black Lives.

Early Pioneers

More than a century before the Unitarians and Universalists merged in 1961, the American Unitarian Association (AUA) had an opportunity to embrace an African American minister and perhaps spread liberal religion beyond the confines of its largely white, middle class membership. In 1860, Reverend William Jackson, African American minister of the Salem Baptist Church in New Bedford, Massachusetts, spoke before the AUA autumnal convention, which was meeting in his city. On the last day of the convention, Thursday, October 11, 1860, Jackson stood up before the assembled ministers and laypeople and announced that he was a new convert to Unitarianism and intended to preach its doctrines in his congregation moving forward. A collection was taken up to help settle the debt that his church owed, after which he was sent on his way. Reverend Jackson received no word of encouragement, and the Unitarians present did not use this opportunity to try and evangelize African Americans. It appears they wanted to keep their faith the province of a select few. Reverend Dan Harper, formerly the minister of the First Unitarian Church in New Bedford, notes that the response Jackson received "prefigured the course of Unitarian race relations for the next century."[2]

Other African Americans were attracted to liberal religion in the nineteenth century but they were few and far between. Francis Ellen Watkins Harper became a member of the First Unitarian Church of Philadelphia in 1870 and remained one until her death in 1911. Yet she never wrote about or publicly acknowledged her Unitarianism and she also maintained her membership in (Mother) Bethel AME Church. She likely kept her ties to the AME church for social and political reasons, as she was a frequent speaker and worked with Black churches in social reform movements ranging from abolitionism to temperance to women's rights. Peter H. Clark, a Black schoolteacher in Cincinnati during the mid-to-late nineteenth century, has a similar story as Harper. He began attending Cincinnati's First Congregational Unitarian Church in 1857 and became a member in 1868. Clark, who had been an early admirer of Thomas Paine, was attracted to the minister's deism and abolitionism. Yet he too kept his ties to a Black church with his membership at Allen Temple, the largest AME church in the city. Like Harper, this likely allowed Clark to remain involved in the Black community's social and political life.[3]

Fannie Barrier Williams was another early Black convert to liberal religion. Born in upstate New York in 1855, she grew up in a mostly white town and attended schools that were all white with the exception of her siblings. After getting married and moving to Chicago, Fannie and her husband S. Laing Williams joined All Souls Unitarian Church, led by the radical freethinking minister Jenkin Lloyd Jones. Jones criticized institutional Christianity and much of Christian doctrine, and he was a strong supporter of civil rights and women's equality. Williams, along with a white female Unitarian minister named Celia Parker Woolley, founded the Frederick Douglass Centre in Chicago. This was modeled after Jane Addams's Hull House and provided lectures, classes, and social services in the South Side. Demonstrating the influence of Reverend Jones on her theology, Williams noted in an 1893 speech at the Columbian Exposition that what African Americans need from religion was "more religion and less church. . . . Less theology and more of human brotherhood, less declamation and more common sense and love for truth."[4] Williams would go on to become a pioneering Black leader, helping to found the National Association of Colored Women, an organization that provided services such as childcare, job placement, and education to Black women across the country.[5]

The early twentieth century would see the emergence of the first Black Universalist ministers. Joseph H. Jordan started a Universalist church in Norfolk, Virginia, in 1887, and he would be succeeded as minister by an unrelated man with the same name, Joseph Fletcher Jordan. The latter Joseph Jordan also started a school for African American children, the Suffolk Normal Training School, later renamed the Jordan Neighborhood House. While the Norfolk church had folded by 1910, the Suffolk school continued into the 1970s and was led by Annie Willis, Joseph F. Jordan's daughter, after 1929. Willis was not a minister, yet the school nevertheless was part of the Universalist church's mission to the African American community, begun in the late nineteenth century, and provided both education and services such as a medical clinic to the Black community in the tidewater region of Virginia.[6]

Along with these African American Universalists, multiple Black ministers started their own Unitarian congregations. Egbert Ethelred Brown began adulthood as a treasury clerk in Kingston, Jamaica, a position he served in until 1907. He then traveled to the United States to study for his Master of Divinity at Meadville Theological School in Pennsylvania before returning to Jamaica and starting a Unitarian congregation in Montego Bay. That congregation struggled to establish a solid foothold, with Sunday services attracting between ten and twenty-five people, who met in Brown's home. Brown then returned to the United States and established the Harlem Unitarian Church in 1920. At the beginning of his ministry he aimed "to prove not to the world, but to Unitarians, that Negroes are capable of becoming Unitarians, and that therefore Unitarianism is a universal religion."[7] While many white Unitarians may have believed Blacks were too lost in superstition and emotionalism to embrace the faith, Brown believed otherwise and approached his work with incredible zeal. But he faced many difficulties along the way. For one, he could not find work as an accountant in New York like he had enjoyed in Jamaica, thus he worked as an elevator operator, an office secretary, and a speaker for the Socialist Party, jobs that did not pay very well. He likewise faced numerous personal challenges, including a wife and son struggling with mental illness and another son who died by suicide. And his church and ministry received little support or encouragement from the American Unitarian Association. Despite these challenges, Brown pressed on and, as Juan M. Floyd-Thomas notes, his Harlem Unitarian Church "provided all interested parties in Harlem with an extraordinary venue in which to engage in open debate, social activism, and spiritual awakening through a radical brand of Black Christianity deeply infused with humanist principles."[8]

W. H. G. Carter faced even more of an uphill battle than Brown did in establishing his church. Carter was born in 1877 and had planned to become an AME minister like his father and grandfather but chose not to do so because he did not believe in the divinity of Jesus. After leaving the church, he held various jobs, including postal worker, mural painter, photographer, and real estate speculator. Carter was very politically active, running for city council twice, and he founded the Grand Order of Denizens to provide food and services to the Black community of Cincinnati. In 1918, Carter formed the Church of the Unitarian Brotherhood in Cincinnati, probably the first Black Unitarian church in the country. The church was a small storefront one in operation for twenty years before the American Unitarian Association even learned of its existence. When the association did become aware of his church, they sent the Reverend Lon Ray Call to check out the congregation. He reported on the poor neighborhood conditions and the fact that two local white Unitarian ministers had received a poor response to their sermons and suggested the AUA not recognize or fund the church, a suggestion the organization followed. This, combined with the fact that Carter could not even get his own family members to join his church (his wife worshipped at a different congregation and only one of his fifteen children became a Unitarian) led to Carter's congregation closing down by 1940, although he remained active in the political life of the Black community in Cincinnati.[9]

Lewis McGee had a much shorter ministry at his Black Unitarian Church than Brown or Carter did, yet his was arguably more successful. McGee's Free Religious Fellowship in Chicago grew out of conversations between him, his wife Marcella McGee, and their friend Harry Jones at the Society for Ethical Culture. McGee had been an AME minister and an Army chaplain but eventually accepted the tenets of religious humanism during the 1920s. After World War II, McGee enrolled in Meadville Lombard Theological School in Chicago, where he greatly impressed his faculty members, one of whom noted McGee "seemed to me to be a widely educated and thoroughly liberal personality. He gives the distinct impression of ability and stability." McGee's route toward starting the Free Religious Fellowship took a much different path than Carter's or Brown's. He had been a social worker, so he proposed to conduct a survey among African Americans in Chicago to determine the feasibility of a liberal church there. He concluded that such a congregation could indeed thrive on the South Side and he formally launched the church on April 25, 1948, with fifty-three charter members. Nicole Kirk states that "the theology espoused by the McGees and Jones in sermons and advertisements was a religious humanism that focused on freedom as an opening to new possibilities and the rejection of intellectual imperialism."[10] Their church attracted primarily middle-class and highly educated African Americans, as well as a smattering of whites from other local Unitarian churches that came to offer their support. McGee remained minister of the church until 1953, after which he took a position with the American Humanist Association before becoming the associate minister of the First Unitarian Church of Los Angeles in 1958. Three years later, McGee accepted a call as senior minister of the Unitarian Fellowship of Chico, California, making him the only African American senior Unitarian minister in the country.[11]

Black Power and Unitarian Universalism

While Lewis McGee was beginning his ministry anew in California, an increasing number of African Americans were drawn to Unitarian Universalism. Hayward Henry was one such individual. He grew up in New Orleans, where he was attending Dillard University in the early 1960s. Reverend Albert D'Orlando, minister of the First Unitarian Universalist Church of New Orleans, invited Henry's choir to come sing at his church, a progressive move at a time when white churches did not usually extend such invitations. Henry was also impressed with the church because he was studying biology and evolution, a topic that was off limits at his own Baptist church, yet "the Unitarian Universalist church was willing to allow discussions of Darwinian evolution in a church. That really impressed me." As was the case for Black Unitarians at Egbert Brown and Lewis McGee's churches, Henry appreciated the emphasis on intellectual freedom that he found in Unitarian Universalism. He did not join the church as an undergraduate student, but when he began graduate school at Boston University in 1967, he started attending the Second Unitarian Church of Boston after hearing Jack Hamlin preach on controversial topics such as "Is God Dead?," war and peace, and civil rights. He was heavily involved in the civil rights movement, having been a member of the Student Nonviolent Coordinating Committee and the NAACP Youth Council, yet he kept these involvements to himself, initially. People at Second Unitarian knew where he stood intellectually and theologically, but they did not yet know of his growing commitment to Black Power.[12]

Hayward Henry would be instrumental in what has come to be known as the "Black Empowerment Controversy" within the UUA, including the formation of the Black Unitarian Universalist Caucus, of which he was the first president. Henry posits that the genesis of BUUC was in 1966 when Willie Ricks and Stokely Carmichael began articulating the philosophy of Black Power during a march in Greenwood, Mississippi. After this development, as well as the assassination of James Meredith and riots in Harlem and Watts in the mid-1960s, "us youngsters are saying, you know, the old peace and the old tactics are wearing thin." In October 1967, the UUA called an Emergency Conference to respond to issues of racial unrest in the nation. Roughly 140 people attended the conference, 37 of them African American. Thirty of these Blacks heeded the call of Black Unitarians for Radical Reform, a group centered in the First Unitarian Church of Los Angeles, and formed the Black Unitarian Universalist Caucus, which, as Kerry Pimblott points out in Chapter 2, was one of ten such caucuses formed in white churches during the 1960s and 1970s. BUUC then drew up a list of demands for the Emergency Conference to consider, including the formation of a Black Affairs Council (BAC), whose membership would always include a majority of Blacks and would be elected by BUUC, the funding of BAC at $250,000 a year for four years, and complete control over how those funds were to be spent. The conference adopted these proposals, which were then passed on to the UUA Board of Trustees.[13]

One of the primary goals in creating the Black Unitarian Universalist Caucus was to eliminate racism from the denomination and foster African American self-determination, making the efforts of BUUC similar to those of the Black Catholics that Matthew Cressler examines in Chapter 1. Mtangulizi Sanyika (formerly Hayward Henry) notes that "we had Black clergy there who were telling us they had difficulty getting appointments, getting fellowships . . . getting pulpits. We didn't see many Black people on any committees; we didn't see Black people in their religious ed. curriculum." Even as African Americans were joining Unitarian Universalist churches in greater numbers than ever before, they were still vastly underrepresented in leadership roles in the denomination and felt they had no voice in what was supposed to be a democratic process of decision making. A related goal was pushing the denomination toward "the prioritization of the external agenda against racism in society." While the UUA was probably ahead of many denominations in its response to racism both within the denomination and in fighting it in American society, Sanyika notes that white leaders of the church "had exclusively appropriated unto themselves the right to determine the nature of a racial justice agenda in society." He and other members of BUUC felt that "only the African American community had the right to articulate and implement the racial justice agenda in this church in the future." In pushing the denomination toward focusing on implementing an external racial justice agenda, Henry and other supporters of BUUC made it clear they did not want that agenda "focused on the traditional desegregation approach but self-determination and empowerment." Hayward believed that "in ghettoized communities the problem wasn't Black people and white people not being together, the problem was Black people didn't have any power over housing decisions, economic decisions, education decisions, political decisions, cultural decisions."[14]

After the UUA General Assembly fully funded the Black Affairs Council (BAC, BUUC's financial arm) in 1968 at $250,000 a year, both organizations got to work implementing their main goals. First, BAC deposited $150,000 of its $250,000 in the Industrial Bank of Jenkintown, Pennsylvania, because it had "aggressive and just employment, loan and mortgage policies toward Black people." Other initiatives included sending a group of African American children from Syracuse, New York, to Zambia to study art and dance; job training for ex-gang leaders in Philadelphia; the establishment of Black-owned businesses under a new corporation named Ghetto Enterprises, Inc.; and the production of short films aimed at undermining racism in American society. All this had been set in motion by November 1968, just six months after the UUA General Assembly approved their funding.[15]

Both BUUC and BAC would be short-lived due to both financial issues within the UUA and lingering disagreement over "racial separatism," yet the movement nevertheless had an important impact on the denomination while it was in existence. Mtangulizi Sanyika posits that the founding and work of the Black Unitarian Universalist Caucus "changed the paradigm. It changed the way white and Black people in the denomination understood the relationship between the races in the church in a very fundamental way. Secondly, it opened the conversation about power and participation that had not been opened." John Hurley notes that in the 1930s, St. Lawrence University, a school affiliated with the Universalist Church of America, recommended Jeffrey Campbell, an African American graduate, to the ministry largely because it could not face the contradiction between the denomination's liberal principles and belief in salvation for all with continuing racial discrimination. A similar situation characterized the Black Empowerment saga of the 1960s. Sanyika states that "we exposed Unitarian Universalists to themselves. I think it exposed them to themselves and helped them to see a reality about themselves, and that I think they were sleeping through a revolution and didn't know they were asleep. So it helped them change how they saw reality." Additionally, in Sanyika's view, members of BUUC and BAC opened the doors of the denomination to greater participation and power sharing for lesbians and gays, women, and youth. "We opened the door for all oppressed groups in that church, and most people were oppressed, which was another contribution we made: open the door for all oppressed modalities to become freer in their expression of their faith because they saw in us the courage we had to stand up to power and principality."[16]

Black Lives UU

While forty-five years passed between the defunding of BUUC and the founding of Black Lives of Unitarian Universalism, the latter group has built on the legacy and, in many ways, carried on the work that its predecessor began. Like BUUC, BLUU is an organization committed to radical inclusion and self-determination, as well as social responsibility. Its founders were gathered together for an activist meeting, not a religious one, and the struggle for Black liberation is central to all of its work. BLUU's name, leaders, ideology, and work in the world are all aimed at affirming the central slogan of today's civil rights movement: Black Lives Matter.

Probably the main driving force behind the founding of BLUU was Leslie Mac, an activist who founded the Ferguson Response Network after the murder of Michael Brown in August 2014. Shortly after Darren Wilson killed the unarmed teenager, Mac got into a conflict with the UU minister of her Cherry Hill, New Jersey, congregation. He had written an op-ed in a local newspaper calling the protests in Ferguson a race riot, a characterization with which Mac strongly disagreed. She did not like the fact that the minister was representing the congregation to the public in the way he was, and the minister "got in his feelings, and it turned into this whole big thing." Mac notes that she ended up leaving the church "because the more Black liberation work I was doing, the less inviting the church became to me." Mac was surprised and excited to find a number of other Black Unitarian Universalists present at the Movement for Black Lives convening and they shared similar experiences with her. "I remember Royce James," she states, "who was one of the founding members of BLUU. He was there with his daughter Isis and he said 'well you know, I've just gotten to the point where I'll drop the kids off, and I really can't go in there anymore.'" Lena Gardner, who would become the executive director of BLUU, expressed a similar sentiment, noting "'as soon as I started doing that work, it became, every time I go into church, somebody wanted to confront me; somebody wanted to ask me or tell me what I should or shouldn't be doing, and it stopped being a safe place for me.'"[17]

Mac points out that even with this small sample, she kept hearing the same stories and the same experiences and decided something should be done to address this situation. "One of the things we kept talking about was how we saw the seven principles of Unitarian Universalism directly connected to our work as organizers and activists for Black Liberation; we didn't see a separation between the two," Mac claims. Takiyah Nur Amin, who joined the BLUU Organizing Collective in August 2016, expressed a similar sentiment, noting that "for most Black UUs that we engage with in the group, we don't see that faith perspective of Unitarian Universalism as separate from the work we do in the world, right. It's like they're one and the same. It's like I believe in this free and responsible search for truth and meaning which also calls me to protect the dignity of other human beings, which includes those who are most marginalized, and in many instances, those are poor Black folks, right. So it's all connected for us." Building off this idea, Mac, Lena Gardner, Kenny Wylie, and others decided that "if we came up with the seven principles of Black Lives that would, kind of, tie directly to our principles as Unitarian Universalists and kind of make this statement that like, look, this is a part of UUism too. This notion of liberation for Black people is really important and should be important to all Unitarian Universalists."[18]

Lena Gardner was another driving force behind the founding of BLUU and reflects well the dual goals of providing space for Black UUs while also helping forward the Movement for Black Lives. Gardner's religious upbringing was decidedly noninstitutional, largely because of her grandfather, a conservative Baptist preacher who espoused a theology where "women were evil . . . dancing was evil, everything was evil and everybody was going to Hell." Her father, traumatized by his early church experiences, tried to shield her from that and introduced her to "spirituality and God as sort of in nature and also in community, and sort of to be really honoring the divine in every person and every individual," values that would mesh well with Unitarian Universalism (as well as the religious naturalism Carol Wayne White discusses in Chapter 4), which she was introduced to shortly before starting a Master's degree in justice and peace studies at the United Theological Seminary in Minnesota. Even as she was drawn to the faith, she still struggled with "how white the denomination was and how white the congregation was." She really loved the theology of Unitarian Universalism, but struggled culturally. Nevertheless, Gardner notes, "there are no open and affirming Black churches in Minneapolis . . . and identifying as a queer person, I just made a choice that I would rather put up with the racism and the whiteness at the UU congregation . . . than the patriarchy and the homophobia at the Black churches around here."[19]

Gardner's experience at the First Universalist Church of Minneapolis would end up being similar to Leslie Mac's and would propel her to take a leading role in Black Lives of Unitarian Universalism. Gardner was one of the founders of the Black Lives Matter chapter of Minneapolis in 2014 and she states that once the movement there began "that tore up my soul a little bit because, you know, I would go to church and, you know, these white people would say the most ridiculous things, and I was like, man, I don't think I can do this anymore. You know they had these political analyses that are void of an understanding of structural and systemic oppression . . . they pull out of an ahistorical vacuum." Like Leslie Mac, the lunch that Gardner attended at the BLM convening in Cleveland with other Black UUs was eye opening and raised an important question that remains a central one for BLUU: "How can we make a home that is unapologetically Black and makes room for a diversity of Black experiences and ... perspectives and viewpoints and is also theologically UU?" This question led Gardner, Mac, Wylie, and others to found BLUU in August 2015. "We started it by putting our UU principles through the lens of Blackness." she posits. "That means our first principle was Black lives matter."[20]

In a short time, Gardner, Mac, and other leaders of BLUU would develop their own seven Principles, in a riff on the seven Principles of the Unitarian Universalist Association. The first Principle of the latter organization is "the inherent worth and dignity of every person." If the denomination actually believes this, BLUU members note, then they should have no problem with affirming that "all Black lives matter," the first Principle of BLUU. BLUU's second Principle is "Love and self-love is practiced in every element of all we do." For members and leaders of BLUU, "love and self-love must be drivers of all our work and indicators of our success. Without this principle and without healing, we will harm each other and undermine our movement," both within the denomination and in the Movement for Black Lives. The third principle, "Spiritual growth is directly tied to our ability to embrace our whole selves" likewise links the theological and the political, as the organization states that "the spiritual growth of UUs of color is directly tied to our ability to stand in the truth that Black Lives Matter." The fourth and fifth Principles of BLUU respectively state, "Experimentation and innovation must be built into our work" and "Most directly affected people are experts at their own lives." This latter Principle relates to the point Mtangulizi Sanyika made about BUUC in the 1960s, namely that Black liberation should first and foremost center the needs and desires of Black people, who could make positive choices for their own lives. BLUU's sixth Principle calls for "Thriving instead of surviving," as their vision "is based on the world we want, and not the world we are currently in. We seek to transform, not simply to react. We want out people to thrive, not just exist." Finally, BLUU recognizes the necessity of a "360 degree vision" in their seventh Principle. This vision looks to the wisdom of elders like Mtangulizi Sanyika as well as ancestors such as Toni Morrison in guiding their work. BLUU likewise argues in this Principle that "acknowledging the ways in which a Supremacist society diminishes us ALL is a critical part of the work of the Movement for Black Lives. When the most marginalized of our society is free, then we will ALL truly be free." Every principle at the heart of BLUU as an organization speaks in some way to the tie between religion and Black Lives Matter and demonstrates their belief that Unitarian Universalism can be a guiding force in this political movement.[21]

The twin goals of providing spiritual care to Black UUs and helping to forward the Movement for Black Lives have been at the heart of BLUU's work from the beginning. In early 2018, Mykal Slack joined the leadership team, or Organizing Collective, of BLUU as its new Community Minister with the charge to address both of these key goals. Slack had been working at a UU congregation in Raleigh, North Carolina, and, as had been the case at earlier positions he held at UU churches, he experienced both racism and classism. Finally, in early 2018, Slack, who had been ordained at the Metropolitan Community Church in New York but never pastored his own church, came to the realization that he could no longer work in a primarily white congregation. This realization was a scary one because nearly all Unitarian Universalist churches are primarily white, but just two weeks later, in March 2018, Lena Gardner called and asked him to join the Organizing Collective. For Slack, expanding the power and capacity of Black Unitarian Universalists in the faith "means that we remind each other in all the ways that we can that we're not by ourselves. This is sometimes an isolating faith as a Black UU. . . . Sometimes you're the only person in a church and building the power and capacity of folks is a reminder that you're not by yourself in this faith." For Takiyah Nur Amin, vice-chair and content director of the BLUU Organizing Collective, building the power and capacity of Black UUs is partly about "making sure that our folks just have the information that exists to do with that what they will." For Amin, this is the first step toward Black self-determination in the denomination. BLUU helps connect Black UUs to resources, grants, and opportunities they might not have known existed. Amin likewise posits that one of the earliest needs that Black UUs expressed "was unmet pastoral care and spiritual needs. This was Black UUs who were in congregations but didn't feel like their ministers or faith leadership was adept at providing culturally relevant pastoral care."[22]

BLUU aimed to address this situation with Mykal Slack's hiring and with the creation of the BLUU Ministerial Network, or BLUU-Min. BLUUMin's central goal is providing pastoral care to Black UUs in need. There is a phone line that individuals can call and leave a message, and a pastoral care volunteer or a minister like Mykal will return the call and either talk with the person or provide referrals. BLUUMin volunteers likewise scroll through the pages of the closed Facebook group, which consisted of 760 members as of August 2019, and contact anyone who posts something indicating they need pastoral care or some other type of assistance. BLUU has also created the BLUU Affirmations Ministry, where people can sign up to receive daily affirmations each morning at eleven. Takiyah Amin notes that "it seems like a small thing, but those affirmations are really important, again, because we are all so spread out across the country and it's a way of keeping us connected."[23]

This sense of connection is key to BLUU's online worship that Mykal Slack initiated shortly after joining BLUU's board. Once or twice a month, Slack leads a worship service via the online video conferencing platform Zoom for Black UUs around the country to come together, listen to music by Black people, and engage in worship specifically created for Black people. Reflecting on the significance of Black-only spaces such as BLUU's online worship service, Slack states "we get really used to the white guys, and it has an impact. It can have an impact on how we kind of show up in a space, what we do or don't say, how we do or don't posture ourselves. Being in a space where that is not a consideration at all is just like "okay" [sigh of relief]. I can just kind of breathe and just say whatever. Whatever my spirit would call me to say, and now I don't have to stress about what that's going to look like to somebody else, or how they're going to treat me later on, right." And BLUU is serious about ensuring this is a Black-only space. While AME or Black Baptist churches welcome anyone who enters their doors, Mykal begins each BLUU online worship service by first asking if everybody present identifies as Black. He notes that there are other spaces for those who do not identify as such, but this service is not such a space. In doing this, Slack ensures that all members present feel they can be completely open and honest about what they are going through, especially if those issues relate to their physical congregations comprised primarily of whites.[24]

Along with providing pastoral and spiritual care to Black UUs, Black Lives of Unitarian Universalism was explicitly created to forward the Movement for Black Lives. Lena Gardner notes that goal is "the one area where all of us are very aligned as far as on the OC [Organizing Collective]. Like we must be working as part of a broader Movement for Black Lives, and, you know, that's just very important to us . . . and in solidarity with other movements for justice." One way they do this is simply showing up and being there for protests, demonstrations, and other activities that are part of the movement. Another way is by using their funds to support people and organizations in need. BLUU donated $5,000 to the Highlander Center in Tennessee and likewise provided $90,000 in disaster relief after Hurricane Harvey (2017), most of which went directly to Black women who were affected by the storm. BLUU leaders note that in addition to them being influenced by BLM, they are in turn trying to shape the movement. As Leslie Mac claims, "this belief in the inherent worth and dignity of all people, when you put that in the context of Black liberation, that means that all Black people have to be considered when you're organizing, when you're planning, when you're thinking what you're going to do."[25]

Showing up and actively contributing to the Movement for Black Lives is BLUU's indirect way of proselytizing and growing its membership. According to Takiyah Amin, "UUs were never good at the whole proselytizing thing. But if there is any proselytizing, it's through the work. And I think people seeing us show up as folks of faith to work and not to pass out pamphlets that say 'Come to my church' has been really effective in terms of getting folks in the movement interested in what we're doing over here." Leslie Mac expressed a similar sentiment, noting that "we have so many people that we lovingly refer to as BLUU adjacent, so they're not technically UUs, but they continually come to our events, they come to our spaces, they connect with us, and I think they see us living out our faith in a way that's in alignment with the cause of Black liberation, and it speaks to them." An ultimate goal of this approach is for BLUU to become the spiritual home of activists in the Movement for Black Lives. While many of these activists are wary of traditional religious institutions and religious authorities, BLUU's leadership, which consists predominantly of queer-identified and trans individuals, is not just open and affirming toward those groups, but actually reflects much of the leadership of Black Lives Matter, many of whom also identify in similar ways. Takiyah Nur Amin posits that "in my dreams, Unitarian Universalism could become sort of the faith of the future for those of us who are committed to this kind of justice and liberation thing."[26]

Conclusion

Black Lives of Unitarian Universalism has built on the legacy of its predecessors in the denomination in very important ways, while also carving out its own identity and making its own mark in the world in just a few short years as of this writing. Like individual Black Unitarians such as Fannie Barrier Williams and Egbert Ethelred Brown, as well as groups such as the Black Unitarian Universalist Caucus, BLUU aims to foster Black liberation through the prism of Unitarian Universalist theology. BLUU has effectively made use of tools such as Facebook, Twitter, and Instagram to build community among Black UUs around the United States, and has begun to transform online relationships into physical ones by bringing Black UUs to the denomination's General Assembly and by hosting the Harper-Jordan Memorial Symposium in October 2019, an event that consisted of panels on Black UU history and theology, a worship service, and fellowship opportunities. One of BLUU's founders, Leslie Mac, now sits on the board of the UUA and has the opportunity to shape the future of the denomination, while current BLUU leaders such as Lena Gardner, Mykal Slack, and Takiyah Amin remain active in both the denomination and struggles for social justice, representing well the ties between race, religion, and Black Lives Matter.

NOTES

1. Black Lives of Unitarian Universalism, "7 Principles of Black Lives," accessed August 6, 2019, https://www.blacklivesuu.com/7-principles.

2. Dan Harper, "A Cold Shoulder for William Jackson" in *Darkening the Doorways: Black Trailblazers and Missed Opportunities in Unitarian Universalism*, ed. Mark D. Morrison-Reed (Boston: Skinner House Books, 2011), 14–16, 7.

3. Qiyamah Rahman, "Francis Ellen Watkins Harper, 1825–1911," in Morrison-Reed, *Darkening the Doorways*, 18–22; Bruce Beisner, "Peter H. Clark, 1828–1925," in Morrison-Reed, *Darkening the Doorways*, 24–27; Sankofa Working Files Collection—Individuals. Box 1, Folder 12: Peter H. Clark, Meadville Lombard Theological School Archives and Special Collections; for more on Clark see Nikki M. Taylor, *America's First Black Socialist: The Radical Life of Peter H. Clark* (Lexington: University Press of Kentucky, 2013).

4. Fannie Barrier Williams, "Religious Duty to the Negro," in *The New Woman of Color: The Collected Writings of Fannie Barrier Williams, 1893–1918*, ed. Mary Jo Deegan (DeKalb: Northern Illinois University Press, 2002), 76–77.

5. June Edwards, "Fannie Barrier Williams, 1855–1944," in Morrison-Reed, *Darkening the Doorways*, 30–35.

6. "Chronology of Black Involvement in Unitarianism, Universalism, and Unitarian Universalism," Unitarian Universalist Church of Norfolk Records, 1866–2011, Box 62, Folder 17, Special Collections and University Archives, Old Dominion University; Mark D. Morrison-Reed, *Black Pioneers in a White Denomination*, 3rd ed., (Boston: Skinner House Books, 1994), 31.

7. Rev. Hilary Bygrave, "Report of Trip to Montego Bay, Jamaica" Mark Morrison-Reed Ethelred Brown Research Collection, Box 1, Folder 5, Meadville Lombard Theological School Archives and Special Collections.

8. Morrison-Reed, *Black Pioneers in a White Denomination*, 33–76; quote from Juan M. Floyd-Thomas, *The Origins of Black Humanism in America: Reverend Ethelred Brown and the Unitarian Church* (New York: Palgrave Macmillan, 2008), 1.

9. Bruce Beisner and Walter Herz, "William H. G. Carter: 1877–1962" in Morrison-Reed, *Darkening the Doorways*, 53–55; David Whitford, "A Step toward Racial Reconciliation" *UU World* 16, no. 3 (May-June 2002): 24–30.

10. Nicole C. Kirk, "A Humanist Congregation in Post-War Black Chicago: Lewis McGee and the Free Religious Association, 1947–1953" in *Humanism and the Challenge of Difference*, ed. Anthony B. Pinn (New York: Palgrave Macmillan, 2018), 79.

11. Morrison-Reed, *Black Pioneers in a White Denomination*, 113–32; "Interview between Lewis A. McGee and Dan Huntington Fenn, 1946," Sankofa Working Files Collection—Individuals, Box 3, Folder 13, Meadville Lombard Theological School Archives and Special Collections; Nicole C. Kirk, "A Humanist Congregation," 78–79, 83; Lewis Allen McGee, "Martin Luther King Jr." in *Darkening the Doorways*, 179.

12. Author interview with Mtangulizi Sanyika (formerly Hayward Henry), January 19, 2019.

13. Author interview with Mtangulizi Sanyika (formerly Hayward Henry), January 19, 2019; Unitarian Universalist Association, "Empowerment Controversy Timeline," accessed August 19, 2020, https://www.uua.org/re/tapestry/adults/river/workshop15/178882.shtml.

14. Author interview with Mtangulizi Sanyika (formerly Hayward Henry), January 19, 2019.

15. "Social Responsibility" *Interchange: Newsletter of the Connecticut Valley District of the Unitarian Universalist Association* (November 1968): 2, Unitarian Universalist Association Commission on Religion and Race Records, 1968–1969, Box 1, Folder 1, Andover-Harvard Theological Library.

16. Author Interview with Mtangulizi Sanyika (formerly Hayward Henry), January 19, 2019; John Hurley, "Jeffrey W. Campbell (1910–1984) and Marguerite Campbell Davis (1916–1983)" in Morrison-Reed, *Darkening the Doorways*, 135.

17. Author interview with Leslie Mac, August 30, 2018; Author interview with Lena Gardner, December 18, 2018.

18. Author interview with Leslie Mac, August 30, 2018; Author interview with Takiyah Nur Amin, August 22, 2018.

19. Author interview with Lena Gardner, December 18, 2018.

20. Author interview with Lena Gardner, December 18, 2018.

21. Unitarian Universalist Association, "The Seven Principles," accessed August 9, 2019, https://www.uua.org/beliefs/what-we-believe/principles; Black Lives of Unitarian Universalism, "7 Principles of Black Lives," accessed August 6, 2019, https://www.blacklivesuu.com/7-principles.

22. Author interview with Mykal Slack, September 26, 2018; Author interview with Takiyah Nur Amin, August 22, 2018.

23. Author interview with Takiyah Nur Amin, August 22, 2018.

24. Author interview with Mykal Slack, September 26, 2018.
25. Author interview with Lena Gardner, December 18, 2018; Author interview with Leslie Mac, August 30, 2018.
26. Author interview with Takiyah Nur Amin, August 22, 2018; Author interview with Leslie Mac, August 30, 2018.

PART TWO

Contemporary Connections

CHAPTER 6

Death, Spirituality, and the Matter of Blackness

Joseph Winters

Within the last decade, we have witnessed the emergence of two significant movements that pertain to Black life and death. One goes by the name of Afro-pessimism, a current of thought that, according to Frank Wilderson, acknowledges a fundamental antagonism between Blackness and civil society, or Black people and the domain of the Human. For Wilderson and other Afro-pessimists, the world is structurally organized against Black bodies; violence against Blacks provides the world with coherence and order. Afro-pessimism contends that anti-Black racism is a permanent part of this world; consequently, the end of racism requires the end of the world as we know it. The other development is Black Lives Matter, an international activist movement that was "created" by three Black women— Patrisse Cullors, Alicia Garza, and Opal Tometi. Organized in response to George Zimmerman's acquittal in 2013 and the death of Michael Brown in 2014, BLM has become a loose cluster of groups that advocates direct action in response to State killings of Black people, the unequal distribution of wealth and capital, violence against trans subjects, and other forms of injustice. It would seem as if Afro-pessimism and

Black Lives Matter differ on some fundamental concerns.[1] Whereas the pessimist denies that Black people can be included within the sphere of the Human, BLM "affirms the humanity" of Black people as participants work toward a world "where Black lives are no longer systematically targeted for demise."[2] BLM assumes the very attribute that has been refused to Black people according to Wilderson and the Black pessimists. Because of this, it would seem as if the pessimist dismisses as futile any attempt to work within an order that positions Black people at the edges of being, at the lowest frequencies of humanity. Well-intentioned attempts to bring about police reform, for instance, simply circle around within a legal framework that demands Black anguish. While the pessimist appears to abandon hope, BLM is committed to the achievability of a world without racism.

While these differences are significant, this essay focuses on the affinities and continuities between Afro-pessimism and BLM. I contend that these affinities come into view by examining a shared legacy of Black spirituality. As I describe in detail below, Black spirituality is not reducible to a particular religious tradition or institution, nor is it tantamount to belief in god(s). Black spirituality alludes to practices, modes of being, and forms of asociality that have enabled Black people to endure slavery and its afterlife and to subsist within successive regimes that rely on different expressions of anti-Blackness. If, as Michel Foucault claims, racism is a way to insert a break within the continuum of life between who must live and who deserves to die,[3] then Black spirituality inhabits the break, the space between death and life. Black spirituality testifies to, and mourns, forms of death and erasure that prevailing spheres of life both rely on and disavow; at the same time, it is articulated through cries, silences, refusals, memories, writings, and bodily movements that indicate a living remainder, an excess that prevents us from conflating Blackness and (social) death. Black spirituality has diverse political implications for how we might relate to State power and its appendages, yet it registers experiences, encounters, and traumas that extant political grammars cannot redress. In what follows, I further develop this notion of Black spirituality by drawing on figures like Frederick Douglass and Harriet Jacobs. I then show how authors associated with

Afro-pessimism draw on this legacy—with varying degrees of explicitness and intentionality—to make sense of the violence and death that haunts civil society, nation-state projects, and the domain of the Human. I conclude by showing how BLM practices this spirituality, particularly through the die-in, the calling out of names of Blacks killed by the State, and through the interruption of "proper" political gatherings. While Afro-pessimism and BLM disagree about the possibility of Black people being recognized as human, this disagreement occurs on a common terrain of Black spirituality.

Blackness, Slavery, and Spirituality

In *Black Religion and the Imagination of Matter in the Black Atlantic*, philosopher of religion James Noel provides a helpful description of Black spirituality in the context of the Middle Passage and the violent transformation of Africans into merchandise. Noel draws from the work of Charles Long, an author who contends that any engagement with Black religion in the Americas must rehearse "the involuntary presence of blacks in America" in addition to the multiple expressions of the sacred within Black experience, expressions that are not exhausted by Christianity.[4] Riffing on Long's insights, Noel suggests that spirituality is not the opposite of materiality.[5] Rather spirituality names a surplus or excess that derives from, but is not reducible to, material interactions, encounters, and exchanges. Here we might take Noel to be thinking of the aspects of relationality that are not quite visible or measurable. Or he is alluding to dimensions of life and history that are so overwhelming that they cannot be grasped or made sense of within prevailing grammars and discourses. For Noel, the collective trauma of the Middle Passage, an extended event that hailed Africans to the realm of non-being, was marked by indescribable terror and anguish. To be positioned at the threshold of the human, to be treated as a fungible being available for all kinds of (sexual) violence, involves events and incidents that "defy linguistic expression." Or as Noel puts it, "There was no language, however, to describe what it was like to be submerged in those waters—what it was like, physically and spiritually, to be chained underneath the deck [of the slave ship]. . . . The experience defies description because what was experienced was Non-Being or Nothingness."[6] Language fails in the attempt to describe the terror of non-being, the anguish that permeates a situation in which Blacks are considered embodiments of nothingness, stands-ins for the void that subtends being.[7] But saying that language fails or founders does not mean that attempts have not been made to remember, communicate, and re-enact ongoing legacies of dismemberment. Similarly, while Noel underscores the anguish and horror of transatlantic slavery, he also stresses that "the miracle that occurred . . . was that the captives' being was not [completely] obliterated and swallowed up by Non-Being."[8] Black endurance in the face of anti-Black violence occurs through practices and modes of being, such as music and poetry, that register the break of the Middle Passage, that testify to what Spillers calls the wound of Black culture.[9] Black subsistence for Noel does not translate into some linear slavery to freedom or trauma to triumph narrative. Rather in the aftermath of chattel slavery, Black subsistence lingers in that infinitesimal space between death and life and is articulated in forms of sociality that make room for silence, moans, breaks and cuts, speaking in tongues, moments of stillness, and wounded intimacy. Black spirituality ironically indicates what lives on as rem(a)inders of the racial horror that sustains and haunts the order of things.

Think for instance of Frederick Douglass's well-known description of slave songs or spirituals, a description that highlights the relationship between spirit, refusal, and endurance. Douglass recounts in his slave narrative the tendency of slaves to sing as they made a passage through the woods to the Great House. According to Douglass, while people tend to hear in these songs evidence of the slave's contentment, the cry is actually an expression of melancholy and sorrow. It is a testament to "the death-dealing character of slavery,"[10] to the calculated violence that governs the plantation. Douglass writes,

> I did not, when a slave, understand the deep meanings of those rude, and apparently incoherent songs. . . . They told a tale which was altogether

beyond my feeble comprehension; they were tones, loud, long and deep, breathing the prayer and complaint of souls boiling over with the bitterest anguish. . . . The hearing of those wild notes always depressed my spirits, and filled my heart with ineffable sadness. The mere recurrence, even now, afflicts my spirit, and while I am writing these lines, tears are falling. To those songs I trace my first glimmering conceptions of the dehumanizing character of slavery. I can never get rid of that conception. Those songs still follow me, to deepen my hatred to slavery, and quicken my sympathies for my brethren in bonds.[11]

There is much to unpack in this passage. For one, Douglass locates the cry of the slave at the intersection of abundance and lack. While the songs are incoherent or sound like nonsense to some, they are full of meaning to the slave community. Similarly, even as the slave song expresses a wound or ineffable sadness, this wound is a space where anguish and tears "boil over." Furthermore, the wild notes and loud tones blur the temporal distinction between past and present. As he is writing about hearing these songs on the plantation, writing as an escaped/fugitive slave, he acknowledges how the past haunts the present, how the songs (and conditions that demand a moan) stay with him, continuing to inform his understanding of the terror of slavery. In fact, Douglass cannot help crying or boiling over as he writes; he cannot help being taken outside of himself as he reflects on the cries that "afflict" his spirit. If the tear indicates a movement from the interior to the outside, then one might draw a connection between the tear and the compassion toward other captive bodies that the slave song engenders. In other words, the wild, improvised sounds provide an occasion to commune through wounds.[12] This communion happened in covert gatherings and rituals such as the ring shout, a ritual in which Black bodies moved together counterclockwise while clapping hands and stomping feet. In a less immediate manner, this wounded intimacy is prompted in written forms of remembrance, like the slave narrative, that express a stubborn attachment to scenes and sounds of terror—in addition to those captive subjects who endured and refused this terror. Consequently, the reader is drawn into Douglass's description of the slave's spiritual practices, pulled into a legacy of moans and utterances that afflict, disturb, and linger.

It is important that Douglass claims that these songs tell a tale or a certain kind of story. This telling departs from the prevailing conception during Douglass's life that "the slaves are the most contented and happy laborers in the world," a conception that has contributed to tendencies to diminish and explain away the severity of flesh mongering.[13] The tale expressed through the moan also departs from academic treatments of the subject matter of slavery. In the 1845 version of Douglass' autobiography, the author indicates this difference when he writes, "I have sometimes thought that the mere hearing of these songs would do more to impress some minds with the horrible character of slavery, than the reading of whole volumes of philosophy on the subject could do."[14] Whereas reading a philosophical account of slavery might provide conceptual arguments and legible reasons for and against slavery, slave songs prompt one to listen to and hear the dissonant notes, chords, and tones that derive from slave experiences and get passed down to successive generations. The cry becomes an invitation to be "impressed" and overwhelmed by forms of horror and anguish that cannot be captured by reason, logic, or ordinary discourse. In the 1855 version of Douglass's autobiography, the author modifies the earlier contrast between the aesthetic moan and philosophical discourse. He claims, "I have sometimes thought that the mere hearing of those songs would do more to impress truly spiritual-minded men and women with the soul-crushing and death-dealing character of slavery, than the reading of whole volumes of its mere physical cruelties."[15] In this passage, I take it that Douglass is not downplaying the bodily torment brought about by the overseer's whip, torture, sexual violence, and being worked to death. He is suggesting, similar to Noel, that the predicament of non-being, the position at the edges of the Human, involves a kind of death that includes, but exceeds, physical pain and perishing. Furthermore, there is something about the acoustic anguish of the spirituals that registers this soul-crushing aspect of enslavement in a manner that historical accounts cannot. The enslavement of Blacks worked to destroy the spirit, to shatter communal and family bonds, to sever selves from religious and cultural traditions, to expose Blacks to incessant humiliation, angst, and fear, and to render Blackness valueless, wretched, and outside the "sacred precincts" of whiteness.[16] The slave's cry is a sonic testament to (and re-expression of) a kind of anguish that is more than physical and that exposes the limits of philosophical and scientific grammars when covering the anti-Black violence of slavery.

And yet the spiritual, according to Douglass, indicates how the "soul-crushing" operations of slavery were never fully successful. Even as Douglass focuses on the melancholic and depressing tones of the slave song, to cut against the image of the idyllic plantation and to foreground protest and complaint, he claims that the spiritual combines "the highest joy and the deepest sadness."[17] While he insists that slaves sing when they are most unhappy, he also describes the effect of collective slave gatherings as "melancholic relief,"[18] as a temporary outlet and expression of what has to be contained under the surveillance of the overseer. Instead of privileging the joy over the sorrow, or vice versa, one might think of these expressions as a "meeting of extremes" as Douglass describes it. In other words, the spiritual is defined by a tension-filled interplay between anguish and exaltation, or exhaustion and resilience. In fact, the gatherings of the enslaved in the dense woods generated utterances and movements that blur the distinction between affective contrasts like joy and pain. As Saidiya Hartman points out, this blurring gives the slave song an opaque quality, "which troubles distinctions between joy and sorrow and toil and leisure."[19] In Du Bois's postbellum reflection on the sorrow songs, he describes the cry of the enslaved as an articulation of "death, disappointment, and suffering" while maintaining that "through all of the sorrow there breathes a hope."[20] Similar to Douglass, Du Bois suggests that Black spirituals invoke affects and emotions that we usually imagine as opposite, including sorrow and hope. And the fact that Du Bois associates hope with breath, with a sigh, with a subtle aspiration, means that possibilities for a different world remain indeterminate, elusive, and beset by arrangements that choke and strangle, that forced Eric Garner—and later George Floyd—in his final moments to exclaim "I can't breathe."[21]

Consequently, the sorrow song includes and surpasses the very distinction between optimism and despair.

As mentioned above, Douglass speaks about being haunted by the slaves' songs after he has escaped from the plantation. In a similar manner, Du Bois describes the musical epigraph before each chapter of *Souls* as a "haunting echo" of songs that, ever since childhood, have "stirred him strangely."[22] What is crucial to elaborate on here is the link between Black spirituality and haunting. Haunting alludes to ghosts, afterlives, the stubborn presence of the past, and the ways death permeates our social worlds (including the social death that makes the reproduction of life possible).[23] Consider for instance Harriett Jacobs' 1861 autobiography *Incidents in the Life of a Slave Girl*. In the text, Linda Brent (Jacobs' pseudonym) describes being constantly harassed by her master Dr. Flint, a predicament that compels her to hide out for seven years in her grandmother's garret. Insofar as the garret resembles a living tomb, as well as the confined space on the slave ship, Brent's loophole of retreat demonstrates the intimacy between freedom and death, and escape and constraint. The only response in this case to social and political death is a kind of retreat, a kind of death within life, a self-willed confinement, that provides some relief from the sexual advances of Flint while separating Brent from her children, a source of anguish and longing.

As Erin Forbes points out, *Incidents* is written against the backdrop of a nineteenth-century religious movement called Spiritualism, a movement that "sought tangible contact with the dead in order to create a more perfect society."[24] The Spiritualist commitment to maintaining a relationship between the living and the dead helps to illuminate a poignant scene in the text when Brent visits the graves of her parents. Brent writes,

> I went to make this vow at the graves of my poor parents, in the burying ground of the slaves. . . . 'There the prisoners rest together; they hear not the voice of the oppressor; the servant is free from his master.' I had received my mother's blessing when she died; and in many an hour of tribulation I had seemed to hear her voice, sometimes chiding me, sometimes whispering loving words into my wounded heart. . . . As I

passed the wreck of the old meeting house, where, before Nat Turner's time, the slaves had been allowed to meet for worship, I seemed to hear my father's voice from it, bidding not to tarry til I reached freedom or the grave.[25]

Quoting the biblical book of Job, Brent associates the graveyard with a strange freedom, or temporary liberation from the terror and agony that slavery normalized. The cemetery is a site of solace and intimacy, a place of communion with the dead that remain; it is a heterotopia that enables Brent to connect with absent loved ones that still speak or whisper. In fact, Brent describes the graveyard as a "sacred" space that she regularly visits. But here we should not think of the term *sacred* as a signifier for purity and wholeness. Rather the sanctity of the grave-yard is, as Brent describes, marked by a "death-like stillness," longing and mourning, "obliterated" grave markings, wrecked meeting houses, and the conjuring of failed insurrections. The fact that her mother's ghostly voice occasionally chides Brent is a reminder that haunting brings about discomfort and unease as well consolation. Finally, even as the image of ghosts would seem to gesture beyond the physical, Brent reveals the somatic quality of her interaction with her dead parents. For instance, she kneels down and kisses the eroded letters on the board that marks her father's grave, a moment that underscores physical intimacy with death, loss, and remains.

The theme of haunting that reverberates throughout Jacobs' narra-tive is prevalent in contemporary Black studies and literature. Most notably, Toni Morrison's 1987 novel *Beloved* pivots around a commu-nity of the formerly enslaved that is plagued by the return of a child who was killed by her mother (Sethe) in an attempt to defy enslav-ers. Inspired by the life of Margaret Garner, Morrison's novel begins with a piercing epigraph, "Sixty Million and more," which is in part a tribute to the kidnapped Africans at the bottom of the Atlantic Ocean. The epigraph, which registers an excess, or "more," signals how the text and the reader of the novel are haunted by unmourned Black bodies, by a trans-Atlantic operation that converted Africans into merchandise, that made the bottom of the ocean a both a grave-yard and an escape from torment. In line with Morrison's insistence about the spectral presence of the past, Saidiya Hartman contends that there is an afterlife to slavery. As she puts it, "Black lives are still imperiled and devalued by a racial calculus and a political arithmetic that were entrenched centuries ago. This is the afterlife of slavery—skewed life chances, limited access to health and education, premature death, incarceration, and impoverishment."[26] The very language of "afterlife" and "still" signals the continuation of conditions and arrangements that are supposedly behind us, that we have ostensibly overcome and advanced beyond. The elimination of chattel slavery in the United States brought about the birth or emergence of new ways of containing, surveilling, and dismembering Black subjects. In response to this predicament, being haunted by the afterlife of slavery carries ethical and political significance.

Thus far, I have developed a notion of Black spirituality by drawing from slave narratives and authors influenced by this genre. This conception of Black spirituality is in no way meant to be exhaustive. It simply enables me to identify and accentuate key themes and tropes that pertain to Black freedom struggles. Black spirituality registers the limitations of ordinary grammar in the face of Black anguish, the interplay between ecstasy and agony within Black life, and the intimacy between life and death, an intimacy experienced through haunting and embodied especially by those hurled to the edges of social recognition, or positioned as not quite human and worthy of full life. In what follows, I use the notion of Black spirituality to trace connections and affinities between Afro-pessimism and BLM.

Afro-pessimism as Spiritual Thought

In his provocative text *Red, White, and Black*, Frank Wilderson riffs on Hartman's afterlife of slavery motif, contending that Blackness, within the current order of things, is tethered to the specter of the Slave. This fundamental claim propels Afro-pessimism. More specifically, the Afro-pessimist argues that "the structure of the entire world's semantic field—regardless of cultural and national discrepancies—is sutured by anti-Black solidarity."[27] While Blacks can be acknowledged

a project that both endorses immediate, practical attempts to change laws and policies but also sees this short-term change as ancillary to the less determinate activities, practices, and ways of remembering that aim for the end of the world as we know it.

This call for a two-trains approach to organizing resonates with his position on the slavery reparations debate. In an interview with Percy Howard, Wilderson reveals that he supports the reparations movement, not because he thinks that slavery and its afterlife can be repaired but because of the emphasis on movement. As he puts it, "I support the movement because I know it is a movement toward the end of the world; a movement toward a catastrophe in epistemological coherence and institutional integrity—I support the movement aspect of it because I know that repair is impossible. [I support] a movement toward something so blindingly new that it cannot be imagined. This is the only thing that will save us."[32] Here Wilderson indicates that incessant movement and kinetic energy directed toward a radically new world is more important than the achievement of some concrete goal. What can "save us" is something that is at the limits of the Human, that points to the other side of the Human and its appurtenances. At this point, one can only talk about this other side in apophatic terms—not this world, not capital, not anti-Blackness, etc. For Wilderson, movement gestures toward some time or place that cannot be configured within language, a set of images, or a list of political demands. This does not mean that political demands, for reformed policing, universal health care, or a living wage, for example, are not vital. It simply means that these goals are overrun by a broader set of energies, desires, and strivings that aim for what cannot be actualized in this world's arrangements. The insistence on movement resonates with the realm of the spirit, with what exceeds but is connected to material interactions and perceptible objects. Motion, or the movement of spirit, alludes to what cannot be converted into a thing, what cannot be subordinated to discrete ends or limits. While Wilderson does not make this connection between movement and spirit directly, he does admit, "I believe in the Spirit world; that is to say I believe that the African ancestors are still with us and can be consulted from time to time."[33]

Whereas Wilderson remains somewhat reticent about elaborating on Black spirituality, Calvin Warren makes a decisive turn to the spiritual in his articulation of Afro-pessimism. In "Black Nihilism and the Politics of Hope," Warren contends that political hope is a form of "cruel optimism," a device that keeps Black people attached to ideals, fantasies, and arrangements that rely on Black suffering.[34] To put it more precisely, Warren argues that the parameters and features of political life (similar to the Human for Wilderson) reject Black being. He writes, "the logic of the Political—linear temporality, biopolitical futurity, perfection, betterment, and redress—sustains black suffering. Progress and perfection are worked through the pained black body and any recourse to the Political and its discourse of hope will ultimately reproduce the very metaphysical structures of violence that pulverize black being."[35] As Warren points out, the violent relationship between progress and the Black body can be heard in speeches and addresses by celebrated Black leaders—King's insistence on Black suffering as the conduit toward the American dream; Obama responding to George Zimmerman's acquittal by assuring listeners that every generation advances. In these cases, the political and its key concepts don't just diminish the severity of Black suffering; investment in progress, hope, and betterment actually requires Black anguish, in addition to a kind of disavowal of the violence attached to linear time and triumphant accounts of history. For Warren, the grammar of the political "will never obviate black suffering or anti-black violence"; it will simply reproduce these conditions.[36] Hope in the political spells disaster for Black people.

Yet Warren does not abandon hope talk altogether. In fact, he makes a crucial distinction between political and spiritual hope, prioritizing the latter. According to the author, "To speak of the 'Politics of Hope' is to denaturalize or demystify a certain *usage* of hope. Here I want to make a distinction between 'hope' (the spiritual kind) . . . and political hope."[37] For Warren, spiritual hope refers to dispositions and inclinations toward those aspects of existence that defy the limits of reason, that cannot be captured by scientific discourse. The problem for him is when spiritual energy, which can be "invested in various aspects of existence," is forced to find its end in the political. In other words, hope becomes cruel and debilitating as subjects are disciplined to think that hope must have a destination in the political, to think that in order to be hopeful, one must be committed to the political and its anti-Black strategies. Consequently, "to reject the politics of hope . . . [is to reject] certain circumscribed and compulsory forms of expressing, practicing, and conceiving of hope."[38] To rescue spiritual hope from the political is to affirm those energies, attachments, modes of being, and forms of intimacy that enable Blacks to endure and subsist in a world where Blackness is relegated to the peripheries of being, to the limits of the Human. This includes music, worship, practices of care, laughter, and something as simple as a hug, activities that the political treats as relatively insignificant. As Warren further elaborates in his text *Ontological Terror*, Black spirituality is associated with endurance, rather than progress or freedom. Or as he puts it, "Endurance is a spiritual practice" with different aims than political hope.[39] Endurance must face the reality of terror and social death without the consolations promised by the political.

Warren seems to be much more averse to the domain of politics than Wilderson. Similarly, he is less sympathetic to BLM than Wilderson, who has participated in workshops with BLM groups. At the beginning of *Ontological Terror*, for instance, Warren suggests that the very phrase "Black Lives Matter" both conjures and conceals a set of questions: Does Black life matter? What is the relationship between Blackness and life, Blackness and being? Can Blackness be recognized within a domain, the Human, that needs Blackness to signify death, terror, and nothingness? For Warren, the very phrase in question assumes a relationship between Blackness, humanity, and value that cannot exist; the term "Black Lives Matter" is incoherent and contradictory. In light of his strong distinction between spiritual and political hope, I imagine Warren would accuse BLM of being committed to ideals—redress, recognition, equality—that both buttress and veil the conditions of anti-Blackness. At times, Warren's stark contrast between the spiritual and the political forecloses a more fraught, tension-filled, and generative way of thinking about the relationship between Black spirituality and political resistance. In response to

Warren, I read BLM as a site where spiritual practices—vigils, naming of the dead, die-ins—cut against the common sense of the political while working within and at the edges of this domain. Furthermore, I take the broader Movement for Black Lives, a coalition of groups that includes BLM, as an example of Wilderson's insistence on the power of movement, or the kinetic energies that propel and exceed particular goals and ends. In the final section, I trace these connections and possibilities.

Black Life, Black Death, and Practices of Liminality

Much that has been written about Black Lives Matter has attempted to situate this set of movements within the legacy of anti-Black racism and Black liberation strivings. While BLM might seem like a spontaneous development of protests, marches, and demands in response to recent police killings of Black people, several authors have traced the continuity and discontinuity between BLM and previous movements, organizations, and struggles. Keeanga-Yamahtta Taylor, for instance, locates the emergence of BLM within the persistence of racism under the Obama regime and the incapacity to sustain the fantasy of a post-racial America. For Taylor, BLM intentionally opposes the hierarchical and respectability politics of establishment liberals like Al Sharpton and draws energy from activists—such as Bayard Rustin and Angela Davis—who have embraced grassroots style organizing with an intersectional analysis of race, class, gender, and sexuality.[40] Barbara Ransby reminds us that BLM was preceded and inspired by AIDS activism in Black communities, prison abolition movements, and organizations like INCITE! that were established to resist violence against women of color. What stands out for Ransby is that "Black feminist politics and sensibilities have been the intellectual lifeblood of this movement and its practices."[41] For Christopher Lebron, BLM riffs on an ongoing insistence that Black people are human beings and worthy of respect and dignity.[42] In opposition to the Afro-pessimist, Lebron revisits monumental figures like Frederick Douglass and Audre Lorde who assume that the category of the human is capacious enough to include Black people. According to Lebron, Black people's long struggle for recognition and respect underlies and animates BLM's concrete demands for police reform or economic justice.

One author who thinks specifically about the religious and theo-logical implications of BLM is Rima Vesely-Flad. For Vesely-Flad, Mary Douglas's categories of purity, dirt, and contamination are help-ful to understand how Black bodies have been positioned (symboli-cally and materially) with respect to the social order. As she writes, "Anthropologist Mary Douglas explains how societies respond to people associated with social pollution. . . . In an effort to impose order, societies separate, purify, demarcate, and punish those who transgress boundaries or are associated with pollution."[43] For Doug-las, the organization of social space requires the marking of certain kinds of entities and bodies as a perpetual danger to the coherence of that space. Dirt is matter that cannot be easily placed or contained, which is why so much effort goes into the containment of that which signifies dirt. The very threat of contamination is a byproduct of social ordering, of a world that compels our attachments to stable norms, laws, and borders. And yet the contaminating threat also betrays that social conventions and demarcations are not as stable as they appear. While Douglas does not think much about race and coloniality, Vesely-Flad mobilizes the purity/danger relationship to trace tendencies within the modern order to criminalize and punish Blackness. She writes, "Indeed, in a social sphere deeply affected by the European transatlantic slave trade and colonialism, Douglas's theories illumine how Western societies distinguish between dark and light skin color, and consequently penalize dark skin."[44] While Christianity has contributed to the alignment of Blackness with con-tamination, non-being, promiscuity, and excess, Vesely-Flad turns to the liberation strand of theology to challenge and invert these associations. By reminding the reader that Jesus was executed and tortured by the state and that he cared for the pariahs and undesir-able members of first-century Palestine, she urges us to "see Jesus in Michael Brown," to rediscover Jesus in Black flesh. Similarly, the clergy who have conspired with BLM are committed to the notion that God's undergoing of suffering and death (being punctured and wounded by the powers and principalities) carries implications for how Christians should orient themselves to the state, law, and the persecuted.

While Black liberation theology informs BLM, other religious and spiritual traditions have figured into the movement, including the West African tradition of Ifa. For instance, BLM co-founder Patrisse Cullors describes in her memoir that she "lives in the tradition of Ifa, the African spiritual practice that originated with the Yoruba people of Nigeria at least 8,000 years ago. . . . In Ifa we believe that all living beings, all elements of Nature, are interdependent and possessing of soul. . . . In Ifa, we also recognize and believe our Ancestors are always with us and must be honored and acknowledged."[45] Not unlike Calvin Warren, Cullors reveals that "the spirit" (experienced partly through Ifa practices) has sustained her in the midst of the State's war against poor Blacks in her Los Angeles neighborhood. She writes, "We lived alongside the steady buzz of anxiety. I turned ever more toward the spirit, toward that which I could not see but could feel at all times, in order to manage my emotions."[46] Without conflating Ifa and my conception of Black spirituality, we can identify some continuity. For instance, Ifa underscores the interdependence of life and death, the living and the ancestors. The habit of acknowledging the dead, especially Black ancestors who would otherwise remain unmourned or ungrievable, suggests that remembrance and mourning exist at the intersection of absence and presence; honoring the ancestors affirms the life that remains after physical perishing as well as the death and partial loss that always hangs alongside precarious life. In a predicament where Black death and loss make the continuation of social life possible, where Black suffering is partly the result of an imaginary that creates a separation between those worthy of life and those tethered to death, Ifa-inspired spirituality and its commitment to liminality has indirect political possibilities. Similarly, in a world strongly influenced by linear notions of progress that pressure us to leave the past and the (living) dead behind, Black spirituality is a kind of interruption into the temporal order of things, an intervention related to Carol Wayne White's chapter about naturalism's possibility of altering material conditions for Black people.

This Black spirituality is enacted and performed in some of BLM's distinctive practices and strategies. Consider for instance the insistence on calling, shouting, and chanting the names of Black subjects killed by the police during protests and marches. Here I am also thinking of Twitter hashtags (e.g., #SayHerName), posters emblazoned with the names and images of Sandra Bland or Michael Brown, and writings that list and conjure recent victims of State violence. It is also important to keep in mind that BLM was a response to the killing of Trayvon Martin in 2012 and the acquittal of George Zimmerman in the summer of 2013. In other words, while the movement celebrates Black life, the demand to value Black life is tethered to death and grief, in addition to remembering the painful relationship between law, property, and Blackness—stand your ground. The movement for Black lives, in other words, is haunted by the accumulated deaths that brought the movement into being. The particular relationship between naming, subjectivity, and death is complicated and deserves some attention. As Louis Althusser points out, individuals become legible, recognizable subjects through processes and occurrences that are already underway before any individual is on the scene.[47] One becomes a discrete subject, an "I" with certain ascribed capacities and properties, because one is part of a social world that recognizes the subject as such, that calls an individual by his/her/its name. Names and categories—gender, race, nation, citizenship—precede the individual's birth and help bring her into existence and enable her to carry on in the world. And yet the name also exceeds the individual's life span. By calling out the name of the deceased at a rally, members of BLM "keep alive" memories and traces of those who have been erased by the State and its extrajudicial agents. Chanting and calling out the name of dead/killed Blacks gives a kind of posthumous recognition or value to bodies that the prevailing order did not value. The repetition of the name, the shout, the sound, the cry, is a way of communicating with the dead—or allowing the dead to haunt us—and protesting the refusal of recognition that defines social death and anti-Blackness.

The practice of "saying her name" also resists tendencies to privilege certain kinds of Black death over others as catalysts for the movement for Black life. Young cisgender Black men seem to be more worthy of compassion and grief than Black women or Black transgender subjects who are routinely exposed to violence. As Afropessimist Patrice Douglass points out, in response to the SWAT killing of Korryn Gaines in 2016, "Black women are subjected to forms of police violence most often associated with and thought of as only affecting Black men. However, it is far less likely that the cases of Black women become a part of mass public discourse and debate. While the names of a few Black men killed by police in the months preceding Korryn are widely known, their cases commonly discussed, she and other Black women do and did not experience the same public interest."[48] It is important that Douglass tells the story of Gaines' home invasion by SWAT and then pauses to accentuate for the reader: "Her *name* was Korryn Gaines."[49] By calling her name, Douglass is not simply attempting to include Korryn in the domain of the recognized dead. She is reminding us of what events, bodies, and strivings cannot be easily incorporated into and mobilized for political movements and public protests, including the Women's March in January 2017. Taking seriously the intersection of Blackness and gender also directs attention to the queer Black women founders of BLM, to the ways in which Garza, Cullors, and Tometi participate in a Black feminist tradition that rejects totalizing notions of Blackness or the conflation of Blackness with Black male experience. Black spirit is cut, wounded, and dispersive; Blackness is performed through a variety of subject positions and experiences even as each of these positions is affected by the thrust of anti-Blackness. Uttering the names of Sandra Bland, Korryn Gaines, and other non-Black-male victims of the State points to, and registers, the fact that even in death recognition is distributed unequally.

Invoking the names of the dead is part of BLM's practice of intruding on "proper" political gatherings and rallies. Think for instance of the moment in August 2015 when BLM activists Marissa Johnson and Mara Willaford interrupted a Bernie Sanders rally in Seattle.[50] After arguing with the rally's organizers and grabbing the mic from Sanders, Johnson addressed a contentious crowd, calling on the senator and the audience to remember painful realities—gentrification, displacement of poor people, racial profiling, the building of a new $210 million dollar jail to "imprison black children"—that beset what Sanders calls one of America's most progressive cities.[51] What stands out in Johnson's speech, as she repeats the mantra "Welcome to Seattle," are her mentioning that the political event is taking place on indigenous Duwamish land and her requesting a five-minute moment of silence for Michael Brown, who was killed just a year earlier. Recall Frank Wilderson's argument that anti-Black violence and appropriation of Native peoples' land constitute foundational modes of violence, antagonisms that provide US civil society with its coherence and continued existence. Johnson's speech act enables these antagonisms to temporarily intervene into public discourse, and not simply as a talking point or an agenda item. Furthermore, this intervention breaks with the norms and terms of civility that define certain political gatherings. The sound of Michael Brown's name is juxtaposed with Johnson's demand for silence in a manner that registers the inadequacy of words in the face of gratuitous violence. The dissolution and transition of speech into silence invites contemplation of an absence that haunts the general mood and affective resonance of a rally. When Johnson's speech unexpectedly turns into a momentary cry while she is honoring Brown, the audience must again confront the limits of ordinary speech in the face of absurdity. There are instances when ordinary language breaks down and emotions cannot be held back. We hear traces of a musical cry when BLM activists chant songs like Kendrick Lamar's "Alright" during protests. Echoing Frederick Douglass' description of slave songs, the cry communicates more than volumes of political philosophy and discourse ever could.

If the moment of silence responds to and honors death and absence, the die-in re-enacts and simulates the loss of life. While BLM protests are often associated with loud assertiveness, repeated chants, tense confrontations, and kinetic interactions, the die-in introduces what Kevin Quashie calls "quiet." In opposition to the tendency to describe Blackness as expressive and dramatic, Quashie redirects attention to the quiet aspects of Black cultural and political strivings. Quiet alludes to the inner life, or the threshold between the inner and public life; quiet refers to "the full range of one's inner life—desires, ambitions, hungers, vulnerabilities, and fears."[52] Here I do not take Quashie to be offering a reified distinction between the public/external and the private/internal. Rather I take him to be gesturing toward forms of resistance that make room for the expression of vulnerability, grief, and yearning. While this notion of quiet might illumine the stillness of bodies lying on the floor imitating death, one should not ignore the disruptive, unsettling potential of a die-in. Whether performing a die-in at a student or faculty meeting on a college campus or at a shopping mall, the image and sound/silence of death cuts against the smooth flow of things, the everyday processes and transactions that protract the order of things and its prevailing sensibilities. The die-in does not simply show us that life is haunted by (Black) death; it enables participants to take on, embody, and approximate the death that makes social life possible. Consequently, it can be construed as a kind of riff on Harriet Jacobs' experience in the graveyard connecting with her deceased parents. As a practice of Black spirituality, the die-in enables the simulating subject to communicate with the dead, through the descent and fall of the body rather than through speech.

Conclusion

I can imagine a suspicious reader asking a series of questions about my attempt to trace features of Black spirituality through contemporary Black thought, especially Afro-pessimism, and the Movement for Black Lives. Haven't I focused too much on death, haunting, the imperceptible, and the limits of language? Inversely, haven't I downplayed the significance within BLM of concrete demands and goals like reparations or the removal of police from schools? This essay does not diminish the importance of the practical, concrete goals of BLM and grassroots organizing more generally. Rather it refuses any binary relationship between the concrete and the spiritual, since Black spirituality is always expressed or intimated through the flesh— Jacobs kneeling down to kiss the gravestone; Marissa Johnson placing her body before a contentious crowd to request a moment of silence. Black spiritual practices register and indicate what cannot be incorporated or redressed by the current political order, what haunts the political, what Wilderson calls the gap between antagonism and conflict, even as the spirit propels Black struggles and strivings for a radically different world. With Warren and Cullors, Black spirituality is a mode of endurance, a mode of subsisting in a world that for centuries has been organized, in a multitude of ways, against Black people. While this spiritual endurance cannot be reduced to, or confined by, political ends, it does have implications for how we comport ourselves to the political.

Furthermore, by juxtaposing Afro-pessimism and BLM, and by elaborating on Black spirituality, this essay contributes to this volume's efforts to expand conventional understandings of religion and forms of contemporary Black protest. As Anthony Pinn argues, the qualifier "religious" is not reducible to organized religions and institutional expressions. Pinn contends that at its basic level, religion is a kind of striving in the face of dehumanization and anguish.[53] Black spirituality is another way of naming this striving, this endurance in the face of violence, this energy that connects with the dead and points toward a radically different world.[54] Not only does Black spirituality give us a different way of thinking about contemporary theoretical and activist movements; it invites us to think differently about religion, the relationship between religion and politics, and the blurred line between the sacred and profane.

NOTES

1. See for instance Calvin Warren, *Ontological Terror: Blackness, Nihilism, and Emancipation* (Durham, NC: Duke University Press, 2018), 1–25. Also see Frank Wilderson, Samira Spatzek, and Paula von Gleich, "The Inside-Outside of Civil Society: An Interview with Frank B. Wilderson III," *Black Studies Papers* 2, no. 1 (2016): 4–22.

2. "Herstory," Black Lives Matter, accessed August 19, 2020, https://blacklivesmatter.com/about/herstory.

3. Michel Foucault, *Society Must Be Defended: Lectures at the College of France, 1975–1976*, trans. David Macey (New York: Picador, 2003), 254.

4. See Charles Long, *Significations: Signs, Symbols, and Images in the Interpretation of Religion* (Aurora, CO: The Davies Group Publishers, 1999), 188.

5. James Noel, *Black Religion and the Imagination of Matter in the Atlantic World* (New York: Palgrave, 2009), 2.

6. Noel, 70.

7. Calvin Warren's *Ontological Terror* looks at the relationship between being and Blackness. I discuss this more later in this essay.

8. Noel, 73.

9. Hortense Spillers, "Moving On Down the Line: Variations on the African-American Sermon," *Black, White, and in Color* (Chicago: University of Chicago Press, 2003), 262.

10. See Frederick Douglass, *My Bondage and My Freedom* (1855; New York: Dover, 1969), 98.

11. Douglass, 99.

12. On this notion of intimacy through cuts and wounds, see Georges Bataille, *Inner Experience*, trans. Leslie Anne Boldt (Albany, NY: SUNY Press, 1988).

13. Douglass, *My Bondage and My Freedom*, 99.

14. Frederick Douglass, *Narrative of the Life of Frederick Douglass, an American Slave* (1845; New York: Barnes and Noble Classics, 2003), 11.

15. Douglass, *My Bondage and My Freedom*, 98.

16. Here I am riffing on Orlando Patterson's well-known conception of social death. See Patterson, *Slavery and Social Death: A Comparative Study* (Cambridge, MA: Harvard University Press, 1982), 1–17.

17. Douglass, *Narrative of the Life of Frederick Douglass*, 11.

18. Douglass, *My Bondage and My Freedom*, 100.

19. Saidiya Hartman, *Scenes of Subjection: Terror, Slavery, and the Self-Making in Nineteenth Century* (New York: Oxford University Press, 1997), 36.

20. W. E. B. Du Bois, "The Souls of Black Folk," in *Three Negro Classics* (New York: Avon Books, 1965), 386.

21. See Ashon Crawley, *Blackpentecostal Breath: The Aesthetics of Possibility* (New York: Fordham Press, 2017).

22. Du Bois, 378.

23. Here I am indebted to Avery Gordon's understanding of hauntings as a site of discomfort, pain, and unsettlement. See Gordon, *Ghostly Matters: Haunting and the Sociological Imagination* (Minneapolis: University of Minnesota Press, 2008), 23.

24. Erin Forbes, "Do Black Ghosts Matter?: Harriet Jacobs' Spiritualism," *ESQ: A Journal of Nineteenth Century American Literature and Culture* 62, no. 3 (2016): 444.

25. Harriet Jacobs, "Incidents in the Life of a Slave Girl," in *Slave Narratives* (New York: Library of America, 2000), 836.

26. Saidiya Hartman, *Lose Your Mother: A Journey along the Atlantic Slave Route* (New York: Ferrar, Straus and Giroux, 2007), 6.

27. Frank Wilderson, *Red, White, and Black: Cinema and the Structure of U.S. Antagonisms* (Durham, NC: Duke University Press, 2010), 58.
28. Wilderson, 38.
29. See Michel Foucault, *Madness and Civilization: History of Madness in the Age of Reason*, trans. Richard Howard (New York: Vintage, 1988), preface.
30. Wilderson, 2.
31. Frank Wilderson, Samira Spatzek, Paula von Gleich, "The Inside-Outside of Civil Society: An Interview with Frank B. Wilderson III," *Black Studies Papers* 2, no. 1 (2016): 18.
32. Frank Wilderson and Percy Howard, "Frank B. Wilderson, 'Wallowing in the Contradictions,' Part 1," *A Necessary Angel* (blog), July 9, 2010, https://percy3.wordpress.com/2010/07/09/frank-b-wilderson-"wallowing-in-the-contradictions"-part-1.
33. Wilderson and Howard.
34. The term comes from Laruen Berlant's *Cruel Optimism* (Durham, NC: Duke University Press, 2011).
35. Calvin Warren, "Black Nihilism and the Politics of Hope," *New Centennial Review* 15, no. 1 (Spring 2015): 218.
36. Warren, 243.
37. Warren, 218.
38. Warren, 219.
39. Calvin Warren, *Ontological Terror: Blackness, Nihilism, and Emancipation* (Durham, NC: Duke University, 2018), 172.
40. See Keeanga-Yamahtta Taylor, *From #BlackLivesMatter to Black Liberation* (Chicago: Haymarket Books, 2016), 173–77.
41. Barbara Ransby, *Making All Black Lives Matter: Reimagining Freedom in the Twenty-First Century* (Oakland: University of California Press, 2018), 3.
42. See Christopher Lebron, *The Making of Black Lives Matter: A Brief History of an Idea* (New York: Oxford University Press, 2017), xiii.
43. Rima Vesely-Flad, *Racial Purity and Dangerous Bodies: Moral Pollution, Black Lives, and the Struggle for Justice* (Minneapolis, MN: Fortress Press, 2017), xix. Also see Mary Douglas, *Purity and Danger: An Analysis of Concepts of Pollution and Taboo* (New York: Routledge, 2000).
44. Vesely-Flad, xxi.
45. Patrisse-Khan Cullors and Asha Bandele, *When They Call You a Terrorist: A Black Lives Matter Memoir* (New York: St. Martin's Press, 2017), 151.
46. Cullors and Bandele, 112.
47. See Louis Althusser, "Ideology and Ideological State Apparatuses," in *Lenin and Philosophy and Other Essays* (New York: Monthly Review Press, 2001), 115–20.
48. Emphasis added. Patrice Douglass, "Black Feminist Theory for the Dead and Dying," *Theory and Event* 21, no. 1 (2018): 2.

49. Douglass, 1.

50. See "Activists Disrupt Bernie Sanders Speech," Lovelyti TV, posted August 10, 2015, https://www.youtube.com/watch?v=7VbHUI1R3IA.

51. I am grateful to conversations with Laura Grattan about this event and its implications for Bernie's racialized notion of the "people."

52. Kevin Quashie, *The Sovereignty of Quiet: Beyond Resistance in Black Culture* (New Brunswick, NJ: Rutgers University Press, 2012), 6.

53. See especially Anthony Pinn, *Terror and Triumph: The Nature of Black Religion* (Minneapolis, MN: Fortress Press, 2003).

54. Perhaps, as Biko Gray points out, this radically different world means pursuing the impossible. See Gray, "Religion in/and Black Lives Matter: Celebrating the Impossible," in *Religion Compass* 13, no. 1 (January 2019): 1–9.

CHAPTER 7

"A Song That Speaks the Language of the Times"

Muslim and Christian Homiletic Responses to the Black Lives Matter Movement and the Need for a Spiritual Vocabulary of Admonition

Marjorie Corbman

In a radio interview in February 2016, Patrisse Cullors, one of the founders of the Black Lives Matter movement, elaborated on her vision of the "spiritual" core of the movement. Standing on the side of Black lives, Cullors averred, is "spiritual work," a "healing work." This transformative commitment, she went on, makes it possible to imagine Black life: "Our imagination has only allowed for us to understand black people as a dying people. We have to change that. That's our collective imagination. Someone imagined handcuffs; someone imagined guns; someone imagined a jail cell. Well, how do we imagine something different that actually centers black people, that sees them in the future? Let's imagine something different." As such, the movement represents more than a campaign for changes in policy. In its objective, in Cullors's description, of "rehumanizing" the dehumanized collective imagination, Black Lives Matter is grounded in the "deeply spiritual" work of "healing justice." At the same time, Cullors referred to the complicated relationship between main-stream Black institutional churches and contemporary activists in the Black Lives Matter movement, many of whom, as women or as LGBTQ+ individuals, have "been pushed out of the church."[1] Cullors's statements here are consistent with Almeda Wright's analysis of the continuity of the Black Lives Matter movement's ambivalent relationship to religious institutions with historical Black social activ-ism, despite popular conceptions of the civil rights period. Wright demonstrates both that the Black activist movements of the 1960s had a more complicated and at times antagonistic relationship with religious institutions than is commonly narrated and that Black youth activists today are actively engaged in drawing connections between faith and activism even despite these difficulties.[2]

Cullors's interpretation of the work of "rehumanizing" the dehu-manized imagination as a Black spiritual praxis that can occur in concert with or independent from traditional mainstream Black religious institutions shares much in common with religious scholar Anthony B. Pinn's description of African American religion as a "quest for complex subjectivity" not primarily defined by the centuries-long history of white American objectification of Black humanity.[3] Pinn defines this longing for "complex subjectivity" as the desire to break free from the "fixed forms of identity" derived from Ameri-can racial hierarchies in order to cultivate a sense of multidimen-sional personal and communal identity liberated at heart from the ever-present "ghosts of dehumanization" haunting Black conscious-ness.[4] Pinn argues that by framing study of Black religious institu-tions, beliefs, and practices in this way, scholars can avoid reducing Black religious identity to its historically dominant "institutional and doctrinal manifestations," highlighting to the contrary the rich and variegated creativity of Black communities in America in envision-ing a broader "life meaning" for Black people than that assigned to them by American racial violence and domination.[5]

Pinn's framework for interpreting Black religion, like Cullors's in the 2016 interview, and this volume on the whole, offers an expansive understanding of the religious dimensions of contemporary Black-led social movements regardless of affiliation with institutional religious bodies such as churches or mosques. In this volume, contributors have made use of this expansive interpretive framework to place the rhetoric and practices of the Black Lives Matter movement *themselves*, independent of religious affiliation, in conversation with religious or spiritual orientations and praxis. Thus, for instance, Carol Wayne White's essay situates the Black Lives Matter movement's assertion of the inherent value of Black lives and its nonbinary vision of resistance within the framework of religious naturalism, and Joseph Winters, in conversation with Afro-pessimist thinkers, shows how in the Black Lives Matter movement, "the demand to value Black life is tethered to death and grief," reflecting Black spirituality's inhabiting of "the space between death and life."[6]

This essay utilizes the "'capacious' understanding of religion" (as described in the editors' introduction) adopted by this volume in order to situate institutional religious communities' varying responses to the Black Lives Matter movement in a context of religious discourses that transcend institutional religious affiliation. Particular figures' and communities' usages of religious narratives, scripts, and symbols occur within broader cultural contexts, in which specific religious traditions are used by communities as "vehicles," in the framework of the Islamic scholar Sherman Jackson, for broader religious projects. In *Islam and the Blackamerican: Looking toward the Third Resurrection* (2005), Jackson argued for the existence of a category of Black Religion, which is not synonymous with "African American religion" broadly speaking, but rather an important "subset of the aggregate of black religious expression in America."[7] Black Religion, argues Jackson, is centered around "the desire to annihilate or at least subvert white supremacy and anti-black racism," regardless of the religious "vehicle" (e.g., Christianity or Islam) that gives it its particular shape.[8] Jackson's formulation of the existence of religious "vehicles of appropriation" helps explain the widely varying responses of both predominantly Black and predominantly non-Black religious bodies (within the same broader religious traditions such as Christianity and Islam) to the discourses and practices of the Black Lives Matter movement.[9]

With this framework in mind, this essay argues that predominantly white and/or non-Black Christian and Muslim communities have frequently assumed a perceived *incompatibility* of Christianity or Islam with confrontation and anger as expressed by the Black Lives Matter movement, whereas many Black religious leaders and predominantly Black Christian and Muslim communities have utilized resources from within Christianity and Islam to demonstrate their inherent *compatibility* with the language and tactics of the Black Lives Matter movement. Both Christianity and Islam can serve—and have served—as powerful vehicles of a religious approach centered around the destruction of anti-Black racism. At the same time, predominantly white or non-Black communities have used these same traditions as "vehicles" for their own interests, at times violently opposed to the liberation of Black people and the elimination of anti-Black racism.

This essay focuses on expressions of anger and pain on the part of the Black Lives Matter movement, both because of the crucial role these affective expressions play in the movement itself, and because they have particularly inspired resistance and discomfort within white and non-Black communities. Brittney Cooper describes in *Eloquent Rage: A Black Feminist Discovers Her Superpower* (2018) how white Americans "fixate on the anger and rage that feels palpable at Black Lives Matter protests," and "view this rage with a studied indifference and a willful ignorance that is about not seeing or validating black people's fear and right to be afraid."[10] In the early 1960s, James Baldwin painted a similar portrait of the "willful ignorance" of white American progressives in response to Black expressions of rage and grief, in particular as expressed by the confrontational rhetoric of Malcolm X and the Nation of Islam. Baldwin's explanation for white liberals' confusion in response to Black anger was that they were incapable of seeing Black people as fully human. "Any attempt I made to explain how the Black Muslim movement came about, and how it has achieved such force, was met with a blankness that revealed the little connection that the liberals' attitudes have with their perceptions or their lives, or even their knowledge—revealed, in fact, that they could deal with the Negro as a symbol or a victim but had no sense of him as a man."[11] For Baldwin, this manifestation of "the incredible, abysmal, and really cowardly obtuseness of white liberals" was a result of an inability to understand Black people as people.[12]

This essay examines the ways the confrontational tone of the Black Lives Matters movement, rooted in empathetic response to the suffering and deaths of Black people in the United States, has been expressed in the context of various established faith communities. It will be demonstrated that while religious communities primarily comprised of or led by non-Black members have typically failed to voice a fully "humanized" response to the destruction of Black lives, the Black Lives Matter movement has facilitated development of counter-examples in religious rhetoric by Black religious figures and communities.

This essay will examine four Christian sermons and four Muslim khutbas that have been made publicly available through the digital outreach of the religious communities at which they were delivered or by the preachers themselves; these homiletic addresses are exemplary of the "rehumanizing" spiritual work of contemporary Black social activism as described by Cullors. As Wright has demonstrated, contemporary Black activists are creatively reenvisioning the relationship between faith and social movements. Wright's own discussion of a sermon preached by Reverend Nyle Fort (a different sermon than the one examined in this chapter) as an example of how Fort "imbues elements of Christian worship and sacred liturgy with new meaning" is an important indication of the insights that can be drawn from examination of how the Black Lives Matter movement has been expressed in religious language.[13] These examples build upon this work and have been selected especially in order to highlight the ways Christian and Muslim religious resources have been utilized to express the painful and outraged response typically denied by American cultural consciousness to Black Americans.

No argument is made here that these sermons and khutbas are necessarily representative of overall trends in Black Christian or Muslim religion in the United States; the overall paucity of digitally available preaching expressly on the topic of the Black Lives Matter movement rendered the sample here necessarily limited. It should be noted, for instance, that all of the examples given here are from northern or western cities. Without making an argument for the representativeness of these homiletic examples, this essay rather portrays attempts across religious lines, but *within* a shared legacy of what Jackson calls "Black Religion," to interpret the Black Lives Matter movement by way of the religious vocabularies available to Christian and Muslim preachers.

This essay will characterize the approach of these eight homiletic examples as indicative of the development of a confrontational, oppositional spiritual vocabulary of admonition. This term is inspired by the words of Nyle Fort in his statement that religious communities that have no capacity to name and curse the evils of racism have an "insufficient vocabulary" for defending the lives of the unjustly murdered.[14] In referring to admonition as a necessary mode for religious communication, I acknowledge the long tradition of exhortatory preaching in both the Christian and Muslim (as well as other) traditions, in which, in the words of medieval Muslim scholar Ibn al-Jawzi, those who live in wealth and luxury must be met with "admonition and fright" in preaching, "just as a patient suffering from chill needs to be treated with heat in order to counterbalance his condition."[15] Preaching that is capable of expressing profound outrage, fear, and loss at times serves as a tool for affectively reorienting those who have become desensitized to endemic injustice. As the homiletic addresses examined here show, Christian and Muslim communities already have powerful resources at their disposal, as they have been reimagined via the legacy of what Jackson terms "Black Religion," for constructing theologies that communicate both curse and blessing, lament and consolation, admonition and good news.

Responses to BLM and the Need for a Spiritual Vocabulary of Admonition

In response to the Black Lives Matter movement, many religious communities have asserted their support for the struggle against systemic racism in the United States. Predominantly white, progressive Christian denominations have approved anti-racist motions or policies that reflect engagement with the current movement, have included extensive resources about racial justice and Black Lives

Matter on their websites, and/or have dedicated resources to anti-racist education and organizing in their communities.[16] As Christopher Cameron's essay on the Black Lives of Unitarian Universalism in this volume indicates, this has at times occurred as a result of concerted organizing on the part of Black members of these predominantly white communities. In addition to the involvement of mainline Protestant denominations, the increasing national attention to the persistence of racism in America has led the United States Conference of Catholic Bishops (USCCB) to establish an ad hoc committee focused on "addressing the sin of racism in our society, and even in our Church, and the urgent need to come together as a society to find solutions."[17] Similarly, influential Muslim organizations have outspokenly supported the growing movement.[18] Muslims within the past few years have also founded coalitions dedicated solely to this purpose, such as the Muslim Anti-Racism Collaborative (MuslimARC) and Muslims for Ferguson.[19] Among Muslims, as Iman AbdoulKarim's chapter in this volume also shows, religion and activism find impactful convergence in both individual and organizational efforts.

Despite the openness of many Christian and Muslim religious communities to learning from and supporting the Black Lives Matter movement, predominantly non-Black religious communities, even ones that have made organizational commitments to promote racial justice, have at times struggled to express uncompromising opposition to racist anti-Black violence in the language of their faith traditions. A striking illustration of this problem can be seen in a news story by Michael J. O'Loughlin, published on August 14, 2017, in *America*, which detailed the remarkable transformation over the course of a weekend of Catholic bishops' statements about the gathering of white nationalist demonstrators in Charlottesville, Virginia.[20] The initial statement of the USCCB, released on Saturday, August 12, had called for calm in response to acts of violence that had occurred, without explicitly naming the ideological grounding of these attacks. The bishops described these "acts of hatred" as "an attack on the unity of our nation," and called for a response of "fervent prayer and peaceful action."[21] The statement was met with backlash from those angered by the weakness of the bishops' condemnation of white supremacist violence and their failure to identify specifically the racist ideology that had led to the death of Heather Heyer and the injury of many others. After individual bishops began to speak out in a more specific and oppositional manner, the USCCB released a second statement on Sunday. This time, the bishops were clearer: "we stand against the evil of racism, white supremacy and neo-nazism."[22]

The stress in the bishops' initial statement on calm, peace, and unity was not exceptional. The statement echoed, for example, what Phillip Luke Sinitiere has identified in his examination of evangelical Christian responses to the murder of Trayvon Martin as an "anti-structural," individualistic framework in discussing racial injustice, exemplified by calls for "renewed dialog, deeper discussions, and the expression of more passionate prayers to overcome the color line."[23] This approach was also characteristic of the responses of many Christian communities to the uprising in Ferguson, Missouri, following the August 9, 2014, killing of Michael Brown. Brown was an unarmed Black teenager who had been shot at least six times by a police officer, Darren Wilson, and then left in the street for four and a half hours after his death. By Tuesday, August 13, SWAT teams dressed in riot gear and carrying automatic weapons were on the streets of Ferguson, attacking protesters with tear gas and rubber bullets.[24]

Calls for calm, unity, and peacefulness were central to most predominantly white or white-led Christian denominations' responses to the protests. The Catholic archbishop of the St. Louis archdiocese wrote a letter counseling those "struggling to find peace in the chaos" to themselves become instruments of peace.[25] The presiding bishop of the Evangelical Lutheran Church in America (ELCA) similarly called for prayer and peacefulness, asserting that "in Christ, there is no 'them,' not Michael Brown, not the community, not the police. All are one. All are 'us' and all are Christ's."[26] The official statement of the Presbyterian Church (USA) did acknowledge that the unrest in Ferguson was in response to "years of disenfranchisement and hopelessness" of Michael Brown's community and articulated the need to work to end systemic racism. At the same time, the statement also emphasized that the faithful should remain calm "as work is done by state and federal officials to seek answers and bring justice."[27] The United Methodist bishop of Missouri highlighted the peacemaking efforts of Methodists in Ferguson—including the governor, "an active United Methodist himself." The bishop pledged to "continue to hold in our prayers all those who have most personally and painfully been affected by the violence" and "to bring a ministry of healing to a community that has been deeply hurt."[28]

Similar struggles to voice the outrage and pain felt by many in Black communities over repeated injustices can be seen in the responses of predominantly non-Black Muslim organizations to anti-Black racism and police killings. A parallel controversy to that which occurred over the USCCB's Charlottesville statements occurred within the Muslim community, in which the Islamic Society of North America (ISNA) was widely criticized for a statement it released in response to the protests that had followed the death of Freddie Gray on April 12, 2015. Gray was a twenty-five-year-old Black man who died after he received extensive injuries while in the custody of the Baltimore police. The ISNA statement condemned what they called "wanton destruction, thievery, looting and arson" and asserted that rioting would make "com[ing] together" with the police "to resolve these issues in a constructive, peaceful manner" more difficult. Two days later, in response to criticism, ISNA released a second statement that recognized the "underlying issues of racism and disenfranchisement" behind the protests, but doubled down on its condemnation of vandalism.[29] Manal Omar, in an article for the *Islamic Monthly*, situated ISNA's responses within the context of "a long history of mainstream Muslim organizations failing to offer productive solidarity to urban populations, including Black Muslims."[30]

Even many left-of-center, predominantly non-Black communities have in many cases emphasized the need for calm over outrage, prophetic condemnation, and lament in their responses to the killings of Black individuals. One of the many factors that reinforce barriers to empathy in religious communities that consist of predominantly non-Black members and leadership is a perception that negative or unpredictable emotions like anger represent less religiously appropriate reactions than appeals to calm and the maintenance of unity. The following sermons and khutbas preached in response to the Black Lives Matter movement offer abundant resources for the development of deeply caring, loving, grieving, angry, and healing anti-racist religious thought.

Christian Sermons

The four Christian sermons examined in this section were preached by Reverend Nyle Fort at Shiloh Baptist Church in Trenton, New Jersey; Bishop John Richard Bryant, senior bishop of the African Methodist Episcopal (AME) Church, at Greater Allen AME Cathedral in Queens, New York; Reverend Traci Blackmon at the Riverside Church in Harlem; and Reverend Renita J. Weems, also at Riverside. The first two sermons were delivered at churches affiliated with historically Black denominations, while the two sermons at Riverside were preached to a racially diverse congregation at a landmark church (affiliated with both the United Church of Christ (UCC) and the American Baptist Association) that has historically been associated with predominantly white, liberal Protestantism.

Fort's and Weems's sermons were preached as part of "7 Last Words: Strange Fruit Speaks" services, a practice Fort himself originated,[31] in which preachers use the last words of one of seven Black individuals killed by police, security officials, or vigilantes as their texts.[32] Bishop Bryant delivered his sermon on Black Life Matters Sunday on December 14, 2014, a date that Bryant himself had selected and invited other Christian leaders to honor.[33] Despite the differing contexts and audiences of the four sermons, they powerfully express faith in the God who will act to tear down the structures of abusive authority and save and heal those who have been abused by them.

The Blessing in the Curse: Reverend Nyle Fort

The first sermon examined here was preached by Reverend Nyle Fort, a minister, academic, and activist whose time in Ferguson led to his development of the "7 Last Words: Strange Fruit Speaks" liturgical services commemorating the victims of police and vigilante violence.[34] "I am not here to preach to you," he begins his sermon at Shiloh Baptist Church on October 24, 2014.[35] Fort goes on to say that his sermon was already preached in the last words of Jordan Davis, a seventeen-year-old boy shot and killed at a gas station in Florida after refusing to turn down his music. His final words ("fuck that, n----, turn that shit up!"), Fort says, are the "gospel of Jordan Davis," the good news proclaimed from the "American cross of white supremacy" (01:21). Fort, in an interview with Almeda Wright, described the difficulty in planning to deliver this very sermon, when questions were raised about preaching with Davis's profane language. "Fort and the planning team decided," Wright concludes, "that honoring the words of Jordan was a nonnegotiable."[36] The "miracle" of Davis's last statement, per Fort, can be seen in his freedom to do what the Church has failed to do: to "call out the demon of white racial supremacy in the name of justice." Fort criticizes the inadequate "vocabulary" of faith that has no capacity for cursing (03:22), that is unable "to tell the truth about the hell we're catching as Black people living under the yoke of this American empire" (04:17). He laments what he describes as many Black religious communities' acceptance of the norms of white supremacy, particularly as reflected in the shunning of young Black people "because our music is too loud and our pants are too low and our language just a little bit too real" (05:59). Fort draws upon the example of Malcolm X to make a case for the necessity of language as "real" as that of Jordan Davis's (07:24). Rather than "sweet-talking" the enforcers of white supremacy, in Malcolm's words, Davis was brave enough to "talk back" (12:49).

"Woe unto us," Fort says (06:50). Later, he repeats this lamentation: "Woe to those of us who remain silent in the face of institutionalized injustice!" (08:00). Fort uses the prophetic language of "woe" in order to frame unwillingness to challenge white violence unequivocally as a sin that demands communal repentance. Davis's courage functions, in Fort's sermon, to expose the lack of similar bravery and resistance in the Church. The power to curse, so vividly illustrated by Davis's refusal to turn down his music, opens up new possibilities for action and resistance. Fort argues that the freedom to curse racism, patriarchy, homophobia, transphobia, and any other evil must be followed with a commitment to enter into new ways of being.

> What does it look like in real life . . . to curse white supremacy and police brutality? Well, every time we love on one another, we curse white supremacy. Every time we reject individualism and organize our communities, we curse police brutality. Every time we don't allow ourselves to become a token in and by the system, we curse capitalism and its neoliberal nature. Every time Black brothers and sisters can hug on each other, then we curse plantation politics. Every time we fight against mass incarceration, we curse the history and legacy of slavery. . . . Every time we challenge oppressive legislation, we curse the criminal injustice system. Every time work together, every time we buy Black, every time we grow our own food, we curse the oppressive powers that do everything possible to keep us from loving and supporting one another. (10:05–11:12)

The ultimate end of cursing "oppressive powers" is embodied love for human beings that are systematically and violently devalued by those powers themselves.

Fort's sermon offers a vision of love that cannot bear to be silent and equivocal in the face of systemic brutality. The blessing that emerges from the curse is the destruction of barriers to life, wholeness, healing, and care. Fort ends by reshaping Davis's last words into a call to resistance: "It's time to turn up for justice! It's time to turn up for freedom. . . . It's time to turn up for Black kids being able to listen to the music we like without being shot down in cold blood" (11:54). Anger, lament, and mourning animate Fort's sermon, but it is also eminently hopeful, offering a glimpse into the life "that God intends us to live" through Jordan Davis's example of courageous defiance (13:05).

Learn How to Fight and Cry at the Same Time:
Reverend Renita J. Weems

The second sermon examined here was preached by Reverend Renita Weems, a scholar of the Hebrew Bible and an elder in the AME

Church. Like Fort's sermon, Reverend Renita J. Weems's "[Scream]," delivered at the Riverside Church on February 20, 2015, starts from the last utterances of a Black teenage boy killed by a vigilante.[37] Weems, however, unlike Fort, had no words to interpret as her text: only a scream. Weems reminds those present at the Riverside Church that seventeen-year-old Trayvon Martin's mother was asked to identify her son's voice based on the sound of his final screams. "Imagine," she says,

> being made to sit as Trayvon's mother was, there on a stand, and being asked to listen with poise and dignity at the sound of your child screaming for help, and imagine knowing that your child cried out for help and no one bothered to come to his rescue. . . . This is the tragedy. And I don't know how to make sense of the unanswered cries for help of a boy in Sanford, Florida. (02:42)

Weems's sermon reflects on the theological value of weeping, wailing, and screaming. In the face of senseless evil that we simply cannot accept, she says, "the Bible has a way of handling things that make no sense: you *scream* and you cry out!" (06:42). Weems gives powerful voice to the tradition of lament in the Bible. She encourages her listeners to embrace the emotional instability of so-called hysteria, with all its gendered connotations. "Let each woman teach her daughter a wail," she proclaims, "for *death* has come into our windows and snuffed out our lives. Sometimes crying and weeping and wailing are the only appropriate things that can be done for Trayvon. And so, as a seventeen-year-old young boy . . . his last words were a *scream*! A boy screamed because he was a child. And children in trouble *scream*" (07:52). It is this wailing in the face of the absurdity of total evil, Weems explains, from which jazz and the blues emerged. "It is the blues of our people. It is the ability to take pain to take sorrow to take grief and to turn it into theology of crying out to God, because some things make no sense" (09:53).

Weems challenges her hearers to take the value of Black lives seriously enough to be reflective about their own presence at The Riverside Church, a community that has a long history of supporting progressive causes, but which does not, according to her, resemble the spiritual homes of "those who are being choked to death and those who are screaming" (14:12). Weems's sermon dramatizes the reality and gravity of the crimes she describes; she refuses to allow pain and anger to be subsumed into a theology of consolation or comfort. Her words militate against the familiarity with which Americans have come to greet the destruction of Black lives:

> For crying out loud, who kills the unarmed and leaves their bodies in the street for hours? For crying out loud! Who kills unarmed grandmothers sitting in their homes, reaching for their canes? For crying out loud! Who kills nine-year-old little girls lying on the sofa and being mistaken for a drug dealer? For crying out loud! Who kills a man and chokes him for selling cigarettes? For crying out loud! Who kills someone simply because he's queer? Makes me wanna holler, throw up my hands. It makes you wanna holler. And throw up both your hands. Makes you wanna holler and throw up both your hands. (17:29–18:43)

The movement from crying to throwing up both hands—a gesture of protest—anticipates the conclusion of the sermon, in which Weems advises her hearers to "learn how to fight and cry at the same time" (24:52). She recalls that, according to Genesis, God heard the cries of Hagar's child as she wept over him (Genesis 21:8–21). "God says, 'I have heard the cries of the little boy.' Thanks be to God; God heard Trayvon's cry" (25:06). In her preaching, Weems attempts to awaken attention to the unbearableness of what has happened to Trayvon and far too many others. Fighting back, however, becomes possible because of God's attentiveness to this needless, outrageous suffering.

A God Who Knows How to Bring Down Strongholds: Bishop John Richard Bryant

The theme of God's sovereign power as a source of hope in the struggle against racial injustice is articulated even more strongly by Bishop John Richard Bryant in his sermon given at Greater Allen AME Cathedral on December 14, 2014.[38] The central message of Bishop Bryant's sermon is "You are precious in God's sight because Black lives *matter!"* (05:23). While Bryant starts with an acknowledgment that "we *mourn* with the mothers who mourn" (06:07), this grief also witnesses to the joyful knowledge that in bringing this lament to God,

> We've got a resource greater than a badge, greater than a night stick, greater than handcuffs. We've got something greater than an out-of-order criminal justice system. We've got a God on our side—hallelujah!—who can make a way out of no way. We've got a God on our side who knows how to bring down strongholds. We've got a God on our side who can set at liberty those who are captive. And when we as God's people cry out to God, *watch out!* Because when God gets ready to move, we gonna rise, shine, and give God glory! (09:41–10:46)

The heart of Bryant's sermon is God's involvement in the struggle, the "battle" that everyone in the church must be ready to fight (09:33, 10:56). "We want the world to know," he says, "that police who are out of order have taken the lives of our future, and we don't take it lightly! We mourn, we mourn. We cry, Lord have mercy!" (06:31). Confrontation of evil, in Bryant's sermon, is always combined with prayerful appeal to God.

Bryant, who had issued a universal invitation to Christian leaders to join in the celebration of Black Life Matters Sunday, notes as he calls the men to the altar for a concluding prayer that not only historically Black, but also historically white congregations in denominations such as the such as the ELCA and the UCC had responded enthusiastically to his request. "God's got more disciples than you know about," he proclaims, "and we simply got to call on those disciples" (12:11). The struggle is unequivocally against "those systemic evil perpetrators that would try to take life from us and from our seed" (18:02), but true repentance and reconciliation is not only possible but a powerful witness to God's great power and love for those who are being oppressed.

Bryant ends with prayer on behalf of the community. In concluding his prayer, he asks the community to embrace each other in a similar way that Fort had in his call to "hug on each other" as a way of cursing white supremacy. "Every brother hug a brother," Bryant says. "Praise the Lord" (19:46). Love and care for the community, in Bryant's sermon, are paired with the need to fight and to "stand" against those who destroy and devalue Black lives.

A Song That Speaks Truth to Power: Reverend Traci Blackmon

Similarly to Bishop Bryant's, Reverend Traci Blackmon's sermon, "We, too, Sing Freedom," given at the Riverside Church in Manhattan on December 21, 2014, is a celebration of God's love for the oppressed and His power to save.[39] Blackmon is the executive minister of the UCC's Justice and Local Church Ministries and has also served a prominent role in the Black Lives Matter movement.[40] Blackmon's sermon focuses on text of the Magnificat (Luke 1:46–55), which she describes as a "song of freedom" (08:36) and "the announcement of God's revolution" (11:11). Contrary to the "syrupy sentimentality" of Christmas preparations in American culture (06:49), Blackmon proclaims the "revolutionary nature" of what Christmas represents (07:10), which is in fact God's choice to be born as "the Afro-Semitic son of a poor teenage mother" (07:18), reversing absolutely the world's order of values. Drawing on the symbol of resistance used in the Ferguson protests, Blackmon describes Jesus as being born "with his hands up" (09:26), declaring in the midst of a world which seeks to kill him, "See me! I do you no harm" (09:44).

Blackmon emphasizes an aspect of the Magnificat that is often overlooked by Christian preaching, even in progressive congregations: that Mary's "freedom song" sings of "a world which will one day be turned upside-down" (10:09). Mary sings about a God who sends the rich away empty and brings the powerful down from their thrones. However, she cautions, God does not want oppressors to be punished, but instead wants them to repent (21:04). In Jesus, she says, one can see clearly that confrontation of those who are hurting and killing others is part and parcel of God's healing, restorative justice-making (23:54). Blackmon's sermon is above all a proclamation of God's victory, a triumph best expressed through song, one that "sings the language of the times," one that is desperately needed (24:57). "We sing because without our song we have no hope" (27:34).

Blackmon, who preaches her sermon, like Weems, at the racially diverse but historically predominantly white community of Riverside, invites her hearers to recognize their own longing for God's revolutionary action in the world. "I am sitting on the edge of my seat," she says, "waiting to hear why the birth narrative of Jesus is good news to people around the globe who are still suffering"(29:03). Turning to the congregation, she asks, "has God's freedom song begun to stir in you? Can you feel God's revolution happening in you?" (31:28). Blackmon communicates the realities of "outrage," "grief," and "fear," but the gospel of Luke's portrayal of Mary serves as an example of someone capable of singing a freedom song about the "saving acts of a revolutionary God, who always intervenes in the midst of injustice"(18:35). As with the other homiletic examples, Blackmon describes confrontation and anger as necessary aspects of openness to faith in the God who acts to save, defend, and protect those whom the world has abandoned.

Muslim Khutbas

Like the Christian sermons, the four khutbas I will examine in this section are drawn from communities with differing historical backgrounds and ideological orientations. They were delivered by Imam al-Hajj Talib Abdur-Rashid of the Mosque of Islamic Brotherhood, Inc. in Harlem; Dawud Walid at the Masjid as-Salam in Detroit; Hajjah Abrafi S. Sanyika at the Women's Mosque of America in Los Angeles; and Sister Nayawiyyah Muhammad, also at the Women's Mosque. Imam Talib's khutba was delivered at a predominantly Black Muslim community descended directly from Malcolm X's Muslim Mosque, Inc.[41] Muhammad's and Sanyika's khutbas were delivered at the (predominantly non-Black) first women's mosque in America, and were both followed by a discussion circle on Black Lives Matter as part of a three-week series. The four khutbas that follow, despite their different areas of emphasis and varying audiences, share assertion of the opposition of Islam to all forms of oppression and the necessity of both restorative justice and healing.

Freedom and Oppression: Imam al-Hajj Talib Abdur-Rashid

Imam al-Hajj Talib Abdur-Rashid's khutba "Freedom from Oppression" was delivered on Friday, August 15, 2014, at the Mosque of Islamic Brotherhood, while the protests in Ferguson and the militarized response of the police were at their height.[42] Imam Talib's advocacy against police brutality dates back significantly further than the current movement; in response to the police killings of a number of Black Muslim men in the 1990s, Imam Talib became a community leader in voicing opposition to police brutality and racially targeted law enforcement tactics such as stop-and-frisk.[43] Imam Talib himself embraced Islam in his twenties as a direct result of reading *The Autobiography of Malcolm X* and encountering the theology of Malcolm and the Nation of Islam, and he emphasizes the historic connection between Islam and the struggle against anti-Black racism in the United States.[44] The khutba itself does not focus solely on the protests in Ferguson. Rather, Imam Talib places the events in Missouri within the much broader context of the struggle for freedom against oppression in world history.

The Qur'anic text Imam Talib uses for his khutba is from Surat ar-Rum, which Imam Talib reminds his listeners means "the Roman Empire" (04:30). He focuses on the forty-first ayah (verse) of the chapter: "mischief, evil, has appeared on land and sea because of what the hands of men have earned, in order that Allah may give them a taste of some of their deeds, or perhaps that they might turn back from evil" (04:25). To pair with this verse, Imam Talib cites a hadith (report of a saying of the Prophet Muhammad) narrated by Abu Dhar al Ghifari, in which the Prophet gives his companions a message from God: "O my servants, I have forbidden oppression for you. I have forbidden oppression for myself and have made it forbidden for you or amongst you. So, do not oppress one another" (05:24). Using these two texts, from the Qur'an and the hadith, Imam Talib explains that there are "two mighty sociological forces that we find in lives of men." These forces are freedom and oppression (06:23).

God commands believers to turn away from oppression because it militates against the very nature of created things: freedom. Oppression is "a darkness of the heart and of the mind . . . the result of the absence of the light of the Creator of the heavens and the earth" (09:05). The denial of divine guidance manifested in oppression is not limited to human beings, but cosmic in its scope, resulting in the suffering of all creatures, the air, the waters, and the earth itself (18:48). Yet the evils of oppression are unsustainable, Imam Talib claims, because "freedom from captivity and oppression is the nature of created things" (22:58). Even a bird locked up in a cage, as soon as the door is mistakenly left open, will rush to escape in flight (22:21). Oppression must hit a breaking point, because it will necessarily "whiplash" back at the perpetrators (20:40). In this sense, the inevitable fall of oppressive empires is the result of the "wrath of Allah" (21:20).

Imam Talib describes the ongoing events in Ferguson within the context of this "great battle going on throughout the earth" between the forces of freedom and oppression (07:35). He condemns the militarized response of the police to the protesters:

> People—innocent, nonviolent men, women, and children gather in the street for nonviolent protest in order to say that the life of the young man who was killed there, Michael Brown, his life is precious to us, and we're not gonna let you just keep killing innocent people. We're gonna raise our voices up in an act of nonviolent jihad. . . . The people say, "okay, even though we have this ongoing problem here in our town, and the police function like an occupying army, keeping injustice, we're gonna keep it nonviolent." . . . And so what do they do? [The police] attack the people who are sitting in the road nonviolently with their hands up in the air. And you know, you can look around the world and see all kind of examples of this same kind of thing, all over Africa, all over Asia, all over Europe, same thing, ain't no different, in the global struggle for *hurriya* [freedom] and against *zulm* [oppression]. (30:10–30:47, 35:00–36:48)

The battle for freedom and against oppression cannot be fought without empathy for all other living beings. Imam Talib refers to a hadith in which the Prophet Muhammad described the *ummah* (Muslim community) as like a human body, "characterized by compassion and love for one another and empathy for one another" (39:54). It is necessary to feel others' suffering—including the suffering of non-human animals—throughout "every cell of your body" (40:32). In order to become a community that acts for freedom, believers must ask God "to move our hearts closer to one another" first (43:40). Imam Talib relates a vision of uncompromising Muslim resistance to oppression, based in the conversion to empathy and compassion that divine guidance effects in the human heart.

Restorative Justice: Dawud Walid

In his khutba, Imam Talib interprets of the words of the Prophet Muhammad (related in the hadith) as pointing to the absolute, cosmic inevitability of the fight against oppression. Dawud Walid's khutba, "#ICantBreathe—From Bilal to Today," delivered at Masjid as-Salam on December 5, 2014, uses the life of the Prophet Muhammad as articulated by the traditional sources of Sunni Islam to make a similar argument.[45] Walid, the executive director of the Michigan chapter of the Council on American-Islamic Relations (CAIR), starts by asserting strongly the need to recognize "our responsibility as Muslims to be people of justice amongst ourselves and to work to establish justice in any society in that we live in." He describes the context of systemic racism in the United States and specifically the ways the history of anti-Black oppression in America informs current instances of police brutality and killings. He gives the names of numerous Black men and boys who have died at the hands of police, including Amadou Diallo, Malice Green, Michael Brown, Eric Garner, Rumain Brisbon, and Tamir Rice, and argues that their deaths must be understood in the context of the "systems" and "structures" implemented from the beginning of the United States "to hold down in particular two groups," Black and Indigenous peoples.

In order to formulate a response to this continued violence, Walid offers lessons from the life of the Prophet Muhammad, whom he describes as providing "the best example" for how to deal with structural racism. In particular, Walid characterizes the Prophet's transformation of his society as dismantling the foundations of "structural tribalism," "structural racism," and economic exploitation.

In the midst of these realities of oppression, Walid argues, using a term frequently used within Black liberation movements including the Black Lives Matter movement, the Prophet Muhammad "built a beloved community that had never been seen in the history of the world." Walid encourages his hearers, when thinking of their own role in American society or the world to consider carefully the implications of the way of life practiced by the earliest Muslim community.

Walid focuses especially on the story of Bilal, one of the companions of the Prophet, using his relationship with the Prophet Muhammad to demonstrate the latter's direct confrontation with the racism of pre-Islamic Arab communities. "Those people used to abuse him, enslaved him . . ." Walid says of Bilal. "Just like we have many people here in America who are descendants from ex-slaves. I want you to make the connection. . . . He used to be tortured. He used to be abused. He came from a group of people who were abused." Recognizing this, the Prophet Muhammad gave Bilal particular honors. Most importantly, when the early Muslim community returned to Mecca following the exile in Medina, it was Bilal who was given the honor of ascending the Kaaba to give the call to prayer. "Think of what [the Kaaba] represents," explains Walid. "The center of life, the center of commerce, the center of pilgrimage for all the Arabs . . . and this man who was once put down, seen to be as nothing but trash, tortured, owned, got on top of the most prestigious place for the Arabs and called the *adhan* [call to prayer]." Bilal on top of the Kaaba represents the "restorative justice" instituted by the Prophet, and indicates the "obligation" all Muslims have to "stand up against injustice, to stand up against racism."

Walid describes the continued existence of both structural injustice and racism in Muslim communities throughout history, but is careful to note that there have always been Muslims ready to speak out and act against oppression, even at the risk of their own lives. "When they saw deviations in society, when they saw injustice, they would speak out against it, even if it meant them being imprisoned or killed or martyred. . . . This is what the early Muslims did." In this khutba, Walid provides an interpretation of Islam as fundamentally representing a threat to the structures of oppression and a hopeful beacon for those in need of restoration. He exhorts his hearers repeatedly to do more to stand up against injustice, to embrace their call as Muslims to lead "in the moral, intellectual, and ethical revolutions" of their societies.

The World Cannot Stand on Untruths: Hajjah Abrafi S. Sanyika

In his khutba, as has been discussed, Walid portrays Muslim opposition to injustice as rooted in the history of the earliest Muslim community. Hajjah Abrafi S. Sankiya, drawing upon Afrocentric thinkers in her khutba "Standing on Truth, Stepping Out in Truth," delivered at the Women's Mosque of America on January 27, 2017, grounds the history of resistance to oppression even further back, in ancient Africa and especially ancient Kemet (Egypt).[46] Sanyika tells her hearers, a racially diverse group of mostly Muslim women, that it is crucial that Muslims recognize that the primary principles of Islam were taught many generations before the birth of Muhammad and were first recorded in texts written in Africa. The foundational ethical worldview of Islam and of other religions, she says, was given expression long before the birth of these faith traditions. Sanyika explains that she is not arguing that Islam "somehow borrowed from those ancient African religious traditions" (12:10), but rather she sees the similarities between Islam and pre-Islamic African ethical and spiritual thought as "confirming what Islam has taught us: that there is only one God and one humanity and that God brought guidance to God's creatures from the beginning of human life in East Africa. And God has sent successive prophets with the same message over and over because humankind continually lapsed and had to be reminded" (12:20).

Recognizing this history is essential, claims Sanyika, for counteracting the "concerted, deliberate agenda to discredit the history of Africa" which has obscured the perception of Africa and people of African descent for centuries (12:50). This historic and systemic devaluation of Black people and culture, she says, "is the source of all the trauma we are presently experiencing" in the United States

(13:00). While the "Western" world may reward Muslims for forgetting the history of colonialism and slavery, some younger Muslim scholars now realize that they "must develop a liberation theology that benefits Muslims rather than regurgitating their Western training" (16:59). These young thinkers are not afraid to draw connections between the devastation currently being experienced in the Arab world and the suffering of people of African descent: both examples have their roots in colonialism and the lies about history and civilization that are told in order to uphold it (17:13).

Exposing these lies, she asserts, is necessary for Muslims, who are bound to speak the truth—because the "world cannot stand on untruths" (22:53).

> With the past five hundred years of brutal enslavement of African people, this society has come to the brink of genocide and that is what has caused the Black Lives Matter movement. I submit to you that we, all of us, have an obligation to tell the truth and I submit that we as women may well be the vanguard to right this wrong. Why? Because Black lives matter. (17:48–18:20)

Sanyika argues that acknowledging the achievements of people of African descent and their specific contributions to the knowledge and well-being of the world is necessary for undoing the racist mindset that hundreds of years of colonialism and the erasure of African existence created. But in addition, it is also what is required by the fundamentally universal orientation of Islam. "We are all one humanity, one creation, in submission to one God, and God has commanded us to tell the truth" (23:07). Sanyika reminds her listeners that Islam is not based in any isolated cultural context, including that of the Prophet Muhammad, but rather in God's relationship with all living beings. A true commitment to the belief in God's universal care for creation would require "honor[ing] those who are now reviled" and asserting unapologetically that Black lives matter (22:56).

Consciousness-Raising and Nurturing the Soul:
Sister Nayawiyyah Muhammad

Sister Nayawiyyah Muhammad's khutba, delivered at the Women's Mosque of America on August 26, 2017, is not solely focused on Black lives or resistance, though it was given in advance of a discussion circle moderated by Muhammad at the Women's Mosque on the Black Lives Matter movement.[47] The primary focus on Muhammad's khutba instead is the history of the place of women in the mosque. However, throughout the khutba, she draws upon her own experience growing up within the Nation of Islam in order to demonstrate the importance of addressing the negative self-worth of devalued persons and prescribe a way for women "to take ownership of their lives, of our lives" (28:46). Muhammad says that the Nation of Islam's "strong call for Black unity, and its push for Black people to know their worth and to do for self, could be considered an early example of a Black Lives Matter movement" (17:56). Attention to the cultivation of self-worth and self-care is crucial, Muhammad demonstrates, for both women and Black Americans.

Muhammad grounds her conviction of the need for self-nurturing in the Qur'anic account in Surat ash-Shams of "God instill[ing] an oath on the creation, through a beautiful description of the sun, the moon, the night, the day, the sky, the heavens, and the earth" (24:10). God's oath is not exclusive to the beauties of the physical world, however, but extends "to include our souls . . . our souls were given proportion, order, and enlightenment" (24:22). The Qur'an speaks unequivocally of the intrinsic goodness of the human person. Each soul contains a "seed of what it means to act with virtues of justice, of mercy, and forgiveness," and this seed must be cultivated and nurtured in order to grow into its full maturity (25:45).

Muhammad describes her own experiences of racism as having previously devastated her sense of self-worth. "Fear, doubt, false thinking, injustices to ourselves and to others, and feelings of unworthiness will stunt your soul" (26:15). In response, one must know one's true worth as grounded in the Creator of all things. Muhammad describes this knowledge of self-worth and cultivation of self-love as becoming possible in spaces that are safe for "consciousness-raising" such as the Women's Mosque (26:45). Similar to Fort's description of the oppressed community loving on each other as resistance to white supremacy, Muhammad asserts that self-nurturing and communal care can have radical social and political implications.

> Transcending social issues historically has consisted of navigating disparities in this tug-of-war of power imbalances. The nurturing of your souls, of yourself, is so critical to our existence, to our quality of life, how we see ourselves collectively and individually. If we desire to heal ourselves, our communities, our nations, and ourselves and our environment, we must begin to heal our thinking by healing our thoughts, and the thoughts we think about ourselves and others. The power to heal these imbalances in our lives lies within us. (28:02–28:47)

Muhammad powerfully envisions community healing, rooted in personal connection with God and all other created beings, as the motivation for resistance to all forms of injustice.

Conclusion

The final khutba examined here underscores an important theme that runs throughout all of the homiletic examples discussed above. While many of the other addresses more vividly convey the need for condemnation of evil, Muhammad's khutba highlights what makes such confrontational rhetoric necessary: the pervasive dehumanization of Black people in the United States. Muhammad's portrayal of communal self-nurturing as rooted in a vision of the soul as beautiful and enacted in public challenges to power imbalances mirrors Pinn's depiction of religion as, at best, enabling "the flexible reorganization of psychic, social, economic, cultural, political, geographic, and intellectual space."[48] Condemnation of evil alone is not sufficient; it must follow from a healing re-imagination of the self and the community as not defined by the "ghosts of dehumanization." However, this "rehumanization" necessarily results in the expression of pain, anger, and committed opposition to ongoing injustice.

The sermons and khutbas examined here, read together, offer a complex vision of what the "healing justice" work described by Cullors at the beginning of this essay looks like. The homiletic examples draw upon diverse lineages of thought and religious practice—for example, the legacy of the Nation of Islam and Malcolm X in American Islam, discourses rooted in the Methodist and Baptist congregations historically predominant in Black Christianity, the tradition of Black liberation theology, the insights of Afrocentric scholars and figures, and the sources of traditional Sunni Islam—but these "vehicles" are utilized in the expression of a shared religious outlook rooted in the struggle against anti-Black racism. Notably, this religious discourse normatively incorporates Black anger, grief, and pain.

Together, the homiletic examples paint a vivid picture of a spiritual practice grounded in cursing the demons of white supremacy and injustice (Fort), screaming and wailing with Trayvon Martin (Weems), mourning with the God who is on the side of Black lives (Bryant), proclaiming God's revolution (Blackmon), striving in the cosmic battle against oppression (Talib), claiming the oppressed one's right to the central place of prayer (Walid), exposing the lies of anti-Blackness (Sanyika), and cultivating a healing collective space (Muhammad). Shared by all of the speakers is a commitment to the vision of the full humanity of Black people asserted uncompromisingly by the Black Lives Matter movement. The witness of the movement, whether expressed explicitly in religious language (or practice as AbdoulKarim's chapter elucidates) as in these examples, or communicated in more "secular" idioms, is a profoundly "rehumanizing" force that can serve as a model for religious communities in the United States. In addition, careful attention to these examples demonstrates that predominantly non-Black religious communities must reexamine fundamental premises of their religious worldviews in order to issue unequivocal support for the statement "Black lives matter." In order to give these words meaning, non-Black religious communities must allow their religious language to register the pain and outrage of Black people; moreover, they must commit to ongoing and uncompromising confrontation of the forces mobilized against Black life.

NOTES

1. Patrisse Cullors, "Patrisse Cullors and Robert Ross: The Spiritual Work of Black Lives Matter," interview by Krista Tippett, *On Being*, orig. airdate, February 18, 2016, https://onbeing.org/programs/patrisse-cullors-and-robert-ross-the-spiritual-work-of-Black-lives-matter-may2017.

2. Almeda Wright, *The Spiritual Lives of Young African Americans* (New York: Oxford University Press, 2017), 154–97. Similar arguments stressing the continuity between the Black Lives Matter movement's relationship to religiosity and that of earlier Black social movements are made by contributors to this volume, as in Matthew Cressler's and Kerry Pimblott's essays.

3. Anthony B. Pinn, *What Is African American Religion?* (Minneapolis, MN: Fortress Press, 2011), 62.

4. Pinn, 79, 75–76.

5. Pinn, 92–93.

6. Joseph Winters, "Death, Spirituality, and the Matter of Blackness," in *Race, Religion, and Black Lives Matter*, ed. Christopher Cameron and Phillip Luke Sinitiere, 149–74.

7. Sherman Jackson, *Islam and the Blackamerican: Looking toward the Third Resurrection* (New York: Oxford University Press, 2005), 29.

8. Jackson, 29.

9. Jackson, 28.

10. Brittney Cooper, *Eloquent Rage: A Black Feminist Rediscovers Her Superpower* (New York: St. Martin's Press, 2018), 210.

11. James Baldwin, *The Fire Next Time* (New York: Vintage Books, 1993), 58–59.

12. Baldwin, 58.

13. Wright, *The Spiritual Lives of Young African Americans*, 168–71.

14. Nyle Fort, "Jordan Davis Sermon," YouTube video, posted by Nyle Fort, November 7, 2014, https://www.youtube.com/watch?v=MKQ6c12G4sQ, 3:22.

15. Quoted in Tarif Khalidi, *Arabic Historical Thought in the Classical Period* (Cambridge, UK: Cambridge University Press, 1994), 201.

16. See, for example, "Support the Black Lives Matter Movement," Unitarian Universalist Association, July 1, 2015, https://www.uua.org/action/statements/support-black-lives-matter-movement; "Black Lives Matter," Evangelical Lutheran Church in America, accessed February 13, 2018, http://elca.org/blacklivesmatter; "Racial Justice," Evangelical Lutheran Church in America, accessed February 13, 2018, https://www.elca.org/Resources/Racial-Justice; "Racial Justice," The United Church of Christ, accessed February 13, 2018, http://www.ucc.org/justice_racism; The Office of the General Assembly of the Presbyterian Church (U.S.A.), "Facing Racism: A Vision of the Intercultural Community Churchwide Antiracism Policy," Presbyterian Church (USA): Presbyterian Mission, May 21, 2016, https://www.presbyterianmission.org/

resource/facing-racism-vision-intercultural-community-churchwide-antiracism-policy.

17. "U.S. Bishops Establish New Ad Hoc Committee against Racism," United States Conference of Catholic Bishops, August 23, 2017, http://www.usccb.org/news/2017/17-149.cfm. On November 14, 2018, as a result of increasing national pressure to address racial injustice, the USCCB also approved a statement, published as "Open Wide Our Hearts: The Enduring Call to Love, A Pastoral Letter against Racism." ("U.S. Bishops Approved 'Open Wide Our Hearts: The Enduring Call to Love, A Pastoral Letter against Racism,'" United States Conference of Catholic Bishops, November 14, 2018, http://www.usccb.org/news/2018/18-186.cfm). Catholic theologians MT Davila and Eric Martin, responding to the letter publicly through Political Theology Network, criticized the USCCB's letter for its emphasis on "personal conversion at the expense of structural transformation" (MT Davila, "The Conversion of Hearts and the Sin of Racism," Political Theology Network, February 22, 2019, https://politicaltheology.com/the-conversion-of-hearts-and-the-sin-of-racism) and for its inadequate "vacillating constantly between vague admissions of fault and specific self-praise, understandings of racism as structural and merely individual, awareness of power difference between races and claims that all are accountable for racial injustice" (Eric Martin, "Blackface and White Comfort: Reading the Bishops' Letter from Charlottesville," Political Theology Network, February 15, 2019, https://politicaltheology.com/Blackface-and-white-comfort-reading-the-bishops-letter-from-charlottesville).

18. "Structural Racism," ICNA Council for Social Justice, accessed February 13, 2018. http://icnacsj.org/structural-racism; "MPAC Track Record on Addressing Police Brutality and Racism in America," Muslim Public Affairs Council, December 23, 2014, https://www.mpac.org/blog/mpac-track-record-on-addressing-police-brutality-and-racism-in-america1.php; "CAIR Calls for National Action on Racism after Ferguson Grand Jury Decision," Council on American-Islamic Relations, November 25, 2014, https://www.cair.com/press_releases/cair-calls-for-national-action-on-racism-after-ferguson-grand-jury-decision; "#BLM: Statements and Resources," CAIR-Chicago, accessed April 15, 2021. https://www.cairchicago.org/blm.

19. Muslim Anti-Racist Collaborative, accessed February 12, 2018. http://www.muslimarc.org; Muslims for Ferguson Facebook page, accessed February 12, 2018, https://www.facebook.com/Muslims4Ferguson.

20. Michael J. O'Loughlin, "How the Catholic Response to Charlottesville Moved from Pleas for Unity to Condemnations of Racism," America, August 14, 2017, https://www.americamagazine.org/politics-society/2017/08/14/how-catholic-response-charlottesville-moved-pleas-unity-condemnations.

21. "President of U.S. Conference of Catholic Bishops Calls for Calm Amid Vio-

lent Protests in Charlottesville," United States Conference of Catholic Bishops, August 12, 2017, http://www.usccb.org/news/2017/17-143.cfm.

22. "USCCB President and Domestic Justice Chairman Call for Prayer and Unity in Response to Deadly Charlottesville Attack," United States Conference of Catholic Bishops, August 14, 2017, http://www.usccb.org/news/2017/17-144. cfm.

23. Phillip Luke Sinitiere, "Will the Evangelical Church Remove the Color Line?: Historical Reflections on *Divided by Faith*," *Christian Scholar's Review* 43, no. 1 (Fall 2013), 60–63.

24. See Jamelle Bouie, "The Militarization of the Police," *Slate*, August 13, 2014, http://www.slate.com/articles/news_and_politics/politics/2014/08/police_in_ ferguson_military_weapons_threaten_protesters.html; Jamelle Bouie, "How a Demonstration Turned Into a Disaster," *Slate*, August 14, 2014, http://www. slate.com/articles/news_and_politics/dispatches/2014/08/ferguson_police_ attack_protestors_with_tear_gas_rubber_bullets_on_site_reporting.html.

25. Archbishop Robert J. Carlson, "Archbishop Carlson's Letter on Ferguson," *St. Louis Review*, August 20, 2014, http://stlouisreview.com/article/2014-08-20/ archbishop-carlsons.

26. "ELCA Presiding Bishop Urges Prayer, Peace amid Outrage over Shooting Death," *Evangelical Lutheran Church in America*, August 15, 2014, http://www. elca.org/News-and-Events/%207691#sthash.KkYESKWq.dpuf. The full press release of the ELCA expressed the wish that the Ferguson community work with law enforcement to hold police accountable, stated the need to end racial profiling, and criticized the justice system for devaluing Black lives.

27. "PC(USA) Leaders Call for Calm and Prayer in Ferguson Crisis," *Presbyterian Church (USA)*, August 19, 2014. https://www.pcusa.org/news/2014/8/19/pcusa-leaders-call-calm-and-prayer-ferguson-crisis.

28. Bishop Robert Schnase, "Missouri Bishop Releases Statement on Ferguson," *UM Insight*, August 18, 2014, https://um-insight.net/in-the-church/missouri-bishop-releases-statement-on-ferguson.

29. Sheila Musaji, "Controversy over ISNA Statement on Baltimore Uprising— Updated 5/4/15," *The American Muslim (TAM)*, May 4, 2015, http:// theamericanmuslim.org/tam.php/features/articles/controversy-over-isna-statement-on-baltimore-uprising/0020395.

30. Manal Omar, "Baltimore Protests: Muslims Must Say and Do the Right Thing," *Islamic Monthly*, April 30, 2015, http://www.theislamicmonthly.com/ baltimore-protests-muslims-must-say-the-right-thing.

31. See Nyle Fort and Darnell L. Moore, "A Black Theological Response to Ferguson and Anti-Blackness," *QED: A Journal in GLBTQ Worldmaking* 2, no. 2 (Summer 2015): 208–14. This article contains the full text of the Jordan Davis sermon discussed below; the quotes used in this chapter, however, are transcribed from the video of the event itself. While the text does not di-

verge substantially from the published version, there are small differences. See also Wright, *The Spiritual Lives of Young African Americans*, 168–71 for a discussion of Fort's development of the "7 Last Words: Strange Fruit Speaks" series in the context of young Black activists' reimagination of Christian worship and liturgy.

32. "7 Last Words: Strange Fruit Speaks," event posted to Facebook by the Riverside Church NYC, accessed February 14, 2018, https://www.facebook.com/events/712380978875307; "7 Last Words: Strange Fruit Speaks," *Shiloh Baptist Church*, accessed February 14, 2018, http://www.shilohtrenton.org/LiveStream/7LastWords-2014-rev4%20(1).pdf.

33. Cora Jackson-Fossett, "Faith Leaders Unite on 'Black Life Matters' Sunday," *Los Angeles Sentinel*, December 11, 2014, https://lasentinel.net/faith-leaders-unite-on-Black-life-matters-sunday.html.

34. Fort is a PhD candidate in the Department of Religion at Princeton University. See Fort and Moore, 214.

35. Nyle Fort, "Jordan Davis Sermon," YouTube video, posted by Nyle Fort, November 7, 2014, https://www.youtube.com/watch?v=MKQ6c12G4sQ, 00:51.

36. Wright, *The Spiritual Lives of Young African Americans*, 168.

37. Renita J. Weems, "Rev. Dr. Renita J. Weems—[Scream], Trayvon Martin," YouTube video, posted by the Riverside Church, February 25, 2015, https://www.youtube.com/watch?v=2gPB-w2XP5Y&t=1172s.

38. Bishop John R. Bryant, "Black Lives Matter," YouTube video, posted by Greater Allen Cathedral Church, December 15, 2014, https://www.youtube.com/watch?v=w9LpNKcUZzk.

39. Rev. Traci deVon Blackmon, "We, too, Sing Freedom—Rev. Traci deVon Blackmon," YouTube video, posted by the Riverside Church, January 7, 2015, https://www.youtube.com/watch?v=qb6WtfygVPk.

40. "Meet Our Officers," *United Church of Christ*, accessed on February 13, 2018. http://www.ucc.org/about-us_meet-our-officers.

41. "Imam Talib: Put on the Whole Armor of God," *Amsterdam News*, June 2, 2017, http://amsterdamnews.com/news/2017/jun/02/imam-talib-put-whole-armor-god.

42. Imam al-Hajj Talib Abdur-Rashid, "Freedom from Oppression," YouTube video, posted by MIB Harlem, August 15, 2014, https://www.youtube.com/watch?v=3jOc-JKdh6M&t=717s.

43. "Imam Talib."

44. "Imam Talib."

45. Dawud Walid, "Audio: '#ICantBreathe—From Bilal to Today' Khutbah," *Weblog of Dawud Walid*, December 5, 2014, https://dawudwalid.wordpress.com/2014/12/05/audio-icantbreathe-from-bilal-to-today-khutbah, accessed February 10, 2015. The link to the audio file of this khutba is unfortunately no longer functional at this web address.

46. Hajjah Abrafi S. Sanyika, "Jumma'a 25 (1/27/17)," Internet Archive, uploaded by WomensMosqueofAmerica on May 18, 2017, https://archive.org/details/QAJan.2017/khutpah+Jan.+2017.mp3#.

47. Sister Nayawiyyah Muhammad, "Jumma'a 20 (8/26/16)," Internet Archive, uploaded by WomensMosqueofAmerica on May 18, 2017, https://archive.org/details/BlackLivesMatter20thJummuah/khutpah+by+Nayawiyyah+Muhammad.mp3.

48. Pinn, 77.

CHAPTER 8

"Islam Is Black Lives Matter"

The Role of Gender and Religion in Muslim Women's BLM Activism

Iman AbdoulKarim

The Black women, members of the queer community, and youth at the forefront of Black Lives Matter (BLM) resist "the mistakes of previous movements, especially the classism and sexism that all too often shaped the direction of older civil rights and feminist struggles" by affirming "the lives of Black queer and trans folks, disabled folks, undocumented folks, folks with records, women, and all Black lives along the gender spectrum."[1] The tension between the historic use of religion to support gender and class conservatism within the Black liberation movement and BLM's disavowal of such conservatism informs this essay's inquiry into Muslim women's activism in the BLM movement. In an era characterized by BLM's mission to unsettle the norms of previous movements, how do contemporary Muslims engage Islam and fashion a Muslim religious identity that supports BLM's Black feminist values?

This essay draws on qualitative interviews conducted in 2016 with Muslim women BLM activists to examine how interlocutors' religious identities support their activism, and how their activism informs the meanings they assign to Islam. Seven interlocutors, whom I refer to as Nadia, Drew, Fatima, Dalal, Magda, Amina, and Sara, contribute to BLM's mission through their work as writers, teachers, grassroots organizers, and/or leaders of their local BLM chapters.[2]

Ultimately this essay affirms Islam's legacy as a Black protest religion in the BLM era, echoing scholarship on Black Muslim influence in the Black Power and Black nationalist movements and Dona Auston's recent scholarship. Yet, not unlike Marjorie Corbman in Chapter 7, I argue that the meanings assigned to Islam and articulations of Muslimness as an embodied mode of resistance to anti-Blackness are evolving alongside discourses on gender and sexuality in the BLM era. The first section of this essay identifies the importance of Muslims' gendered religious identities in resisting racialized oppression in the twentieth century, as noted in the work of Sylvia Chan-Malik, Edward Curtis, and Su'ad Abdul Khabeer. This brief introduction establishes Muslims' long use of deliberately gendered religious identities as an important historical antecedent to contemporary Muslims' BLM activism. The second section examines the religious meanings interlocutors assign to their activism and the use of prayer to support their organizing, as well as the political discourses triggered by their activism and BLM's woman-led and action-oriented organizing strategies. Finally, the last section analyzes interlocutors' critical engagement with Islamic religious knowledge to support the feminist politics at the center of their own worldviews and BLM's mission. By centering the pivotal role gendered religious identities and feminist politics play in supporting their belief that "Islam is Black Lives Matter," I propose that a full rendering of Islam's relevance to BLM must account for both race *and* gender to understand the complex function of religion in the contemporary movement for Black life.[3]

Islam and Blackness: Intersectional Oppression and Resistance

Prior to examining how Muslim women engage Islam to support their activism, it is important to briefly note two approaches for illustrating the relationship between Islam and Blackness in the US. The first approach examines how, as Dona Auston notes, anti-Blackness and Islamophobia are not only "specific manifestations of a similar impulse," but "intimate bedfellows" for past and contemporary US Black Muslims who live at their intersections.[4] The second approach examines the critical role of gender in Islam's legacy as a Black protest religion in US history. Although not exhaustive, these approaches draw on the long and influential history of US Black Muslims as they navigate systems of power and craft unique forms of resistance to anti-Blackness.

The relationship between US anti-Muslim sentiment and anti-Blackness dates back to American chattel slavery. Kambiz GhaneaBassiri examines the paradoxical ways Black Muslim slaves in the Antebellum South experienced "de-Negrofication" and "de-Islamization," which "interrupted prejudicial patterns of cultural stereotypes" associated with their racial and religious identities.[5] Enslaved Muslims' religious identities de-negrofied them by distancing them from connotations of Blackness, while their Blackness de-Islamized their religious identities and distanced them from the "licentiousness and despotism" associated with Islam under the Ottoman Empire.[6] However, constructions of Black Muslims as "friendly foreigners" dwindled in 1865 with Emancipation Proclamation and were replaced by what Edward Curtis refers to as the "Black Muslim Scare" of the twentieth century. The Black Muslim Scare reached its pinnacle during the Cold War Era when the Federal Bureau of Investigation's Counter Intelligence Program (COINTELPRO) placed the Nation of Islam (NOI) and other Black Muslim organizations under government surveillance.[7] Consequently, and as Curtis argues, US Islamophobia stems from national anxiety around rising Black nationalism and "the state's legal and extra-legal attempts to control, discipline, and punish Muslim American individuals and organizations."[8] Current Homeland Security initiatives like Counter Violent Extremism (CVE), which disproportionality targets Muslims, and the FBI's creation of the category "Black Identity Extremists" stem from COINTELPRO and illustrate that contemporary US Black Muslims experience heightened vulnerability to state violence due to anti-Blackness and Islamophobia.[9]

The relationship between Islam and Blackness is also defined by US Muslims' resistance to oppression. Scholarship on Islam in the US adopts a lived religion approach to examine how Muslims' racialized existences inform the meanings assigned to their religious identities. For example, Curtis examines the Islamization of the Black body for NOI members under the leadership of Elijah Muhammad. Ritual activities like no-pork diets, selling *Muhammad Speaks* newspapers, attending Temple meetings, and adopting "zoot suit" dressing served "as a means by which Black men and women could save their bodies from emasculation, violation, and contamination."[10] Based on a gendered analysis of women's involvement in the Ahmadiyya movement and NOI, Sylvia Chan-Malik argues that twentieth-century US Muslim women used Islam to resist gendered and racialized oppression by fashioning a Muslim religious identity "insurgently against" the violence ascribed to their bodies. Popular images of NOI women fulfilling the domestic roles of wife and mother during the Cold War era were characterized by an "insurgent domesticity" that rendered "their acts of 'gendered submission' into forms of religious ritual, political protest, and national threat" that asserted the supremacy of the Black patriarchal family during the Crisis of Masculinity.[11]

Islam's role as a Black protest religion in American history is intimately connected to normative gender roles that function as distinct forms of resistance to anti-Blackness. NOI politics and religious identities were grounded in the performance of an explicitly Black heterosexual masculinity through the figure of the "Muslim dandy" that challenged white supremacist depictions of Blackness as "surplus, excess, and lack."[12] Similarly, NOI women's insurgent domesticity performed the ideological work of challenging negative depictions of the broken Black family through popularized images of the Black nuclear family that emphasized Muslim women's influence in the private sphere.[13] Consequently, Islam's critical impact on the Black liberation movement in the mid-twentieth century was characterized by Muslimness functioning as an embodied form that challenged white supremacy by drawing on normative constructions of gender, patriarchy, and Black masculinity to assert the value of Black life.

The historic use of gender norms to craft a Muslim religious identity in opposition to anti-Blackness does not suggest that Muslim women's religious identities are, or have ever been, disjointed from the Black feminist tradition. To the contrary, Debra Majeed's scholarship introduces the term "Muslim womanism" to construct a philosophical perspective that "draws attention to the varied conditions of Black womanhood as experienced by African American Muslims, and the values of Islam they articulate."[14] More recently, Chan-Malik offered a definition of US Muslim feminism as a "critical strand of gender justice discourses of US women of color, alongside Black feminism [. . .] which encompasses the ways US Muslim women have engaged Islam in various forms in order to secure gendered agency and freedom."[15] Concepts like US Muslim feminism and Muslim womanism account for the ways attention to race and Blackness expands what gendered expressions are considered resistant.

Majeed and Chan-Malik demonstrate that gender and Muslim women have always been integral to Islam's legacy as a Black protest religion, and this legacy serves as the historical backdrop in which contemporary Muslims construct an Islam that aligns with BLM's feminist politics. While interlocutors adopt an approach toward their gendered religious identities that is distinct from their predecessors, their approach toward gender, Islam, and BLM does not signal the irrelevance of Muslim women's religious identities in their resistance to anti-Blackness. Instead, interlocutors demonstrate that Muslim women's resistance to anti-Blackness is developing alongside discourses on gender and sexuality in the Black liberation movement. Ultimately, Muslim women feminists and BLM activists illustrate that pluralism, specifically diversified embodiments of Muslim women's religious identities and engagements with Islamic religious knowledge, is a defining characteristic of Islam's role in the BLM era.

BLM Organizing Strategies and Activism as a Religious Obligation

Keeanga-Yamahtta Taylor argues that the new generation at the forefront of BLM stands in sharp contrast to "old guard" organizing strategies that are "not simply the product of male leadership, but of an older model that privileged leveraging connections and relationships within the establishment over street activism—or using street protests to gain leverage within the establishment."[16] BLM's women-led organizing strategies favor social media, grassroots initiatives, and street activism over models adopted by national organizations "whose mostly male leaders make decisions with little input or direction from people on the ground."[17] As the new generation at the forefront of BLM imagines new, decentralized, and adaptive organizing strategies for Black liberation, the religious rituals and knowledge that support activists' work also take on new meaning. The following section examines how Islamic ritual practices support interlocutors' activism and how BLM's women-led and decentralized organizing principles inform the ideological work performed by Muslim women's activism in the public sphere.

Prayer as Ritual Resistance to Gendered and Racialized Oppression

Interlocutors use prayer to affirm their humanity and resist the dehumanizing nature of gendered and racialized oppression. For example, Fauzia describes her religious identity as going beyond her physical visibility as a Muslim woman and identifies prayer as "what gets me through a lot of my own [hardships]."[18] Likewise, Dalal, who sits on the steering committee for one of the largest BLM chapters, confronts "moments of hopelessness" in the Trump-era political climate through the ritual act of prayer, which sustains her on a "personal and intimate level."[19]

When Drew found herself in physical danger while standing in a protest line in front of police officers who were assaulting peaceful organizers, she began to prostrate in front of officers and pray.

Thereafter, officers took off her *hijab*, or headscarf, and arrested her. She explained her decision to pray by noting that "prayer is like a meditation for me, and it centers me. [. . .] I started praying because I wanted the presence of Allah there. [. . .] They say when you pray you are acknowledging your humanity, so after I prayed I felt clear."[20] Drew noted that prior to praying, her Muslim identity was less visible because of her dress and because her *hijab* was wrapped in a traditionally Black fashion. When photos of her arrest appeared on social media and national news outlets, Drew received contradictory backlash from non-Muslims who accused her of extremism, and from Muslims who accused her of being unrepresentative of the Muslim community due to her embodied religious identity.

Drew, Dalal, and Fauzia's use of prayer to resist the physical, emotional, and mental violence of racialized oppression affirms Auston's argument that Muslims' engagement with BLM "represents one present-day embodiment of a raced spirituality [. . .] that has historically imagined and enacted Blackness and resistance to racism through individual and collective religious praxis" that draws on the long history of the African American freedom struggles, Black protest repertoires, and Islamic mandates for social justice.[21] Drew's act of spiritual resistance and its public reception performs ideological work specific to the BLM era. As Muslim women, interlocutors' activism asserts two distinct gendered discourses that challenge popular narratives on women's participation in the Black liberation movement.

First, Drew's act of resistance challenges what Treva B. Lindsey identifies as Black women and girls' marginal space in "most discussions about Black violability, despite being on the frontlines of protests against anti-Black state violence occurring across the nation."[22] Interlocutors' public activism on the frontlines and experience with police violence requires Black women and gender to be accounted for in conversations on police brutality, a key value of BLM's organizational mission and a sentiment popularized through campaigns such as #SayHerName led by Kimberlé Crenshaw and the African American Policy Forum. Second, the popularization of Drew's image as a Black Muslim woman utilizing prayer to protest white supremacy engages with a form of gendered resistance that has not historically been assigned to Black Muslim women's religious identities in the

Black liberation movement. For example, and as noted above, NOI women's insurgent domesticity performed the ideological work of challenging negative depictions of the broken Black family by asserting the supremacy of the Black patriarchal family.[23] Like the insurgent domesticity embodied by NOI women's gender performance, Drew's prayer challenges white supremacy by asserting her humanity as a Black woman in the face of anti-Black state violence. Yet Drew's gender performance and public activism challenges assumptions that Muslim women's religious identities are exclusively located in the private sphere or reflected in singular modes of dress or embodiment. Putting Drew's gendered resistance in conversation with the pivotal gendered resistance of NOI women does not decontextualize either from the unique socio-political contexts that inform them. Instead, it illustrates that interlocutors' protest activity in the BLM era assign distinct meanings to Islam as a Black protest religion and reflect a plurality in Muslim women's activism. Though they may utilize similar ritualized forms of resistance, such as prayer, their activism undertakes ideological work against white supremacy, male-centered understandings of racialized oppression, singular constructions of Muslim women's religious identities, *and* patriarchy.

Dua versus Doing: Activism as a Religious Obligation

BLM's action-oriented organizing strategies are reflected in the religious meanings interlocutors assign to their activism. Their obligation to resist oppression was not fulfilled through prayer alone but required direct action. For example, Drew argued that "when you are doing activism and you're advocating for the disadvantaged, you are expressing your faith" in a way that embodies the values of fasting during Ramadan and *zakat*, or charity.[24] Interlocutors further articulated the relationship between their religious obligations to uphold social justice and their organizing within BLM by distinguishing between prayer and protest, or what Magda referred to as *"dua* [prayer] versus doing."[25]

Magda, a west-coast BLM activist and poet, defines her religious obligations toward social justice as not only compelling her to acknowledge and speak out against oppression, but to also act out against it through art and organizing. Magda is critical of Muslims who confine their protests to their prayers and distinguishes her approach toward social justice and religion from that of "people who see oppression happening from around the world and all they do is *dua* but no action." Magda criticized approaches that viewed prayer as the only way to end injustice. She argued that people cannot "pray oppression away" and believes she cannot "depend solely on God and think he is going to give [her] everything."[26] She approaches prayer and protest as a "two-way relationship between us and the creator." Magda uses this notion of a two-way relationship to go as far as to say that those who only make *dua* are no different than oppressors: "I want to be doing all of these things for God, to show him that I am following his commands and that I do stand up for the oppressed." Magda's activism and spiritual connection to God are complementary, her obligation to both prayer and direct action validate her social justice work.

Like Magda, Fatima is critical of equating prayer with direct action against injustice. Fatima, a Twin Cities activist of Somali descent, views her approach toward religion and activism as symbolic of generational differences in combating police violence within her local community:

> I wasn't going to be the way my parents taught me, which is, "Oh, this is all part of God's plan, you just duck your head, mind your business, and live your life." I want to call this advice, but it's really demands that our parents made of us. But we all collectively made the decision to say, "No thank you. I'm not just going to sit around and wait for things to sort themselves out. I'm going to do something about it myself."[27]

Fatima contrasts her motivations for leading collective actions against police brutality in her community to her parents' use of religion to frame injustice as a part of "God's plan." She employs this generational distinction to frame her activism as a form of religious resistance equivalent to prayer.

Interlocutors support their activism through the ritual act of prayer while arguing that their obligations toward social justice are not fulfilled by prayer alone. They draw a distinction between *dua* and doing to propose that a combination of prayer and direct action against injustice fulfills Muslims' obligations to uphold social justice. In doing so, interlocutors' activism takes on religious significance as a ritualized form of resistance that animates Islamic social justice principles in their everyday lives. The action-oriented religious meanings interlocutors assign to their activism and the gendered political discourses triggered by their organizing demonstrate that Islam's current role as a Black protest religion is informed by BLM's organizing principles. As further explored in the next section, interlocutors also critically engage with Islamic religious knowledge to support the Black feminist ethos at the center of both BLM and their personal politics.

BLM, Black Feminist Politics, and Islamic Religious Knowledge

Like the critical approach Alicia Garza, Patrisse Cullors, and Opal Tometi adopted to develop BLM's intersectional organizing principles, interlocutors adopt a similarly critical approach toward their own interpretations of Islamic texts and the religious knowledge transmitted in their personal networks and communities. In outlining the herstory of the BLM movement, Garza contrasts BLM's organizing principles to previous Black liberation movements that created space for cis, heterosexual men at the expense of women, queer, and trans people. Consequently, BLM is committed to "placing those at the margins closer to the center" by drawing on the leadership of women, queer, and trans people to resist not only anti-Blackness, but gender, sexual, and class oppression.[28] Their mission echoes Crenshaw's critical race theory of intersectionality in that it aims to build a movement that accounts for the ways gender, sexual, and class identities inform Black vulnerability and resistance.

Interlocutors hold Islamic religious knowledge to the same feminist standards that inform BLM's organizing strategies. They construct an Islam that supports their feminist worldviews by holding

Islamic social justice values in tension with uses of Islamic religious knowledge to undermine women's gendered and sexual agency. The following section explores this tension by examining how interlocutors frame their activism and the BLM movement as an extension of Islam's origins as a protest religion, yet they critically engage with religious knowledge that undermines their intersectional activism. Interlocutors' engagement with Islamic religious knowledge suggests they are taking a distinct approach toward religion's role in the Black liberation movement. Interlocutors approach their Muslim religious identities as evolving alongside their lived experiences as Black and Muslim women of color. Thus, the religious meanings interlocutors assign to their activism and their engagements with Islamic religious knowledge are emerging alongside their engagements with Black feminist politics.

Religious Obligations to Uphold Social Justice and Intersectional Activism

Interlocutors frame their intersectional activism and BLM's commitment to centering the marginalized as a reflection of Islam's historical origins as a protest religion and Islamic text's community-centered approach toward social justice. For example, Amina described the relevance of Islamic history to BLM by noting that "our religion is radical; [. . .] the *ummah* came out of opposition, and I don't think people remember those roots at all."[29] Amina refers to Islamic history as "radical" because the Muslim community, or *ummah*, was originally formed in opposition to oppressive Meccan powers who persecuted the Prophet Muhammad for his revelations. Fauzia draws a similar connection between Islam's inception, her religious identity, and activism. She defined the substance of Islam as "helping people who are being discriminated against." Like Amina, she notes that protest and speaking out against injustice are embedded in Islamic history and are "what Islam is about." Amina and Fauzia reference Islamic history to illustrate the contextual similarities between the persecution of the first Muslim community and the murder of Black people at the hands of police and other forms of state violence.

Interlocutors view the intersectional nature of their activism as embodying Muslims' obligation to take a community, rather than individual, approach toward resisting injustice. Dalal argues that Islam "gives us one of the most beautiful definitions of ways to always stand up and take action against injustice, which is, you are to stand against injustice even if it is not against yourself."[30] Sara also cited Qur'anic approaches toward social justice that extend beyond the individual as motivating her activism and writing on Black liberation:

> I call out injustice because there is that *ayah* [Qur'an verse] that I always go back to: Even if it is your mother, brother, father, or sister, you have to call out injustice when you see it because if you ignore it, Allah sees that you see it and you aren't going to be able to get away from that. [. . .] You should feel it so deeply that you hate it, you act out against it, you speak out against it. So, when I feel like I can't speak out against it, I write out against. I hate it so much that Allah knows.[31]

Sara and Dalal paraphrase Qur'an verse 4:135 to frame BLM's commitment to centering the marginalized as a reflection of Muslims' obligation to advocate for the oppressed, even if the oppressors are members of their personal network. Interlocutors' pairing of their activism with Islamic social justice principles echoes Abdul Khabeer's assessment of what can be considered religious about the BLM movement. She describes BLM's emphasis on community and "duty to love one another" as contradictory to the individualism that defines secularism.[32] Similarly, rather than locating BLM's emphasis on community love "on either side of a sacred/secular divide," Jennifer Nash places the movement within the Black feminist tradition, which enables BLM to transcend binary constructions of religion and secularism.[33] Interlocutors merge Islamic religious knowledge and Black feminist politics by framing their intersectional activism and BLM's commitment to centering the marginalized as an extension of Islamic history and Islamic text's community centered approach toward social justice.

"Journey of Unlearning": Developing an Islam Aligned with BLM-Era Feminist Politics

Interlocutors hold Islamic ideals for community love in tension with historic and contemporary uses of Islamic religious knowledge to undermine their and other women's agency. For example, Nadia described herself as continuously engaged in a "journey of unlearning" as she navigated religious knowledge that undermined her intersectional politics and activism.[34] Yet interlocutors simultaneously framed their activism as a reflection of Islamic social justice principles. This "journey of unlearning" echoes what bell hooks describes as a recognition that "our ways of knowing are forged in history and relations of power" that shape social experiences, performance of community, and lived realities.[35] Interlocutors constructed a vision of Islam divorced from systems of power that undermine their worldviews by directly engaging with the Qur'an and alternative forms of religious knowledge, like queer theology, to produce their own interpretations of Islamic texts. In doing so, interlocutors assess Islam's ability to stand against multiple forms of oppression, specifically the class, gender, and sexual oppression that informs their lives as Black and Muslim women of color.

For example, Sara reflected that she felt intense "shame" in her inability to feel a connection to her religion when she initially became involved in her local activist community. Sara distanced herself from her local Muslim community because she felt her politics made her "not Muslim enough." She felt her religious identity and experiences within her religious community contradicted her evolving feminist politics and activism. Sara later reestablished a connection to Islam by "decoupling patriarchy from Allah" through her own interpretations of Islamic texts:

> For a long time, I blamed Islam for setting up an acceptable patriarchy through gender norms, the mosque, and family dynamics. I was doing the work of decoupling patriarchy from Allah [. . .] when I read some of the interpretations of the Quran, it [was] not comforting [. . .] I hated men for doing that, for interpreting the Quran and limiting where I can move and can be. To the point, if you really think about it, it can be

interpreted that being on video protesting is *haram* [forbidden] because visually you could be turning someone on from five thousand miles away. [. . .] But if you move it into the realm of humanity and human error, [and know] this has nothing to do with Allah, that is man's expectations of me and [activism] is Allah's expectations of me.[36]

Sara unlearned the "acceptable patriarchy" associated with her understanding of Islam by conceptualizing restrictive gender norms as a reflection of "man's ego" and "human error." Sara's critical engagement with Islamic religious knowledge and the distinction she drew between "man's ego" and "Allah's expectations" challenged the barrier she constructed between her activism and religion. Interlocutors' engagement with Islamic texts and religious knowledge to support their activism against race, gender, and sexual oppression blurs the Islam versus Muslim binary. Defined by Kecia Ali, the Islam versus Muslim binary defines Islam as "pristinely religious" and Muslim being "what Muslims actually do." This binary perpetuates the notion that "Islam is not the problem, but Muslims who only imperfectly practice a perfect faith."[37] Ultimately, the binary functions to safeguard Islamic texts and widely held Islamic beliefs from critique. Though interlocutors distinguish between what they feel are real social-justice understandings of Islam and interpretations derived from "man's ego," they utilize this distinction to hold Islamic texts and religious knowledge to the Black feminist standard at the center of their, and BLM's, activism and worldviews.

Like Sara, Amina, a BLM activist and amateur filmmaker, described how an introduction to queer theology challenged the distinction she drew between her feminist politics and religious identity. Amina recalled that when growing-up there was not an "open understanding of who and what could represent Islam" in her household. Amina articulated her religious identity through dress which developed alongside her feminist politics as she became more engaged in queer theology and anti-racism activism. The impact of queer theology on Amina's embodied religious identity demonstrates that interlocutors' changing feminist worldviews and politics influence their approach toward the Islamic religious knowledge transmitted in their homes and communities.

Sara and Amina's experiences illustrate the occasional contradictions Muslim women face in their attempts to support and defend their intersectional activism. On one hand, interlocutors' gender performance and feminist politics can be used to categorize their activism as unrepresentative of Islamic values due to male-centered, patriarchal religious knowledge. On the other hand, interlocutors produce their own and engage with alternative interpretations of Islamic texts to define their activism as a reflection of "Allah's expectations" of them.[38] They navigate the tensions between their activism and religious knowledge that undermines their worldviews by approaching religion as highly individualized, malleable, and evolving alongside notions of oppression, justice, and freedom. In doing so they construct an Islam that aligns with their feminist politics and commitment to centering the marginalized of the marginalized.

Conclusion

Muslim women's ritual forms of resistance, the religious meanings they assign to their activism, and their engagements with Islamic religious knowledge are evolving as strategies for Black liberation account for gender, sexual, and class oppression. Drew, Fatima, Dalal, Magda, Amina, Nadia, and Sara merge BLM's action-oriented and intersectional organizing strategies with Islamic social justice values by utilizing prayer as a form of resistance that affirms their humanity as Black and Muslim women of color; drawing a distinction between *dua* and "doing" to frame their activism as fulfilling a religious obligation to take direct action against injustice; and engaging with Islamic texts to both "unlearn" patriarchal religious knowledge and frame their intersectional feminist politics as a reflection of Islam's community-centered approach toward social justice. Interlocutors' engagement with Islamic rituals and religious knowledge to craft a Muslim religious identity that supports their activism illustrates that they approach religion as individualized and informed by their gendered and racialized experiences; in addition, they illustrate the religious pluralism apparent in the BLM movement.

In examining the ways interlocutors construct a Muslim religious identity and understanding of Islam that supports the feminist and intersectional nature of the BLM movement, it is clear that understanding where and how religion figures into the BLM movement must be approached in tandem with centering women, queer, and trans activists leading BLM. This poses opportunities for examining how BLM and Black feminist politics influence the rituals, gender performances, and Islamic religious texts considered integral to Black flourishing.

NOTES

1. Marcia Chatelain and Kaavya Asoka, "Women and Black Lives Matter: An Interview with Marcia Chatelain," *Dissent Magazine*, Summer 2015, https://www.dissentmagazine.org/article/women-black-lives-matter-interview-marcia-chatelain; "About," Black Lives Matter, accessed January 13, 2019, https://Blacklivesmatter.com/about.
2. Interlocutors names have been anonymized to protect their confidentiality.
3. Nadia, personal interview, August 16, 2016.
4. Donna Auston, "Mapping the Intersections of Islamophobia and #BlackLivesMatter: Unearthing Black Muslim Life and Activism in the Policing Crisis," Sapelo Square, May 19, 2015, https://sapelosquare.com/2015/05/19/mapping-the-intersections-of-islamophobia-Blacklivesmatter-unearthing-Black-muslim-life-activism-in-the-policing-crisis.
5. Kambiz GhaneaBassiri, *A History of Islam in America: From the New World to the New World Order* (New York: Cambridge University Press, 2011), 18.
6. GhaneaBassiri, 22–24, 27.
7. Edward E. Curtis IV, "The Black Muslim Scare of the Twentieth Century," in *Islamophobia in America: The Anatomy of Intolerance*, ed. Carl W. Ernst (New York: Palgrave Macmillan, 2013), 77.
8. Curtis, 76.
9. Emmanuel Mauleón, "Black Twice: Policing Black Muslim Identities," *UCLA Law Review*, 65 (2018): 1326–90.
10. Edward E. Curtis IV, "Islamizing the Black Body: Ritual and Power in Elijah Muhammad's Nation of Islam," *Religion and American Culture: A Journal of Interpretation* 12, no. 2 (2002): 172, doi:10.1525/rac.2002.12.2.167.
11. Sylvia Chan-Malik, *Being Muslim: A Cultural History of Women of Color in American Islam* (New York: New York University Press, 2018), 77, 98.
12. Su'ad Abdul Khabeer, *Muslim Cool: Race, Religion and Hip Hop in the United States* (New York: New York University Press, 2016), 224.

13. Chan-Malik, *Being Muslim*, 77.
14. Debra Majeed, *Polygyny: What It Means when African American Muslim Women Share Their Husbands* (Gainesville: University Press of Florida, 2015), 2–3.
15. Chan-Malik, *Being Muslim*, 185.
16. Keeanga-Yamahtta Taylor, *From #Blacklivesmatter to Black Liberation* (Chicago: Haymarket Books, 2016), 168.
17. Taylor, *From #Blacklivesmatter*, 168.
18. Fauzia, personal interview, October 3, 2016.
19. Dalal, personal interview, September 28, 2016.
20. Drew, personal interview, October 4, 2016.
21. Donna Auston, "Prayer, Protest, and Police Brutality: Black Muslim Spiritual Resistance in the Ferguson Era," *Transforming Anthropology* 25, no. 1 (2017): 14.
22. Treva B. Lindsey, "Post-Ferguson: A 'Herstorical' Approach to Black Violability," *Feminist Studies* 41, no. 1 (2015): 235, doi:10.15767/feministstudies.41.1.232.
23. Chan-Malik, *Being Muslim*, 77.
24. Drew, personal interview, October 4, 2016.
25. Magda, personal interview, September 24, 2016.
26. Magda, personal interview, September 24, 2016.
27. Fatima, personal interview, October 3, 2016.
28. "Herstory," Black Lives Matter, accessed November 14, 2018, https://www.blacklivesmatter.com/herstory.
29. Amina, personal interview, August 3, 2016.
30. Dalal, personal interview, September 28, 2016.
31. Sara, personal interview, September 15, 2016.
32. Su'ad Abdul Khabeer, "We Gon' Be Alright: Black Lives Matter and Black Religion," *Immanent Frame*, September 22, 2016, http://tif.ssrc.org/2016/09/22/religion-secularism-and-Black-lives-matter/#Khabeer.
33. Jennifer C. Nash, "Black Feminism: The Promise of Black Lives Matter," *Immanent Frame*, September 22, 2016, http://tif.ssrc.org/2016/09/22/religion-secularism-and-Black-lives-matter/#Nash.
34. Nadia, personal interview, August 16, 2016.
35. bell hooks, *Teaching to Transgress* (New York: Routledge, 1994), 30.
36. Sara, personal interview, September 15, 2016.
37. Kecia Ali, *Sexual Ethics and Islam: Feminist Reflections on Qur'an, Hadith and Jurisprudence* (London: Oneworld Publications, 2016), 144.
38. Sara, personal interview, September 15, 2016.

CHAPTER 9

The Need for a Bulletproof Black Man

Luke Cage and the Negotiation of Race, Gender, and Religion in Black Communities

Alex Stucky

In the debut trailer for *Luke Cage* (2016), Luke Cage (Mike Colter) abandons his yellow and blue costume for a simple Black hoodie. The trailer draws the viewer's attention to this alteration when Luke pulls the hoodie up and bullets bounce harmlessly off his chest. The powerful imagery evoked the murder of Trayvon Martin, a Black teen killed by George Zimmerman, and the dark hoodie that became a symbol of Martin's murder. The acquittal of Zimmerman led to the foundation of Black Lives Matter (BLM) by Patrisse Cullors, Alicia Garza, and Opal Tometi. As the movement gained momentum in national discourse following the deaths of Eric Garner and Michael Brown, Cheo Hodari Coker began production on the Marvel Netflix series *Luke Cage*. In interviews, Coker denied BLM's influence upon *Luke Cage*'s story, but the series reflected conversations held in Black communities in the wake of violence and injustice following the deaths of people of color.[1] Perhaps in a moment of synchronicity,

Luke Cage foregrounds Black women, rather than the Christ-figure Luke Cage, as the potential salvation of Black communities in the wake of systemic violence against Black men.

In this chapter, I argue that *Luke Cage* season 1 highlights the necessity of Black community engagement and activism to address racial inequality in the United States. Instead of featuring an all-powerful hero, *Luke Cage* highlights the limits of the superhero and Christ-figure by addressing the injustices against Black communities and the importance of Black community activism. First, I argue that Coker situates this Black community in the real world crisis of state-sponsored violence against Black men. By examining the ramifications of systemic violence, Coker establishes a crisis that his Black Christ figure must address to provide salvation while rooting the series and Luke's messianic narrative in Black liberation theology. It is only after noting the far-reaching implications of state violence against Black bodies that we can examine the role of a Christ-figure in a modern Black community. Second, I argue that *Luke Cage* questions the role of religion and attempts to find the limits of a lone savior or Christ figure's ability to combat systemic violence against Black bodies. Coker interrogates the role of religion in current Black activism, noting the absence of religious leadership while wondering if religion and salvation narratives have fostered complacency. Finally, I argue that Coker shifts focus from his Christ figure, Luke Cage, to Black women as the heroes of Black communities. Because of the shortfall of Black masculinity due to systemic racism, Coker positions Black women as the leaders of Black communities and demands community labor to combat social injustice, rather than hoping for a hero. Engaging an analysis of Black women and movement leadership in the realm of popular culture further connects this chapter to themes throughout the second section of this volume.

The superhero genre provides a natural extension to religious metaphors and messianic imagery. In *Super Heroes*, Richard Reynolds notes that as authors debuted new superheroes, they drew upon a variety of theologies to explore the genre.[2] For instance, Ms. Marvel, Kamala Khan, discusses Islamic theology, and the limited series *JLA: The Nail* explores the Amish faith, pacifism, and the role of violence in the superhero genre. Netflix's *Luke Cage* offers a bevy of theological themes. The authors of "Bulletproof Love: *Luke Cage* (2016) and Religion" explore how the television series reflects upon Luke as a Christ figure, his ties to prophetic realism, and his community activism.[3] However, "Bulletproof Love" offers only scant exploration of how religion has shaped Black activism. Because Coker wove prominent theological themes into a narrative that offers significant BLM ties, any analysis of *Luke Cage* must explore both topics. I expand upon the religious arguments in "Bulletproof Love" to examine how *Luke Cage* brings religion into conversation with Black activism. The series makes overt arguments about how a Christ figure cannot solve the mass incarceration of African Americans and about the necessity of community labor, like Black Lives Matter, to challenge the state's perpetuation of violence against Black bodies.

The Black superhero or Black Christ figure is inherently placed in larger conversations surrounding Black identity and racialization in the United States. In Edward Blum and Paul Harvey's *The Color of Christ*, the authors note that depictions of Jesus as Black became inherently embroiled in ongoing conversations about racial identity.[4] Similarly, in *Super Black: American Pop Culture and Black Superheroes*, Adilifu Nama notes that Black superheroes reflect "American racial morality and ethics."[5] Traditionally, whiteness has dominated the role of the Black superhero. These characters, created by white men for white children, offered racialized readings that eschewed Black ideology and experiences. In *Black Skins and White Masks*, Marc Singer observes that these heroes provided a "mixed bag" of affirmation and racism. However, *Luke Cage* provides an original perspective by featuring a prominent Black superhero developed by a Black showrunner, cast, and crew. Originally, Marvel based *Luke Cage* around blaxploitation narratives, but the television series revels in Black culture and provides an unapologetically Black-centered narrative that offers new ground on superheroes written by and for people of color.

Because of the construction of blackness in the United States, analysis of racialization must extend to the site of gender and masculinity. Building upon previous calls for considering gender alongside racial examination, this chapter examines how *Luke Cage* combats notions of dangerous Black hypermasculinity through an emphasis on women in Black communities. In *Black Superheroes, Milestone Comics, and Their Fans*, Jeffrey Brown argues that scholars must examine gender dynamics in Black superheroes because American culture constructs the Black male body as a site of hypermasculinity.[6] Brown warns that the Black superhero runs the risk of becoming an overabundance of hypermasculine signifiers which leads to stereotypes of dangerous Black masculinity.

In this chapter, I use a post-structuralist approach that is not beholden to the authorial intent of the series. While Coker repudiated the idea that *Luke Cage* is in conversation with Black Lives Matter, the audience tied the two together because both discussed systemic violence against Black communities. Despite Coker's denial, the show's audience decoded the series as an exploration of BLM given the larger historical moment in which the series aired.[7] This reading became so prominent that supporters of All Lives Matter denounced the series' political messages as racist.[8] Because of the audience's reading of *Luke Cage*, the series came into direct conversation with the BLM movement and offered a rich site that argues for Black women to be placed into leadership positions in Black communities in the wake of systemic violence against Black men, a site formerly inhabited by Black ministers and religious leaders.

Black Masculinity in a Moment of Crisis

A crisis is often central to the superhero narrative; in *Luke Cage*, the crisis is systemic racism and violence against Black bodies. Throughout the thirteen-episode first season, *Luke Cage* presents a Black community in a fictionalized version of Harlem that has had its young men and boys targeted by the state. Similarly, in much of Western literature, a Christ figure must address some crisis to provide salvation to the masses. Because *Luke Cage*'s crisis is systemic racial oppression, the series becomes rooted in a Black liberation theological perspective that fuses salvation with liberation.[9] As a Christ figure, Luke cannot provide salvation without first addressing this oppression this Black community faces. Due to the conflation of liberation and salvation, I must first address how the series constructs and understands the state apparatus designed to target Black men and the ramifications of this systemic violence; only then can we examine how *Luke Cage* presents its arguments surrounding the role and limitations of the Black Christ figure in America.

Many scholars, politicians, and pundits have argued that there exists a crisis of violence in Black communities. Anticipating the litany of racist arguments about Black communities, Coker targets the most prominent white liberal arguments featured in the famed Moynihan Report. *The Negro Family: The Case for National Action*, written by Daniel Moynihan, became a key text in American cultural consciousness and argued the lack of economic success in Black communities stemmed from a cultural decay rooted in fatherless households. In *Luke Cage*, when a character mentions Moynihan's arguments as an answer to fixing Harlem, he is immediately killed. Because Moynihan's arguments relied on racist and sexist implications about Black single mothers, Coker literally kills Moynihan's argument before it is spoken. Instead of agreeing with the superficial and racist analysis, the series provides a nuanced argument about criminality, positive masculinity, and systemic racism.

Overall, the series argues that criminality stems from a lack of positive masculinity in minority communities. The series emphasizes this through the loss of Black father figures in the show. As Luke talks with Pop, a fatherly barbershop owner, Luke draws a direct comparison between violence and the lack of a paternal figure, "everyone has a gun, no one has a father."[10] Through this conversation, Coker argues violence and crime in urban communities stems from a loss of positive masculinity for young men to emulate. This thread continues in a later episode when another character argues that baseball is a game passed on from fathers to sons and "that's why you don't see no niggas playing. All their fathers are gone."[11] While these conversations are the most straightforward, the series underscores the loss of Black masculine figures through Luke's dating life, but also through the creation of the series' antagonists, as both Diamondback (Erik LaRay Harvey) and Cottonmouth (Mahershala Ali) lacked father figures. The lack of paternal figures is felt throughout the series and is Coker's primary argument for the rise of crime in Harlem.

However, the series shifts past Moynihan's arguments about cultural decline and fatherhood to assert that the mass incarceration of Black bodies has caused the shortfall of positive masculinity. Episode 4, "Step in the Arena," provides Luke's origin in Seagate Prison. By repeatedly mentioning Luke's innocence as the penal system torments him, the series notes that innocence does not matter for Black bodies. Extending this portrayal, the episode emphasizes the role of racism in the penal system through Albert Rackham, a corrupt prison guard and Luke's primary tormentor. For Rackham and other guards, Luke's value is not in his humanity or morality but in his physical labor. While Rackham values Luke's physical prowess and hopes to turn him into a gladiator, a prison fighter, Rackham viciously beats him when Luke turns down his offer. In other words, Luke's body and physical health only have value if Luke works for Rackham. Rather than scapegoat Rackham as merely a racist prison guard, the episode argues that mass incarceration is an extension of slavery and systemic racism, as Michelle Alexander does in *The New Jim Crow* (2010) and Ava DuVernay in *13th* (2016). Luke turns down Rackham's offer to be a gladiator, saying, "slavery was always a good offer to a master."[12] This single episode constructs mass incarceration as a racist institution built upon the framework of slavery, which dehumanizes Black bodies and only values their physical labor and violence.

Building on this argument, *Luke Cage* establishes that the penal system dehumanizes incarcerated populations. First, drawing upon the Tuskegee Experiments, the series notes how the penal system treats incarcerated populations as subhuman. Not only does Rackham nearly murder Luke, but the prison runs experiments, conducted by Dr. Noah Burstein, on inmates. Burstein's experiment saves Luke's life, but only because Dr. Reva Connors pleads with Burstein. This moment of mercy is juxtaposed with Luke learning that he was always going to be experimented on, and Burstein's initial refusal because he thought it would be a waste of resources to try to save

Luke's life.[13] With inmates, guards, and even prison doctors treating inmates as subhuman, Luke initially embraces toxic masculinity, violence, and the belief he is less than human.

The dehumanization of incarcerated people directly causes the development of a toxic and violent masculinity. During Luke's first night in prison, he cries himself to sleep while professing his innocence. This scene offers one of the first moments of vulnerability for Luke and breaks the stoicism he has maintained throughout the first three episodes. During Luke's first group therapy session, Reva warns him against the desire to embrace emotionless strength and toxic masculinity. In *Social Death*, Lisa Marie Cacho directly ties decriminalization with humanization, and "depathologizes nonnormative racial masculinities."[14] Mass incarceration directly constructs toxic masculinity through its dehumanization practices. Because of Rackham's gladiator fights, Luke's isolation develops and he responds by becoming detached and emotionless while viciously fighting and killing other inmates. Both Rackham and Burstein highlight how prisons view inmates as subhuman and cause the development of a toxic masculinity that all but guarantees recidivism.

Only by rejecting toxic masculinity can an incarcerated person escape the vicious cycle of mass incarceration. Through Squabbles, another inmate, and Reva, Luke realizes that he is still human and that emotional vulnerability is not a weakness. After Reva demands to see Luke, she reminds him of his humanity and empathy. The reemergence of Luke's humanity causes him to expose Rackham's corruption. While Rackham nearly murders Luke for doing so, Luke's friendship with Reva causes her to beg Burstein to save Luke's life, which imbues him with superhuman strength. This moment highlights the importance of community to humanize incarcerated populations and prevent recidivism. Through its examination of mass incarceration, these episodes argue the development of community leads to real strength and allows for Luke to not only survive prison but become invulnerable.

After detailing the pervasive violence embedded in mass incarceration, the series argues that state violence is inherent in its institutions. After Diamondback frames Luke for the murder of a police officer, the police conduct numerous raids on the residents of Harlem. As police conduct these raids, Captain Ridley tells the officers to "go easier" on those being arrested. Despite her call to not use unnecessary force, an officer responds, "I been on the job for twenty-eight years, I'm not some idiot who's afraid of Blacks and Hispanics."[15] Anticipating the "bad apples" explanation of police violence, *Luke Cage* argues police will continue to use violence against people of color because these institutions demand it. The scene emphasizes this sentiment as the conversation cuts between shots of young Black men tackled and arrested by police officers. By presenting systemic state violence not derived from individual prejudice, the series indicts law enforcement institutions as inherently problematic and built upon racism. The series emphasizes inherent state violence when police detain Lonnie, a young Black boy. While questioned about Luke's whereabouts, Lonnie mentions his afterschool activities and GPA to construct himself through respectability politics.[16] However, the series notes that respectability politics will not protect Black bodies from state violence, and Lonnie is viciously attacked by the Black police officer. In this moment, the series argues against the often-cited arguments of respectability politics and "bad apples" to instead highlight the pervasiveness of state violence against Black bodies. The scene emphasizes Coker's larger argument, that state violence does not come from racist individuals in institutions but from the institutions themselves.

Thematically, these moments establish Black masculinity under the constant threat of violence. Numerous episodes feature senseless violence against young and old Black men to ask, How does the Black community hope to combat systemic racialized violence? This question becomes the central crisis and highlights the oppression minority communities face in the United States. While Coker does not intentionally engage with Black Lives Matter, the central themes and questions established in the series are the same questions that BLM and Black communities asked following the murders of Trayvon Martin, Eric Garner, and Michael Brown. By firmly establishing this crisis, Coker opens the door to examine how Black communities can find salvation, and *Luke Cage* explores the tension in a superhero that struggles against a society that devalues Black lives.

The False Salvation of Superhero Narratives

By presenting Luke as a Christ figure unable to solve systemic racism, Coker argues salvation narratives provide false hope as he examines the role of religion in Black communities and, ultimately, posits that the superhero fantasy causes complacency. Because Coker worries that religion has made Black communities wait for a Christ figure to lead the charge against systemic racism and violence, he explores how society would react to the emergence of a Christ figure leading Black communities. Coker refutes those hoping for justice and salvation without community labor by underscoring the limits of a Christ figure or superhero in the wake of systemic violence. Because the superhero genre works best as a reflection of modern American culture, the superhero inevitably protects the status quo. This means that Luke cannot upend or remake systems of power in the United States, even those that target Black bodies. While some limits of this Christ figure are inherent to the superhero genre, Coker presents other limitations tied to the violent responses toward Black liberation leaders of history like Martin Luther King Jr., Malcolm X, or Fred Hampton.

First, the series roots Luke in a Christ narrative by emphasizing his work in the margins of society and presenting him as an outsider to Harlem. As an escaped convict, Luke worries that he will be sent back to prison and refuses to engage with the people of Harlem. The series stresses Luke's outsider status when Pop mentions he could pay Luke more if he was willing to accept non-cash payments. Similarly, Luke pays more for his apartment by paying in cash. These brief moments, and Luke's referring to Harlemites as "Reva's people," serve to underline Luke's existence in the margins of society with temporary connections to the community.[17] Like most Christ narratives, Luke exists on the margins of society, an outsider coming into the community to provide eventual salvation.

Luke's marginalization directly stems from his metaphorical baptism, establishing him as a Christ figure. In most savior narratives, the Christ figure undergoes a moment of baptism or transformative experience to fulfill their messianic status. For Luke, this comes from the baptism that provided him with superpowers. Burstein's experiment mimics baptism by not only submerging Luke in water, but also the metaphorical death and rebirth as Luke briefly dies and is born anew. As it did for the apostles, Luke's resurrection causes the hero to change his name from Carl Lucas to Luke Cage as a symbol of his rebirth. By rooting Luke's literal transformation in a moment of baptism, the series draws a visual parallel with the longstanding symbolism of Christianity and being born anew.

However, the series shifts past presenting Luke as a follower of Christ and directly compares Luke to Jesus to emphasize the theme of Luke as a Christ figure. After escaping Seagate, Luke quotes Luke 4:18 for his new name: "The Spirit of the Lord is on me, because he has anointed me to proclaim good news to the poor. He has sent me to proclaim freedom for the prisoners and recovery of sight for the blind, to set the oppressed free."[18] This passage comes from when Jesus reads Isaiah 61:1–2. Not only is the passage key for establishing Luke in liberation theology, but it positions Luke as a torchbearer of Jesus's message of salvation for the marginalized. In the first three episodes, Luke has yet to "come out" as a superhero in Harlem, but the series draws direct parallels to Luke as a Christ figure set to provide liberation for oppressed people. Others, like Cottonmouth, attempt to dissuade Luke from interfering with Harlem by drawing similar parallels but with violent ends. For instance, Cottonmouth says, "it costs to be a savior. Just ask Jesus."[19] The series provides direct comparisons between Luke and Jesus to bluntly articulate that Luke is a Christ figure.

Despite bluntly presenting message of Luke as a Christ figure, the series asks nuanced questions about whether the role of the Christ figure is to provide salvation for the innocent or damnation of the guilty. While superheroes frequently fight villains, Luke concerns himself with saving innocent lives rather than punishing the villains in the show because the show roots Luke in Black liberation theology.[20] The passage of Luke 4:18 ends with Jesus choosing not to complete the verse of Isaiah, "the day of vengeance of our God."[21] By having Luke repeat Luke 4:18 instead of Isaiah, the show argues that a choice must be made between salvation and damnation, and a savior must first provide salvation. This theme becomes displayed in Luke's actions following a gang shooting at the end of the second episode. Luke provides aid to those around him and desperately tries to save Pop's life rather than chase the gunman down. This moment highlights the choice of the Christ figure, that Luke can only provide salvation or damnation, not both, and is reified in Luke's eulogy for Pop, when he vows to "help those in need and protect them from the forces that would do them harm."[22] By focusing on salvation, Luke becomes rooted in a liberation theology and hopes to save the oppressed.

Because systems of power and institutions of inequality provide the main antagonists for Luke, the series argues that there are limits to Christ figures in combating inequality. While Luke shields innocent people from violence, he provides no vision for protecting the people of Harlem from systemic violence. The methods Luke employs to combat this rising violence are entirely reactionary or unfortunate failures. With Luke's help, the police arrest Cottonmouth, but Cottonmouth quickly makes bail, and corrupt police officers refuse to arrest other influential criminals. Like the arguments made about the penal system, the series argues there are institutional failures, not merely a few bad individuals. For every villain arrested, a new villain quickly appears. After Cottonmouth's death, Diamondback quickly assumes control of crime in Harlem. After Diamondback's arrest, season one ends with Mariah Dillard taking control. After Rafael Scarfe, a corrupt cop, dies, another corrupt police officer takes his place. For Coker, a bulletproof Black man can offer momentary protection, but he cannot offer consistent salvation nor solve the issues of state violence against Black bodies. By positioning Luke's antagonists not as people, but as corrupt systems of power, the series argues that a Christ figure can only provide reactionary methods that only change the people involved and not the root of the injustices committed.

Extending these limits further, Coker warns against embracing a Christ figure because of the real world violence committed against Black liberation leaders. Not only does Luke face numerous assassination attempts, which he only survives due to his impenetrable skin, the series name-drops MLK and Malcolm X as dire warnings against traditional leadership structures. In the song "Bulletproof Love," featured in episode 12, Method Man draws parallels between Luke and the assassinations of Martin Luther King Jr. and Malcolm X when he raps, "Look, dog, a hero never had one / Already took Malcolm and Martin, this is the last one."[23] A Christ figure, or any leader of Black communities, will be targeted and assassinated. The series drives this message home in the latter half of the season with the development of the Judas Bullet, a bullet capable of piercing Luke's skin and killing him. With obvious Christ parallels in the name, *Luke Cage* asserts a bulletproof Black man will only cause the system to develop new methods to kill Black men.

The loss of Black male religious leadership is felt throughout the series, as *Luke Cage* examines the importance of religion in shaping Black communities and activist movements. While religious leadership is noticeably absent in *Luke Cage*, this leadership overshadows the series as a force that has drastically shaped the lives of these characters. For instance, Luke is the son of Reverend James Lucas. Reverend Lucas is absent from the first season of the series, except for a brief flashback, which only features his back.[24] Yet James's religious tutelage decidedly shapes the series as a driving force for both Luke and his villainous half-brother, Diamondback. Like leaders of the past, Reverend Lucas's presence is felt, but the lack of religious leadership in the present also highlights an aimlessness of this Harlem community without these traditional leaders. Instead of lingering on Luke and Diamondback, Coker implores the audience to look for new sources of leadership in Black communities, as the heirs of Reverend James's legacy revolve around violence.

Because the superhero provides the fantasy of an effortless salvation, Coker worries that oppressed communities will wait for a savior instead of mobilizing against systemic violence, or respond violently. For the series, problems of liberation theology become apparent in calls for effortless salvation as people solely rely on Luke to solve their issues. Episode 5 features Luke wandering around town helping various residents of Harlem, and without Luke's intervention, some of those residents would be injured or killed. However, the series examines the impacts of these interventions, noting residents of Harlem become complacent or hold Luke in contempt for not saving them. This spirals out of control as Aisha plans to murder Cottonmouth for the theft of her father's championship ring when Luke is not able to provide an easy solution. When he defies Aisha's expectations of an easy intervention, she spirals out of control and attempts to commit violence. While liberation theology preaches to the oppressed, Coker worries that a Christ figure will cause complacency or worse; if the Christ figure is unable to immediately solve these injustices, people will lose hope and resort to violence. This critique of the Christ figure adds to Coker's larger message about the necessity of community labor in seeking to solve these injustices.

While Luke's religiosity provides a basis for his protection of people, Coker uses other prominent characters to highlight how religion often justifies violence. When asked about the teaching of Jesus and turning the other cheek, Cottonmouth responds, "Jesus saves, I don't."[25] This moment places Cottonmouth outside of the gospel, but he continues to evoke the Old Testament. Cottonmouth makes biblical references including eye-for-an-eye judgements and referring to Luke as "dishwasher Lazarus."[26] More versed in scripture, the second villain of the series, Diamondback, almost exclusively speaks by quoting scripture and biblical metaphors for his own nefarious goals. Diamondback quotes Jesus and Matthew 10:34, "I did not come to bring peace but a sword."[27] By having multiple villains justify violence through biblical quotations, Coker argues that religion can help or hinder the Black community but can never fix these systemic issues.

Luke Cage positions the duality of religion as a force of good and evil, as an influence that can offer hope and salvation but also a complacency that undercuts movements for equality or even supports systemic violence. Presenting a Cain and Abel story, the two half-brothers, Luke and Diamondback, use scripture to justify their opposition to one another. After Diamondback ambushes Luke in Harlem, Diamondback quotes 1 Peter 5:18: "the devil walks around seeking whom it can devour," and Luke refers to Diamondback as "his cross to bear."[28] Later, Diamondback argues that Harlem "is worshipping a false idol. You, Carl. You're the golden calf."[29] While the climactic fight in the first season returns to the theme of a lack of positive masculinity for the villain, the events of the series feature a religious echo that can be manipulated. Coker ultimately positions religion as a tool that can help or hinder, but that will not offer actual salvation against systemic violence.

Salvation Found through Community Labor and Activism

Coker dismisses the possibility of a savior changing systemic violence and instead argues for community activism, noting the importance of Black women in these movements. Black women have largely been forgotten in mainstream consciousness when it comes to the civil rights movement and the women's rights movement. Many scholars argue that often "Black" is equated with Black men and "woman" is equated with white women."[30] In an effort to alter this perception, Coker's visionaries are all Black women who take various forms of leadership to change Harlem. Symbolically, Pop's death shifts Luke away from Black male leadership to focus on three women and their competing visions for the Black community. Unlike Luke Cage, Mariah Dillard (Afre Woodard), Misty Knight (Simone Missick), and Claire Temple (Rosario Dawson) are from Harlem, and each offers a unique political positionality to save Harlem.

The three women offer different avenues to effect change in the Black community in response to violence against black bodies. While Luke and other Black men are viciously attacked throughout the series, these three women take control of the situation to enact different forms of leadership. In the season one finale of *Luke Cage*, the titular hero squares off against Diamondback. During the climax of the first season, various characters repeatedly refer to the fight as the "battle for the soul of Harlem." While the brawl operates as the climax to the first season, the actual battle for Harlem's soul occurs parallel to this climax as three women fight for their competing visions of Harlem and its Black community. Despite being titled after its male protagonist, *Luke Cage* offers an introspective look at the role of women in

Black communities. As showrunner, Coker examined how the state's systemic violence and persecution of Black men established women as the leaders of Black communities, and how the response to police violence was shaped by gender dynamics.

Each of these three female characters represents a different political avenue for the Black community to respond to state violence against Black bodies. Broadly speaking, each of the characters represents current political discussions, including top-down political change, system reform, and activism. Mariah Dillard operates from a position of power in Harlem as a city councilwoman and millionaire and desires to help Harlemites from the highest political levels. As a police detective, Misty Knight investigates the murder of Dante Chapman. As a representative of the police, she advocates for reforming the system from the inside and argues that the system can be changed for the better. Finally, Claire Temple serves as a grassroots activist. Claire attempts to help her marginalized community and advocates for people to become involved and challenge systems of power. All three of these women of color offer direct ties to Harlem and articulate how Luke could create societal change for the Black community in America.

Mariah Dillard, a corrupt city councilwoman in Harlem, represents the arguments for a neoliberal, top-down approach for Black politics, which advocates for adhering to traditional capitalist criteria to prove worth and for placing Black people in positions of power to effect change for the black community. One of the first arguments Mariah provides addresses Black Lives Matter: "for Black lives to matter, Black history and Black ownership must matter."[31] Mariah's arguments are built upon proving worth through traditionally defined avenues of success and systemic change once elected to positions of power. Dillard's position reflects the arguments surrounding the election of President Barack Obama. For many, the election of President Obama signaled a change to the typical establishment that continued to be dominated by white men. Similarly, Mariah advocates for Black community members to elect people from Harlem to city positions and for those elected officials to defend their community from outsiders.

On the surface, Mariah appears to value her community and advocate for their best interests, but the series utilizes Black historical figures to foreshadow Mariah's favoritism for institutions of power. The series uses various political initiatives to flesh out Mariah's character including her largest project: the Crispus Attucks Complex, a low-income housing initiative. Mariah intends to use the complex to revive Harlem's businesses and neighborhoods, which she believes will usher in a new Harlem Renaissance. By invoking the name of Crispus Attucks, the series ties Mariah to longstanding narratives of Black bodies and Black sites of resistance whitewashed to reinforce American capitalist mythology. Ta-Nehisi Coates links Crispus Attucks and President Obama as part of a narrative that frequently discards Black radicalism for white comfort. These narratives often point to instances of African American success to argue against systemic racism, depict Black communities in cultural decline, and ultimately uphold systems of racial oppression.[32] When the White House invited Black Lives Matter to speak with then president Obama, the group declined the invitation because they believed President Obama upheld systems of oppression over the lives of Black people and often demanded they change to better suit American capitalist enterprises.[33] Mariah namedrops artists like Langston Hughes and Duke Ellington as key individuals of the Black cultural revolution and development of Harlem's prosperity, but she argues that these figures developed due to Black economic prosperity. Mariah views success through the capitalist lens. She argues that Black communities must adhere to traditional avenues of success and extends her argument to placing members of the Black community into positions of power to change the system from the top down.

Despite Mariah's public persona of helping Harlem, the series warns against reliance upon political figures to truly effect change to systems of power. Early in the show, the tension between Mariah and Cottonmouth comes from an illegal loan she gave her cousin and her need to repay that loan before city accountants audit her office. Her major housing initiative, the Crispus Attucks Complex, also operates as a "Fort Knox" for Cottonmouth and Mariah's illegal enterprises and houses millions of dollars in drug money. Mariah wants to help the people of Harlem, especially in the wake of white gentrification. Despite Mariah's desire to help Harlem, her help is conditional. The show argues, through Mariah, that ultimately those in power will not change these systems to help those suffering because upending traditional power structures will affect them. Mariah spearheads a movement against police brutality following the assault of Lonnie by police officers, but her motivations are entirely self-aggrandizing as she desires more political influence. Mariah hopes to use the assault on Lonnie and the emergence of Luke to promote her political career, and through conversations with her chief of staff, she cynically hopes for the death of Luke because the martyrdom of Luke Cage is just what she needs to take a national stage.[34]

Ultimately, *Luke Cage* argues that because systems of power mar Black communities, communities cannot rely on the people the system imbued with power, even the elected officials of minority communities. When the residents of Harlem learn of Mariah's connection to her cousin Cottonmouth, the city council asks Mariah to resign. Councilman Booker informs Mariah that she has lost all her political capital, and she will no longer be an effective representative for her constituents. Rather than resign, Mariah plots to keep her power and assassinate Booker. Mariah's political career focuses on what will help her first, rather than what will benefit the people of Harlem. *Luke Cage* warns against hoping for elected officials and those in power to challenge the system and argues that top-down activism will never lead to change.

As a police officer, Misty Knight represents the reformist arguments of working within the systems of power to effect social change. While Mariah desires political self-interest, Misty Knight and her captain, Priscilla Ridley, want to help the people of Harlem and work within the police department to reform the systems of abuse that affect Black communities. By presenting Misty as an upstanding member of the Harlem community, Coker offers a sympathetic Black police officer who truly desires to help and improve her community. Both Misty and Ridley attempt to reform the police depart and expel the officers that abuse their power. Following Pop's funeral, Misty admits to Luke that the system is far from perfect but that it works, and she pleads with Luke to help her makes changes from within the system rather than tear it down.[35] As a reformist, Misty provides an uneasy alliance to Luke in the quest to arrest Cottonmouth, Diamondback, and Mariah. However, because Luke operates outside the system, the antagonisms between the two slowly develop over the course of the season. While Misty and Luke unite in the wake of Diamondback, they ultimately desire different things as Luke slowly becomes an activist and Misty remains a reformist.

Like the problems of top-down change, *Luke Cage* critiques reformist arguments through Misty Knight. While Coker completely indicts the systems of violence toward Black bodies, he recognizes that there are people who actively resist these systems from within like Detective Knight. However, Coker's primary critique of Misty derives from Misty's desire for peace and justice. From the first scene, Misty wants to arrest Cottonmouth and bring down his criminal empire, however, this desire comes into conflict with Luke Cage's actions, who Misty feels risks causing violence to break out in Harlem. The internal conflict of Misty's two desires frequently causes Misty to develop a tenuous alliance with Cage throughout the course of the series and causes other characters to question whether she wants peace or justice in Harlem.

Coker asserts that Black police officers can and do uphold systems of racialized violence against Black bodies. The conflict between justice and peace comes to a head following the vicious police brutality against Lonnie. During a heated exchange with Captain Ridley and Misty, Lonnie's mother, Patricia Wilson says, "you'd think a sister in charge would change things. But you're blue, which makes you just as white as anyone else!"[36] Patricia's outcry denounces the police department following the assault of her son as they attempt to placate her rather than address the abuse. The scene insinuates that Black police officers will continue to protect blue lives over innocent Black lives. Through Patricia's outcry, the series rebukes the notion that Black police officers cannot be complicit in systems of racialized violence.

Luke Cage argues that police officers and reformists will protect systems of power to uphold peace even when a system is beyond salvaging. The desire to uphold peace over seeking justice develops in Misty over the course of the season. Initially, Misty believes that with Luke's help, she can help save Harlem and reform the system. However, when it becomes clear that Luke will need to fight Diamondback, Misty becomes far more concerned with preventing the two from fighting. Because Diamondback cannot be arrested due to his political connections, Misty targets Luke Cage. During a police interrogation, Misty becomes more violent in her quest to uphold peace and even goes so far as to choke Claire. While seemingly paradoxical, Coker argues that reformists view violence by the state as an acceptable action to prevent civil unrest.

The dichotomy of acceptable and unacceptable forms of violence takes a deeper role in Misty's narrative as the militarization of the police occurs with the sole goal of killing Luke Cage. Despite her attempts to save Harlem as a police officer, Misty cannot reform a system that desires to hunt down and kill Black bodies. Misty's vision for a safer Harlem comes directly into conflict with the laws she has vowed to uphold when the New York Police Department begins equipping their officers with new, powerful weapons designed to kill Luke Cage. The use of the Judas Bullet by police officers serves solely to kill Cage and Diamondback under the guise of "public safety." Despite numerous characters knowing that Cage is an innocent and lawful citizen, the NYPD decides that both Luke and Diamondback are too dangerous to live. Coker presents the escalation of the NYPD as an extension of systemic racialized violence. The development and production of the Judas Bullet by police occurs because of a bulletproof Black man. Coker offers a sympathetic view of reformists but ultimately argues that reformists will have to choose a side, that they cannot straddle the line between Black communities' safety and the belief that systems of power can be salvaged.

While Mariah and Misty provide methods for reforming the system, *Luke Cage* recognizes the importance of effecting change through activism and community mobilization. Originally introduced in Netflix's *Daredevil*, set in Hell's Kitchen, Claire Temple returns to Harlem for introspection and feels that her community might provide answers to the violence she has witnessed. Claire's return to Harlem underscores the importance of community in response to violence. During her first appearance in *Luke Cage*, Claire discusses with her mother how she hopes to address the emergence of superheroes and the violence against them and to advocate for them in her community. As Stan Lee does in the X-Men comics, Coker briefly uses superpowers as a metaphor to discuss violence against racialized communities, but he quickly returns focus to candid discussions about racism.

Extending Coker's concerns about complacency, Claire's advocacy focuses on shifting apathy to action in the Black community. For the first half of the series, Claire persuades Luke to become engaged with the Black community and move away from his general apathy. When Cottonmouth discovers Luke's history at Seagate, Luke plans to flee Harlem. Rather than aid Luke's escape, Claire chastises him and argues that he must fight for his new community. Claire argues that Luke is a representation of the people of Harlem and notes, "half the people up town have fathers, brothers, uncles, cousins in prison. You're no different than anybody else."[37] Claire argues that with Luke's symbolic stand, the Harlem community will join him. Her argument becomes centered on Luke not being a figurehead of the community, but rather fully joining the community and working with Harlemites to challenge systemic violence. Throughout the series, Claire persuades apathetic and endangered Harlemites to become good Samaritans and help their community. Claire's position favors grassroots activism and builds coalitions across Harlem, which clearly reflects the decentralized activism of Black Lives Matter.

Symbolically, Claire provides an antithesis to Mariah and Misty, both of whom argue that Black lives matter when they adhere to respectability politics. Mariah argues for Black capitalism and Misty demands adherence to the law, but Claire, an ER nurse, argues that lives inherently matter. Due to the systemic gun violence in the show, Claire works tirelessly to save the lives of people shot, from a corrupt cop to the protagonist. When Diamondback shoots Luke, Claire does not question whether he values rule of law or Black business; she attempts to immediately save his life. Similarly, when Cottonmouth shoots the corrupt police detective Rafael Scarfe, Claire risks her own life in her attempt to save him. By having Claire repeatedly save individual's lives, Coker argues that we must value lives over systems of power and propriety.

Mariah, Misty, and Claire represent different political positions in Black communities that attempt to effect systemic change. Coker notes the faults of each positionality, but like Luke Cage, sides with Claire and community activism over top-down change or reforming these institutions of violence. *Luke Cage* argues for community engagement and activism to address violence against marginalized communities. In the wake of state violence against Black masculinity, *Luke Cage* faithfully places its trust in Black women to provide leadership and effect social change.

By first laying the groundwork of how state violence has permeated and dramatically affected Black communities, Coker constructs a very realistic crisis in the Black community, a crisis that imprisons men of color, destroys positive masculinity, and leaves violence in its wake. Because of this realistic crisis, Luke Cage, a Christ figure, cannot solve this problem like he would with a supervillain; instead, Coker argues that state violence must be addressed through political activism like Black Lives Matter. Through this political activism, Coker analyzes three key positions, represented by important women in *Luke Cage*, to construct change in America: top-down change, reformers, and political activists. Through these three women, Coker asserts that change can only come through outside political activism holding those in power and within the system accountable for their actions. Despite not intending to comment on Black Lives Matter, Coker's *Luke Cage* provides a compelling narrative arguing for the necessity of such a movement.

Luke Cage revels in Black history and art, but the series also notes that Black lives inherently have value. While *Luke Cage* spends considerable time examining the role of religion and music in Black communities and dismisses the hope of salvation from a lone figure, the series' central message is its celebration of Black life. In the wake of state violence against Black masculinity, *Luke Cage* offers a necessary message of hope about how much Black lives matter.

NOTES

1. Tristram Fane Saunders. "'Luke Cage Is a Black Hero, Not a Hero Who Happens to Be Black': Meet the Makers of Marvel's Bold New Netflix Series," *Telegraph*, September 30, 2016, https://www.telegraph.co.uk/on-demand/0/ luke-cage-is-a-black-hero-not-a-hero-who-happens-to-be-black-mee.

2. Richard Reynolds, *Super Heroes: A Modern Mythology* (London: Batsford, 1992), 12.

3. Ken Derry, Daniel White Hodge, Laurel Zwissler, Stanley Talbert, Matthew J. Cressler, and Jon Ivan Gill, "Bulletproof Love: *Luke Cage* (2016) and Religion," *Journal of Religion, Film and Media* 3, no. 1 (May 2017): 123, DOI: 10.25364/05.3:2017.1.7.

4. Edward Blum and Paul Harvey, *Color of Christ: The Son of God and the Saga of Race in America* (Chapel Hill: University of North Carolina Press, 2014), 221.

5. Adilifu Nama, *Super Black: American Pop Culture and Black Superheroes* (Austin: University of Texas Press, 2011), 4.

6. Jeffrey Brown, *Black Superheroes, Milestone Comics, and Their Fans* (Jackson: University Press of Mississippi, 2000), 269.

7. Rob Sheffield. "'Luke Cage': Meet the First Black Lives Matter Superhero," *Rolling Stone*, October 5, 2016, https://www.rollingstone.com/tv/tv-news/luke-cage-meet-the-first-black-lives-matter-superhero-112895.

8. Debbie Encalada. "White People: 'Luke Cage' Is Racist," *Complex*, October 3, 2016, https://www.complex.com/pop-culture/2016/10/luke-cage-racist-says-white-people.

9. Blum and Harvey, *Color of Christ*, 222.

10. *Luke Cage*, season 1, episode 1, "Moment of Truth," directed by Paul McGuigan, aired September 30, 2016, on Netflix, 35:08.

11. *Luke Cage*, season 1, episode 5, "Just to Get a Rep," directed by Marc Jobst, aired September 30, 2016, on Netflix, 36:33.

12. *Luke Cage*, season 1, episode 4, "Step into the Arena," directed by Vincenzo Natali, aired September 30, 2016, on Netflix, 10:52.

13. *Luke Cage*, season 1, episode 10, "Take It Personal," directed by Stephen Surjik, aired September 30, 2016, on Netflix, 19:34.

14. Lisa Marie Cacho, *Social Death: Racialized Rightlessness and the Criminalization of the Unprotected* (New York: New York University Press, 2012), 162.

15. *Luke Cage*, season 1, episode 10, "Take It Personal," 14:34.

16. *Luke Cage*, season 1, episode 10, "Take It Personal," 16:28.

17. *Luke Cage*, season1, episode 2, "Code of the Streets," directed by Paul McGuigan, aired September 30, 2016, on Netflix, 6:40.

18. *Luke Cage*, season 1, episode 4, "Step into the Arena," 48:58.

19. *Luke Cage*, season 1, episode 5, "Just to Get a Rep," 20:47.

20. Blum and Harvey, *Color of Christ*, 9.

21. Isaiah 61:1–2 (King James Version).
22. *Luke Cage*, season 1, episode 5, "Just to Get a Rep," 45:35.
23. *Luke Cage*, season 1, episode 12, "Soliloquy of Chaos," directed by Phil Abraham, aired September 30, 2016, on Netflix, 30:01.
24. James Lucas, played by the late Reg. E. Cathy, becomes far more prominent in *Luke Cage*'s second season, as the series shifts away from its exploration of Black Lives Matter to instead examine the forgotten Afro-Caribbean narratives, including Afro-Caribbean religious practices, tied to African American history. The series explores this narrative through John "Bushmaster" McIver, a Jamaican antihero whose family ties to Harlem were erased by the Dillard family in favor of a more sanitized African American–centric narrative.
25. *Luke Cage*, season 1, episode 2, "Code of the Streets," 12:32.
26. *Luke Cage*, season 1, episode 5, "Just to Get a Rep," 20:39.
27. *Luke Cage*, season1, episode 8, "Blowin' Up the Spot," directed by Magnus Martens, aired September 30, 2016, on Netflix, 34:57.
28. *Luke Cage*, season1, episode 8, "Blowin' Up the Spot," 31:22.
29. *Luke Cage*, season1, episode 8, "Blowin' Up the Spot," 37:07.
30. Barbara Smith, *But Some of Us Are Brave* (New York: Feminist Press at CUNY, 1993), xvii.
31. *Luke Cage*, season 1, episode 1, "Moment of Truth," 37:07.
32. Ta-Nehisi Coates, *We Were Eight Years in Power: An American Tragedy* (New York: One World, 2017), 138.
33. Dawn Rhodes, "Chicago Black Lives Matter Activist Declines White House Invitation," *Chicago Tribune*, February 19, 2016, http://www.chicagotribune.com/news/local/breaking/ct-black-lives-matter-reject-white-house-meeting-20160218-story.html.
34. *Luke Cage*, season 1, episode 9, "DWYCK," directed by Tom Shankland, aired September 30, 2016, on Netflix, 31:53.
35. *Luke Cage*, season 1, episode 5, "Just to Get a Rep," 18:16.
36. *Luke Cage*, season 1, episode 10, "Take It Personal," 25:10.
37. *Luke Cage*, season 1, episode 7, "Manifest," directed by Andy Goddard, aired September 30, 2016, on Netflix, 26:44.

CHAPTER 10

The Sounds of Hope

Black Humanism, Deep Democracy, and Black Lives Matter

Alexandra Hartmann

On June 3, 2020, after days of powerful protests following the murder of George Floyd, Sixteenth Street in Washington, DC, became the site of incredible beauty and collective caring born from exhaustion, pain, and struggle. Led in song by local musician Kenny Sway, thousands of Black Lives Matter protesters raised their phones and turned on their flashlights as they sang Bill Withers' "Lean on Me" together. The performance marked an important moment in the protests; it allowed participants to catch a break and to immerse themselves in the outpour of solidarity, the collective resistance to degradation, and the shared commitment to Black lives. In a matter of days, the site would be renamed Black Lives Matter Plaza and decorated with a bold yellow "Black Lives Matter" mural.

Across the United States, the largely peaceful protests were met with a disproportionate level of state-led retaliation. Police in riot gear used rubber bullets and tear gas against protesters, and even the National Guard was deployed to defend the capital. In fact, a mere two days before Sway's performance, protesters had been brutally dispersed from the very same spot on Sixteenth Street to make way for a photo opportunity with the president brandishing the Bible. When asked why he chose to come out to perform that night (after all, in the midst of the COVID-19 pandemic), Sway answered that he felt the protests were lacking a fundamental spiritual element— he found that music was missing. For those present, the collective performance of "Lean on Me" became a means to "show people the real essence of these protests," and a way to "showcase black art and love and passion."[1] In the days that followed, Sway and many other artists returned to stages and accompanied and supported the protests lyrically.

Sway's interpretation of the moment reflects the role of music in African American activism and culture. Music has undeniably been an important life-affirming cultural expression for Black people and a site of resistance even at times of life's most violent denial. Just as Ralph Ellison celebrated the blues as "an impulse to keep the painful details and episodes of a brutal experience alive in one's aching consciousness" by drawing from it "a near-tragic, near-comic lyricism,"[2] Cornel West insists that "the deepest existentialist source of coming to terms with white racism is music."[3] In this light, nihilism resulting from Black existence in a white hegemonic/supremacist society—a world invested in the disciplining and destruction of Black life—has not been allowed to triumph; instead music has enabled people to endure and find meaning in the existential struggle. Throughout history, Black (popular) culture and music have allowed African Americans to "humanize a dehumanizing environment."[4]

While music was central to African American culture as an expression of deepest sorrows and tragic experiences during and after slavery,[5] its essential dual role as a site of both spiritual resistance and political protest was especially pronounced in the civil rights movement of the mid-twentieth century. In fact, it was one of the movement's motivational forces. Not only did protesters in the streets rely on their own voices to speak their desires, counter their fear, and face the violent police and white civilian opposition, but the movement also found outspoken support among artists such as Nina Simone, whose "Mississippi Goddam" creatively and powerfully denounced white supremacy.[6] In the post-soul era over the past fifty years, R&B and hip hop have become the primary musical genres of choice to voice dissent with ongoing anti-Black racism, fight racialized injustices, and grapple with existence.[7]

Social movements and Black music have influenced one another all throughout African American history. Reading Black music as an "expression of black movement politics," Reiland Rabaka notes that there is a "liminal, in-between, and often inexplicable place where black popular music and black popular movements meet and merge." In his writings on the civil rights movement specifically, Rabaka elaborates further: "Black popular movements are more than merely social and political affairs. Beyond social organization and political activism, black popular movements provide much-needed spaces for cultural development and artistic experimentation."[8] Not surprisingly given the close ties between Black social movements and Black popular culture, the current civil rights campaign spearheaded by Black Lives Matter (BLM) and the issues they raise have become recurring and often central themes in contemporary music. They have both animated music and been affected by music in turn. Daphne A. Brooks remarks that "a diverse array of musical voices has emerged in tandem with, in response to, inspired by and occasionally at ideological odds with this new movement."[9] These voices protest the racial, social, and political status quo.

In this essay, I would like to probe protest songs released in the wake of BLM's creation for their religious potentials. In its broadest sense, this chapter follows religious scholar Anthony B. Pinn, who insists religion is the attempt to produce meaning in response to one's lived experiences and conditions. This attempt can find expression in a wide range of cultural practices ranging from literature to music, ritual, and theorizing. The material and sociohistorical facts of existence deeply condition the shape of religion. For African Americans, this has meant existing within an overwhelmingly white supremacist, anti-Black, and thus hostile world.[10] I argue that underlying major parts of BLM and its culture is a *Black humanist worldview*. Drawing on Pinn's research on Black humanism as an (overlooked) form of African American religion, I demonstrate how Black humanism not only serves as a driving ideological force but also as a spiritual, meaning-providing horizon of the movement that pervades the movement at large and permeates the music associated with BLM. Black humanism is a creative response to and an orientation in a world marked by anti-Blackness through which African Americans have wrestled with their lived experiences. Unlike historically more dominant religious orientations such as evangelical Protestantism, Black humanism figures as a primarily nontheistic worldview that places humans at the center of the world. In this worldview, humans are responsible for the conditions of human life and thus in charge of maintaining but also transforming the world. It follows that a measured hope undergirds this ideology and its culture. Not relying on or waiting for supernatural interventions into the course of history, humanists believe transformation to be possible through human commitment even if it is never guaranteed. In the Black humanist tradition, hope is fragile and resides in the struggle rather than the outcome.

While other (religious) traditions certainly play a role in BLM, this essay emphasizes its Black humanist dimension.[11] My analysis primarily focuses on the works of Beyoncé, Kendrick Lamar, Usher, and John Legend that were all released during the first years of BLM between December 2014 and April 2017. These artists stand in a long tradition of African American intellectuals and writers whose works have advanced Black humanist thought, among them Zora Neale Hurston, Ralph Ellison, James Baldwin, Toni Morrison, and Cornel West. While some artists directly support the movement, others implicitly show support by sharing in the intellectual and ethical tradition of Black humanism. Regardless the individual artists' relationships to BLM, contemporary mainstream Black music has once again become explicitly political in the movement's wake.[12]

A Conceptual Triad: Black Lives Matter, Black Humanism, and Deep Democracy

BLM stands in a long civil and human rights tradition of fighting systemic as well as personal injustices against Black people.

As Christopher Lebron writes, among those who have previously claimed that Black lives matter are intellectuals ranging from Frederick Douglass to Audre Lorde, all of them "thinkers and activists who sought to establish for themselves an authority to protect black lives that was not openly given them by society; [if anything,] the authority to seek security was often withheld."[13] While BLM, of course, pushes for legal justice and an end to state violence against Black people, it also seeks greater room for individual freedom and opportunities that acknowledge the beauty, worth, and multiplicity of Black existence often denied in everyday life. Keeanga-Yamahtta Taylor notes that this dual function is already entailed in the movement's name: "The brilliance of the slogan 'Black Lives Matter' is its ability to articulate the dehumanizing aspects of anti-Black racism in the United States."[14] BLM, then, is a rallying cry for justice on a number of levels, both institutional and personal.

Over the past couple of years, BLM has become an umbrella term for a multitude of organizations, protests, and activist groups with both shared and locally specific agendas. Precisely because BLM is decentrally organized with flat hierarchies, it is difficult to arrive at a comprehensive definition of its demands. One of its overarching principles, however, is the struggle for justice in a way that acknowledges the multifaceted his/herstories of oppression. In an online statement insightfully titled "A Vision for Black Lives," *The Movement for Black Lives* (M4BL) declares in this regard:

> There can be no liberation for all Black people if we do not center and fight for those who have been marginalized. It is our hope that by working together to create and amplify a shared agenda, we can continue to move towards a world in which the full humanity and dignity of all people is recognized. . . . This agenda continues the legacy of our ancestors . . . and also propels new iterations of movements such as efforts for reproductive justice, holistic healing and reconciliation, and ending violence against Black cis, queer, and trans people.[15]

Against this backdrop, BLM emerges as an ideology that aspires to justice for all people but especially those who have often been excluded from (Black) human rights efforts of the past. It is more than the struggle against police violence; it is the struggle against structural anti-Black racism and for full collective and individual equality. The emphasis is on putting an end to discriminatory practices so that "healing" and "reconciliation" can begin to take place for all humans.

This is a desire not unfamiliar in Black religious studies and one mirrored in Pinn's concept of "complex subjectivity." Pinn distinguishes between two modes of looking at African American religion, namely 1) a historical perspective that focuses on institutions and movements such as the Black Church and the Nation of Islam, and 2) a perspective that explores the "underlying impulse" of religion as a "quest for complex subjectivity."[16] It is the concept of complex subjectivity that concerns us here. Pinn explains: "This quest means a desired movement from being corporeal object controlled by oppressive and essentializing forces to becoming a complex conveyer of cultural meaning, with a complex and creative identity."[17] As agentic beings, humans can take up the struggle for complex subjectivity and reject the reduction of identity by external powers. This endeavor rests at the heart of Black spirituality in general and of Black humanism in particular.

Black humanism comprises a variety of positions and outlooks that are tied together by a this-worldly orientation. Humans and their well-being are at the center of this worldview. Often marked by religious doubt if not straight-out freethought, Black humanism is a "life orientation that relies on human ingenuity and creativity to achieve greater life options and a greater degree of subjectivity."[18] It recognizes that, given the belief in the absence of a supernatural power, humans are in charge of altering the world for the better. A number of features are typical of a Black humanist worldview and relevant in the context of BLM. The Black humanist tradition emphasizes the continued relevance of the past for the present, not least because it regards human beings as embodied. Embodiment describes the fact that longstanding dominant societal and cultural structures of power are inscribed into people's bodily scripts as habits and find expression in actions, thought, and emotions. Precisely because they are embodied and thus function pre-reflectively, these scripts resist easy change and further impact future possibilities. Consequently, faith in the direct (political) outcomes of human actions is limited.[19] But Black humanism insists on the importance of human agency nonetheless and accepts a responsibility to tend to lived bodies and their needs. Deep, humanistic caring for self and others constitutes community. Based on this, it promotes a fragile hope that a better future is possible though never guaranteed. Change can be pushed for and yet will be inhibited by those in power wishing to maintain the world as it is.[20] Instead of giving in to a nihilist impulse, Black humanists readily embrace an existential struggle since "success [lies] in the process" rather than in outcomes (only).[21] Hope is to be found in the struggle itself. Such a human-centered worldview recognizes both human potentials and shortcomings and holds humans accountable for the status quo. At the heart of the tradition is the desire for unconditional Black equality and for greater possibilities of life.

Both BLM and Black humanism thus aim to transform society to reorganize the psychic, economic, social, and emotional ways of the world from anti-Black to anti-racist. One way to secure social justice and Black equality as well as to support the struggle for complex subjectivity is by pushing for a deep sense of democracy. Such a sense of democracy does not so much regard democracy as a form of government; instead, as Judith Green points out, it is primarily a way of life dedicated to bringing forth the "possibility of more equal, respectful, and mutually beneficial ways of community life and 'habits of the heart'—those characteristic, feeling-based, culturally shaped and located frameworks of value within which we perceive the world and formulate our active responses to it."[22] Put differently, *deep democracy* is shaped by a profound care, by a love ethic, for both oneself and others. Green maintains that such a conception is necessary in order to actually fulfill the frail promise of America's unrealized democratic vision, one which it has violently denied entire groups of people since its founding days. There is a need to actively create deep democracy.

Cornel West, who is part of the deep democratic tradition himself, writes extensively about longstanding African American engagement in the deep democratic tradition.[23] In *Democracy Matters*, West tellingly does not begin his reflections on democracy with the United States' founding fathers but instead identifies two dominant streams of democracy in Black intellectual thought and arts that hold the promise of a deep democratic engagement. First, he discusses an Emersonian tradition that emphasizes the individual's responsibility to actively realize their democratic vision. In this strand, "Man thinking" autonomously, guided by conscience, is central, and West holds that Ralph Ellison and James Baldwin advocate this responsibility of the self in their writings. At the same time, however, they denounce the social wrongs and shortcomings of society, thus highlighting the structural obstacles in the way of true democracy.[24] Second, West traces a tradition that begins with Herman Melville and finds its reenactment in the works of Toni Morrison. This stream exposes the limits and threats that racism and imperialism pose to the democratic potential of individuals as well as of society.[25] African American engagement with democracy thus highlights issues of universal concern while never failing to address racial injustices that tie in with other social justice concerns.

It is in the efforts of the marginalized that the deep democratic tradition has historically been most vocal—however, as a realistic ideal, not a utopian conception. Patrick Deneen advocates human "imperfection" as a viable resource and calls for democratic realism and decidedly not for unbound optimism because the latter tends to inhibit action while the former promotes it.[26] This profound commitment to justice and a fuller mode of being resonates with Black humanism's core elements: humans are responsible for the ways of the world, which accounts for both the possibility of change and the possibility of failure.

Clearly, deep democracy is a Black humanist ideal and practice. African American artists and intellectuals of the Black humanist tradition have been committed to making visible but also to enhancing the lives of those who have been excluded from—if not exploited and devastated by—the democratic experiment of America. In fact, Black humanism has long been present in African American communities, first most visibly in the secular work songs and the oral tradition of the enslaved and later in the literary writings of many African American authors who challenged white supremacy as well as patriarchal and heterosexual norms and fought for fuller modes of existence.[27] BLM stands in that very tradition. Yet, far more explicitly than previous movements, it emphasizes not only Black but also (Black) women's and transgender lives and demands and fights for their civil and human rights. Like their many predecessors, BLM activists take seriously human suffering while striving for human well-being; they acknowledge human capabilities to do good but are also acutely aware of the capabilities of humans to act in harmful ways. And so indeed, if we think of democracy not so much as a political system but as a cultural, philosophical, and ethical outlook, there is a dire need to continue the struggle for its realization. Given the ongoing marginalization of and discrimination against social groups along race, gender, and other lines, a deep sense of democracy does not rule the US despite the nation's often evoked self-conception as the beacon of democracy. In this light, BLM appears as a form of deep democratic activism because it draws attention to the fundamental discrepancy between the idea of America and the (long-standing) reality of America.

As my analysis will show, a Black humanist worldview resonates throughout contemporary BLM music and with it a deep democratic desire. This chapter will primarily focus on lyrics but also take visual material into account to illustrate how many of these artists perform resistance to oppression, denounce the status quo, and imagine alternative life worlds.

Of Being Alright, Breaking the Chains, and Rising to Justice

BLM originally emerged in response to anti-Black police violence. Trayvon Martin's death in 2012, George Zimmerman's acquittal in 2013, and the killings of Eric Garner and Michael Brown a year later quickly turned BLM into a national movement. Yet, the movement fights against anti-Blackness more generally: activists have protested state-induced and -sanctioned abuse and neglect more widely and oppose state violence of any kind. Barbara Ransby cautions that state violence refers "not only to police violence but to the policies that enact physical and psychological harm and are either endorsed or administered by the state (government)."[28] Such policies can be both directly and indirectly inflicted. Many musicians criticize such policies and their underlying politics. Frequently uncovering police violence, systemic injustices, and premature Black death, contemporary Black music denounces the political and social ills of the present moment and often directly references the issues at hand. When Usher repeatedly raps that "We're still in chains," John Legend sings of "All this trouble in this here town," and Kendrick Lamar recalls that "We been hurt, been down before . . . / po-po / Wanna kill us dead in the street fo sho," the artists criticize the lack of progress made when it comes to the struggle against systemic racism and state violence in the US.[29] They refuse to allow anyone to buy into the myth of a post-racial society so readily proclaimed by white America after the election of president Barak Obama. As an image of both the violent past of chattel slavery as well as of what Michelle Alexander has labeled the new Jim Crow,[30] chains symbolize a lack of freedom but also place the twenty-first century in continuity with previous ones. Like Usher's song "Chains," Lamar's 2016 Grammy Awards performance of "Alright," which has become a popular chant with protesters in the street, explicitly plays at mass incarceration and the prison-industrial-complex.[31] Walking out on stage handcuffed as part of a chain gang, his band locked away in prison cells, Lamar vividly places his performance in the ongoing fight against institutional injustice and for Black liberation. For Lamar, this is a global struggle, emblematically visualized by ending the show with the word "Compton" written over an image of the African continent. Lamar's struggle for Black lives thus takes place on multiple levels—local and global, past and present, individual and collective—as he performs race, liberation, and justice.

The lack of progress the artists criticize notwithstanding, a fragile hope is a recurring theme in the music, which is indicated by other key symbols in selected songs: Usher seeks to break the chains,

Legend sings of riding to the penthouse floor, and Lamar speaks of "being alright." In fact, there is an unresolved tension between hope and despair; a tragically hopeful undertone persists in Black humanism's best fashion. Jeff Chang remarks that Lamar "raps in his verses of fighting and in his choruses of freedom."[32] While the verses of "Alright" narrate the daily disappointments and injuries in a white supremacist society, the chorus asserts that, despite all, "we gon' be alright." In Lamar's most famous lines, we are confronted with the affirmation that things will turn out for the better. Interestingly, Lamar addresses the listener directly—reminiscent of a call-and-response pattern—assuring those in doubt whether or not the present moment can be overcome, that yes, they will not only survive, but they will survive with a sense of completeness: "Do you hear me, do you feel me? We gon' be alright." Acknowledging the danger the present moment poses, he nonetheless asks the listener to "please believe when I say . . . But we gon' be alright." He does not naively downplay suffering, but rather claims survival in spite of it. Defying historical and ongoing existential threats to Black life, he pushes for justice by drawing on the deep democratic tradition.

Usher similarly connects defeat and resistance. While he bemoans dreariness in "Chains," "I-I-I-I been so tired of being insecure . . . / I've had enough running," he simultaneously conjures change and demands immediate action: "Light it on fire / I've had enough." Usher recalls prominent Black Americans like W. E. B. Du Bois and Booker T. Washington who fought for racial justice in their respective times,[33] then ties their struggles to BLM in the present: "I spoke to Tamir Rice's mom and she told me 'be strong.'" By referencing twelve-year-old Tamir Rice, who was killed by police in 2014, side by side with Du Bois and Washington, Usher not only highlights the continuity between past and present injustices but also stresses the need to endure in the ongoing fight against anti-Black racism: "be strong" instills the wish to incite change, even though progress is slow as "we still in chains." Accordingly, past, present, and future are all entailed in these lines, undergirded by an unfaltering confidence: "it won't be long 'til it's justice." Usher, however, neither embraces suffering nor sees redemption in it. This is an important recognition because in a Black humanist worldview, "victories are not won because of or through suffering, but in spite of suffering."[34] Usher is sure that "revolution is coming." Change lies ahead, but only because there are people constantly fighting to finally break the chains. The song thus once again emphasizes human responsibility for and agency in dismantling the world as it is.

Lamar's 2017 album *DAMN* partakes in Black humanism in a manner that resembles the best of Black humanist existentialist thought in the tradition of Richard Wright. In "Pride" he raps about the (im)possibility of a perfect world: "See, in the perfect world, I would be perfect, world."[35] However, the world is not perfect. Instead, it is shaped by human interconnectedness and mutuality and this holds both risk and potential. Advancing a tragic notion of love that can trump pride, Lamar warns that "Love's gonna get you killed / But pride's gonna be the death of you and you and me." Lamar distinguishes between being killed and death, thus calling for civil disobedience rooted in a genuine concern for humanity as part of deep democracy. While love offers no definite protection from getting killed, pride is the guaranteed way to existential nothingness because its ungoverned self-interest precludes community. Survival is possible in love, even when it kills, but pride makes survival impossible. Notice how pride not only is the death of you but also of *you and me*, that is, it is the death of human relationships and community. By claiming that "Race barriers make inferior of you and I," Lamar emphasizes the intersubjective nature of humanity and the inextricable connection between Black and white existences. This calls to mind Fred Moten's appeal to build coalitions based on the recognition that anti-Black racism causes the death of Black as well as white people: "I don't need your help. I just need you to recognize that this shit is killing you, too, however much more softly."[36] Having people realize this connection almost figures as a prerequisite for taking the risk of love that Lamar encourages his listeners to take. It is difficult not to hear Baldwin's courageous request "to do something unprecedented: to create ourselves without finding it necessary to create an enemy" echoed here.[37] While "Pride" ends with an emphasis on humanistic caring, a touch of uncertainty remains whether or not genuine care has ever been achieved: "Me, I wasn't taught to share, but care / In another life, I surely was there . . . / I care, I care / Maybe I wasn't there." In this worldview, failure is always also possible.

Typical of Black humanism and deep democracy, human intersubjectivity is also a central topic in Usher's work. On the Tidal platform, the music video for "Chains" asks visitors to turn on their webcams in order to listen to the song.[38] The video, accompanied by the hashtag #DontLookAway, consists of close-up portraits of Black people killed by the police in recent years and covers the circumstances of their deaths. It will only play if visitors look at and linger on the faces. As soon as visitors divert their gaze the music stops, thus forcing them to face the people. This opens up the chance to recognize the persons as individuals and their deaths as grave losses instead of as the death of "just" another nameless, faceless person. Drawing on Nicholas Mirzoeff, Chang writes that "seeing each other fully and mutually is no less than the beginning of community."[39] The video demands spectators to see the person not simply as a victim but as an existence eradicated. This can be the start of community with those who deem the meaningless deaths an intolerable outgrowth of systemic racism that must be confronted. As Judith Butler professes in an interview with George Yancy, "when lives are considered ungrievable, to grieve them openly is to protest."[40] Consequently, BLM protests can become the site of the start of something new and initiate a collective push for deep democracy, that is, for a way of life that recognizes and leaves unquestioned the humanity of all. The #DontLookAway video has great affective potential because it literally makes it impossible not to look at the injustices done on a regular basis. Figuratively, it asks viewers to also face, take account of, and be touched by the deaths that have occurred and are likely to take place again. The video lets viewers become witness to the crimes committed in the name of white supremacy but invites them to become accomplices in the struggle against racism, thus bridging tragedy and hope once again.

Unlike the other artists' work and almost contrary to Black humanism's measured hope, Legend's "Penthouse Floor" (featuring Chance the Rapper) initially sounds overly optimistic not least because of its upbeat tone. At first sight, the song envisions an ameliorated future where people can peacefully coexist and learn from one another; radically different from the present, it is the "Only future I can see, ain't what it used to be." Change is coming, and the chorus calls on the listeners to seize the opportunity thereof: "Let's ride the elevator, they can't keep us out no more / Go to the penthouse floor." However, a closer look reveals Legend's ties to Black humanism and thus also to a tamed hopefulness. Especially the music video provides a political frame of reference in support of the current civil rights movement. The video represents BLM as a race as well as class struggle. Legend plays an employee at a fancy upscale hotel who enters through the back door and works his way up to the penthouse floor. All throughout the video, we are confronted with stereotypical Trump supporters and upper-class white citizens dining at the hotel's restaurant, while BLM protests are going on outside and the demonstrators try to force their way in. The police, batons in hand, stand between the two worlds and are ready to protect property and the status quo, and, relatedly, the guests' way of life at all costs. Accordingly, space holds great meaning and is sharply divided into outside versus inside, downstairs versus upstairs, and into those who are in the know about "the weight of white supremacy in America" and those who can afford to display "deliberate ignorance and willful blindness about it."[41]

When Legend sings "they see us reaching for the sky," this briefly takes on a double meaning as if the movement was reaching for superficial goods such as literally making it to the penthouse floor. Quickly we learn that this is "just in order to survive." We are reminded of protest chants that appeared after the killings of Michael Brown and others such as "Hands up, don't shoot," which object to police violence and the deaths of Black people at the hands of government institutions. BLM presses for recognition of systemic racism—enacted or supported by white individuals—and makes it nearly impossible to deny its existence. It is justice and equality before the law as well as the seemingly simple right to live (with dignity) that they are reaching for. Both the movement and the music address these existential needs.

Toward the end of the video, everyone—ranging from Legend to the Trump supporter, the police, and the protestors—has reached the penthouse. Celebrating together, they seem to have overcome their differences. If the scene reveals a blind optimism and naiveté, these are quickly tamed: the final scene shows Legend alone, playing the piano in the penthouse that had just moments before been crowded with people. His vision has only been a dream at best. Thus, the optimism makes room for realism as we hear the protests continue outside, which are now met with police sirens and commands—sounds that have historically seldom signaled justice.[42]

Legend further stresses the fact that some are still denied access to the penthouse by altering the lyrics of the chorus, "Let's ride the elevator, it's what we've been waiting for," after the third verse, adding a call to action rooted in a long history of activism: "We'll tear down those penthouse doors." The path to the present moment is long and access is still not granted voluntarily but requires collective and forceful effort. The elevator stands for the daily struggle in time and space. The penthouse, then, is not only a symbol of money but also a symbol of time and progress. There has been some progress—boldly put, from slave huts to the penthouse—but this has by far not comprehensively been the case. While the Black elite—"handpicked from bad apples and bad eggs"—has reached the penthouse, this is not true of the average Black citizen fighting in the streets. The fight for the possibility of change is ongoing. The penthouse is not the final stop, and redemption is undoubtedly this-worldly for Legend: "Let's ride the elevator / 'Til we can rise some more." Justice, in line with the deep democratic tradition, is tied to a constant effort in the here and now and can only emanate from human action.

Legend's earlier work for Ava DuVernay's 2014 film *Selma* similarly built on Black humanist elements, especially by connecting BLM to the civil rights movement and thus stressing Black humanism's consistent role in organized Black resistance. Anything but a problem from the past, Legend sings, "Selma is now."[43] The film's theme song "Glory" (featuring Common) praises the human ability to fight for justice but it also illustrates the fact that the reasons for protests past and present are virtually the same injustices: "That's why

Rosa sat on the bus / That's why we walk through Ferguson with our hands up." Once more we see the struggle for complex subjectivity as the fight against essentializing powers to be more than what one is made to be. Since "Freedom is like religion to us [and] / Justice is juxtpositionin' us," Legend asserts that "we'll fight on to the finish" since "the war is not over [and] victory isn't won." In fact, the struggle shapes identity and becomes part of the self—"resistance is us." Resistance works best, though, Legend claims, when it is performed collectively, as a communal and intergenerational project rather than a personal battle fought alone: "No one can win the war individually / It takes the wisdom of the elders / And the younger's energy" to continually push for deep democracy as a realistic ideal.

As different as their musical styles may be, Lamar, Usher, and Legend partake in a Black humanist tradition that believes that humans have what it takes to transform the world: agency, even if determined by sociohistorical circumstances, a sensitive attunement for the past and those who suffer, and the power of the collective. The songs thus oscillate between despair and hope, individualism and the collective, defeat and victory. Instead of progressing linearly, these are alternating and recurring themes. Yet, somehow, to recall Lamar in the spirit of BLM, they vow that "We gon' be alright."

Of Suffering, Redemption, and Transformation: Beyoncé's *Lemonade*

When compared to the other songs, Beyoncé's 2016 album *Lemonade* is most comprehensively Black humanist because it criticizes systemic injustice but simultaneously connects the fight for justice to human well-being and caring on a larger scale. Both are at the hands of human beings. *Lemonade*'s humanism has a distinctively feminist twist. Ransby writes that we must make sense of BLM in the context of a revived interest in and awakening of Black feminist thought, theory, and activism, arguing that "Black feminist politics have been [the movement's] ideological bedrock."[44] At first glance, the album and the sixty-minute film accompanying it deal with the infidelity of the artist's partner and the process of coming to terms with it.[45] They appear more personal than political. Nonetheless, as Chang is right to remark, "*Lemonade* cannot be heard or seen separately from the exigency of the Movement for Black Lives."[46] In fact, *Lemonade* dissects the private in order to address the social. The connection between the two becomes even more apparent when taking Beyoncé's persona into account; it unmistakably adds a political dimension to her work seldom seen before with her. Most notably, the 2016 Super Bowl halftime show comes to mind in which visually, by way of costumes and dance, Beyoncé evoked memories of the Black Power movement and thus placed herself in a long line of Black freedom fighters.

Lemonade includes twelve songs that are connected through and complemented by spoken-word intermissions and voice-overs. An initial look at the chapters of the visual album already reveals that it holds anguish and anticipation in creative tension. Heavily relying on spiritual language—"the religious idiom of the twenty-first century"[47]—the album outlines eleven stages that progress from intuition, denial, anger, apathy, emptiness, and accountability, to reformation, forgiveness, resurrection, hope, and finally redemption. *Lemonade* thus laments the existential crisis of Black life but seeks ways to work against it. The spoken word parts, borrowed from Black British female poet Warsan Shire, especially add a level of heightened attunement to grief and call to mind that the album is at least as much about Black life in general as it is about personal experiences. Covering states ranging from pain and despair to longing and fulfillment, *Lemonade* carries a measured confidence that life can turn out for the better. However, *if*, to evoke Martin Luther King Jr., the arc of history bends toward justice at all, progress toward justice (read redemption) is neither guaranteed nor linear but requires constant effort and dedication. As agentic beings, people can make a difference even though they are always also bound and limited by social structures. Consequently, Beyoncé maintains that it is necessary to make the best of any given situation because giving up is not an option. The wisdom of Hattie White, Jay-Z's grandmother, resonates throughout the album: "I was served lemons, but I made lemonade."[48] This becomes the motto of the album as a whole; it is about the will to persist and the ability to push for more, rooted in a deep love for human beings, tragedy notwithstanding.

The will to persist is based on a profound awareness of the importance of the past for the present. The title *Lemonade* itself already, while indicating transformation, is inextricably tied to lemons as an ingredient that leaves its distinct traces. Throughout the album it becomes more clear that time cannot neatly be separated into past, present, and future. Establishing the importance of the present moment, Beyoncé declares in "Intuition" that "the past and the future merge to meet us here / what luck, what a fucking curse."[49] It is a fact that cannot be changed—and an ambivalent one at that. Being both luck and curse, it offers opportunities to seek change, but these opportunities are often painful, seldom joyous. Every moment, including the present one, she tells us, has the potential to be either transformative or merely restorative; every moment can become a step toward greater justice or a step back when one refuses to be affected by the efforts of those who push for a deeper sense of democracy. This ambivalence nonetheless offers hope, visible for instance in the image of "A flower blossoming out of the hole in my face" painted in the voice-over section so tellingly entitled "Hope."[50] This image grants transformation by merging suffering and beauty as well as death and new life. Two aspects are particularly relevant for transformation: the strength of the collective and genuine love. Their healing qualities will become a recurring theme toward the end of the album.

In "Redemption" then, we hear Beyoncé describe the making of lemonade in technical terms, but the segment quickly takes on a mystical tone as it addresses her "grandmother, the alchemist":

> You spun gold out of this hard life.
> Conjured beauty from the things left behind.
> Found healing where it did not live.
> Discovered the antidote in your own kitchen.
> Broke the curse with your own two hands.
> You passed these instructions down to your daughter.
> Who then passed it down to her daughter.[51]

Beyoncé recalls how her grandmother has transformed hardships into beauty. She has done so actively, she contended with her lived reality and she succeeded. The ability to struggle, that is, "the antidote," is part of what it means to be human. Agency, however limited, constitutes her identity and lies within the self ("in your kitchen"); she cannot rely on external or even supernatural forces. If making lemonade is analogous to making a way out of no way, Beyoncé tells us that the will to resist and the knowledge of how to turn hardships and despair into beauty and meaning not only reside in humans individually but are passed on from one generation to the next. The grandmother's pain and wisdom live on in the granddaughter. Accordingly, the grandmother's traumatic past also holds meaning for the speaker's present.

New trauma theory details that "traumatization can result insidiously from cumulative micro-aggressions" in daily life and inscribe itself into lived bodies and collective identities.[52] For Beyoncé, women especially have this sweet and sour gift of being able to transform traumata. The grandmother's knowledge is not only intergenerational but particularly gendered because, as *Lemonade* purports, it has been Black women who have had to endure the greatest injuries. In one of the first songs, "Don't Hurt Yourself," we hear Malcolm X declaring that "the most neglected person in America is the Black woman."[53] Zora Neale Hurston's bitter grievance that the Black woman "is de mule uh de world" echoes in his words.[54] If this is the case, where then does the strength for redemption come from? The visuals offer an explanation for Black women's agency to resist, persist, and forgive: it is in community, in close relationships with other women where such a kind of power takes root and is fostered. As the film shows Black women working, dancing, and dining together, community emerges as a source of individual and collective agency. In a fashion reminiscent of Alice Walker's *womanism*,[55] *Lemonade* thus celebrates Black womanhood for its strength and its consecutive ability to work toward communal healing. Beyoncé not only honors her grandmother and her personal ancestors but also the (female) Black humanist artists and intellectuals who came before her, celebrating Black humanity and Black womanhood while being attuned to suffering.

The strength of the female collective resides in a deep love for human beings. Not coincidentally, this becomes most obvious in *Lemonade*'s most explicit reference to the contemporary BLM movement ("Forward" / "Resurrection"). It is here where the mothers of Trayvon Martin, Eric Garner, and Michael Brown hold up pictures of their sons, resisting the gaze of the camera with their unfaltering stare. Staring back is a determined and agentic act, as disability studies scholar Rosemarie Garland-Thomson details.[56] Bell hooks further notes that to "look directly [is] an assertion of subjectivity, equality."[57] While grief shows on the women's faces, dignity does so even more, and they remain undefeated. The lyrics play: "Forward / Best foot first just in case / When we made our way 'til now / It's time to listen, it's time to fight."[58] Moving forward, then, is about both vulnerability and strength, it is about acknowledging one's own and someone else's pain just as much as it is about forcing a change. Shortly before we see these women, a woman asks off-screen, "So how are we supposed to lead our children to the future?"[59] The response is simple but strong: "Love . . . 'cause you ain't got another hope."[60] Beyoncé here offers a Cornel Westian rendition of Black humanism. In *Race Matters*, West identifies nihilism as a dangerous existential threat in America, as "the lived experience of coping with a life of horrifying meaninglessness, hopelessness, and (most importantly) lovelessness."[61] The solution he offers sounds almost too simple but is far from it:

> Nihilism is not overcome by arguments or analyses; it is tamed by love and care. Any disease of the soul must be conquered by a turning of one's soul. This turning is done through one's own affirmation of one's worth—an affirmation fueled by the concern of others. A love ethic must be at the center of a politics of conversion. A love ethic has nothing to do with sentimental feelings or tribal connections. Rather it is a last attempt at generating a sense of agency among a downtrodden people.[62]

A love ethic rests at the heart of the Black humanist tradition. It takes seriously and leaves unquestioned every person's full humanity. A love ethic nurtures and requests a changed course of action because, West maintains in an interview, "when you love people, you hate the fact that they're being treated unfairly."[63] *Lemonade* pushes for transformation by promoting a love ethic even in the face of betrayal, tragedy, and terror.

For those who believe that transformation through love is an easy, peaceful, and straightforward process, the speaker has a disheartening response because freedom is not achieved by "turning the other cheek" as Chang notes.[64] Instead, she will claim her liberty by any means necessary, singing:

> I'm telling these tears, "Go and fall away, fall away"
> May the last one burn into flames.
> Freedom! Freedom! I can't move
> Freedom, cut me loose!
> Freedom! Freedom! Where are you?
> Cause I need freedom too!
> I break chains all by myself
> Won't let my freedom rot in hell
> Hey! I'ma keep running
> Cause a winner don't quit on themselves.[65]

The choice of words such as "flames," "chains," or "rot in hell" already underscores both her willingness and need to put up a fight. This is a woman dedicated to her own well-being who will neither be stopped nor give up. Such a celebration of agency and persistence grounded in self-love is not a sentimental or naïve approach. While these self-assertive lyrics talk of individual liberty and an individual existential struggle, they are, once again, contrastively accompanied by images of women of color of all ages living together peacefully and productively. Collective (Black) womanhood has healing and liberating potential. *Lemonade* points out that freedom and community are not mutually exclusive but rather constitute one another. We do not find radical individualism here but instead a plea for tending to the individual in the collective. The visuals suggest that while love is necessary, it is not limited to romantic love but rather includes both self-love and the love of others, that is, the love of the collective.

Ultimately, the Black feminist agenda is vital to everyone's survival, we are reminded when Kendrick Lamar raps in "Freedom":

> But mama, don't cry for me, ride for me
> Try for me, live for me
> Breathe for me, sing for me
> Honestly guidin' me
> I could be more than I gotta be.

Moreover, the song here points to the intersubjective nature of existence once again. The need for unconditional recognition by self and others is inherent in Lamar's plea to his mother. This, then, is precisely where the power to heal and a sense of agency reside. This is also where complex subjectivity finds expression. Pinn contends that such a form of subjectivity "means individual fulfillment within the context of concern and responsibility for others."[66]

Lemonade's grand finale, "Redemption," promises a fresh start. It takes up the thematic thread of love again:

> My grandma said nothing real can be threatened
> True love brought salvation back into me
> And my torturer became a remedy
> So we're gonna heal.[67]

True love will persist, Beyoncé is certain, and it is the cure long needed. Notice how these insights are again tightly connected to women who came before her. Yet again, past experiences are relevant for the present and its transformation. Following her grandmother's wisdom—and (indirectly) *Beloved*'s Baby Suggs' "we flesh; flesh that weeps, laughs. . . . Love it. Love it hard"[68]—Beyoncé embraces the lived body by tending to its physical and spiritual needs in "All Night":

> Found the truth beneath your lies
> And true love never has to hide
> I'll trade your broken wings for mine
> I've seen your scars and kissed your crime.[69]

268 · RACE, RELIGION, AND BLACK LIVES MATTER

It is here, toward the end of the album, where many Black humanist elements come together: hope rooted in love, which is, in turn,
rooted in a genuine sensitivity toward the past and its relevance for
the present and future, and the belief in human ability to push for
change. In the final intermission, "Redemption," the voice-over asserts
that "we're gonna start again."[70] However, we are not let off the hook
that easily. Even though *Lemonade* certainly ends on a hopeful and
reconciliatory note, this hope is fragile at best. It is difficult to pre-
dict how long peace will reign or whether the cycle of betrayal—both
on a personal level and on a social level—will start again. Not least
because of the video's predominantly southern setting that calls to
mind the nation's racist past, the album rejects the notion of linear
progress. The institution of slavery and the anti-Black structures
that became apparent in the aftermath of Hurricane Katrina are both
heavily associated with the region. The circular set-up of *Lemonade*
attests to the continuities so that Beyoncé's initial lament in "Anger"
still quietly continues to ring in the final notes of the album as an
ever-present doom: "Why can't you see me?" She is speaking to her
lover but also to a society that has not only regularly failed to recognize but even violently denied the humanity of Black people.

Conclusion: Where Do We Go from Here?

This essay analyzed how Black humanist ideas echo in the works
of contemporary musicians whose works have both become central to and emerged from BLM. Throughout, I have regarded Black
humanism as a religious orientation and creative response that has
helped African Americans negotiate and make sense of their lived
experiences in a white supremacist and hegemonic world. All artists
emphasize human effort and agency rather than relying on supernatural forces. The artists speak to and simultaneously voice the
deep democratic desires of the people involved in the movement.
Eddie S. Glaude describes "democracy in black" as "efforts to imagine a democratic way of life without the burden of the value gap *or*
the illusion that somehow this country is God's gift to the world."[71]

Black people have unfalteringly fought for a world in which their lives matter equally. This continuous struggle and effort constitute the Black contribution to America, now most visible in BLM—the most recent chapter in the Black liberation struggle. The musicians under consideration here wrestle with suffering and healing, loss and joy, despair and hope. In doing so, they simultaneously bridge these binaries, thus seeking to transform injustice into justice. While transformation is not a definite process, in the words of activist Brittany Packnett, BLM "will have only lost if we lose the will to resist."[72] The will to resist persists, and the resurgence of large BLM protests in the spring of 2020 in reaction to the killings of George Floyd, Ahmaud Arbery, and Breonna Taylor by police officers and vigilantes is vivid prove thereof. Tenacious struggle and the desire to continuously reinvent hope constitute the music's and the movement's Black humanist dimension.

Envisioning the future of BLM, Taylor prophesies: "The long-term strength of the movement will depend on its ability to reach large numbers of people by connecting the issues of police violence to the other ways that Black people are oppressed."[73] Standing in the tradition of Black humanism, the musicians under consideration here have once again begun to relate the institutional violence against Black bodies to a larger historical and systemic picture of violence. As Robin D. G. Kelley remarks, "None of this brutality is new. In my fifty-three years on this planet, I've witnessed not a wave but a continuous stream of police violence that has never let up."[74] In this light, the musicians have illuminated possible ways to fight institutional violence and systemic oppression through organizing, love, and genuine care, thus making room for a fuller sense of being. BLM's goals extend beyond undoing racial inequalities by considering the interlocking systems of oppression, but also by pushing to create better and more complex life options for people. The artists studied here, and Beyoncé most explicitly, push for such multifaceted change as well. Well aware of the lack of radical change that does away with the anti-Black structures at the heart of the American project, they are tragically attuned to failure. Even if uncertain of the outcomes, they nonetheless sound a fragile hope.

NOTES

1. Hannah Natanson, "A D.C. Street Musician Was Troubled by Rioting. He Decided to Save the City He Loved—with a Song," *Washington Post*, June 04, 2020, https://www.washingtonpost.com/dc-md-va/2020/06/04/dc-street-musician-was-troubled-by-rioting-he-decided-save-city-he-loved-with-song.

2. Ralph Ellison, "Richard Wright's Blues," in *The Collected Essays of Ralph Ellison*, ed. John F. Callahan (New York: The Modern Library, 2003), 129.

3. Cornel West, *Hope on a Tightrope: Words and Wisdom* (Carlsbad, CA: Smiley-Books, 2008), 114.

4. Anthony B. Pinn, "Making a World with a Beat: Musical Expression's Relationship to Religious Identity and Experience," in *Noise and Spirit: The Religious and Spiritual Sensibilities of Rap Music*, ed. Anthony B. Pinn (New York: New York University Press, 2003), 3.

5. On the importance of sorrow songs for the (formerly) enslaved, see Joseph Winters, "Death, Spirituality, and the Matter of Blackness" in this book, where he discusses the writings of Frederick Douglass and W. E. B. Du Bois.

6. Claudia Roth Pierpont, "A Raised Voice: How Nina Simone Turned the Movement into Music," *New Yorker*, August 3, 2014, https://www.newyorker.com/magazine/2014/08/11/raised-voice.

7. Two instructive studies of hip hop and its manifold social as well as political agendas are Reiland Rabaka, *The Hip Hop Movement: From R&B and the Civil Rights Movement to Rap and the Hip Hop Generation* (Lanham, MD: Lexington Books, 2012) and Jeff Chang, *Can't Stop, Won't Stop: The History of the Hip Hop Generation* (New York: Picador, 2006).

8. Reiland Rabaka, *Civil Rights Music: The Soundtracks of the Civil Rights Movement* (Lanham, MD: Lexington Books, 2016), 2.

9. Daphne A. Brooks, "How #BlackLivesMatter Started a Musical Revolution," *Guardian*, March 13, 2016, https://www.theguardian.com/us-news/2016/mar/13/black-lives-matter-beyonce-kendrick-lamar-protest.

10. I draw this definition from Pinn's works. See Pinn, *What Is African American Religion?* (Minneapolis, MN: Fortress Press, 2011) for a more detailed explication. Eddie S. Glaude offers a similar approach by discussing African American religion as that which "emerges in the encounter between faith, in all of its complexity, and white supremacy." Eddie S. Glaude Jr., *African American Religion: A Very Short Introduction* (Oxford, UK: Oxford University Press, 2014), 6. Even as this latter definition appears to be broad, Glaude does not explicitly include atheistic, nontheistic, and humanistic orientations but remains committed to the study of more traditionally theistic religious varieties.

11. In 2016, Georgetown University's Berkley Center for Religion, Peace and World Affairs hosted a series of essays in which scholars discuss the many re-

ligious traditions traceable in BLM. For instance, Josef Sorett reads it within the context of Afro-Protestantism ("#BlackLivesMatter and the Heterodox History of Afro-Protestantism"), and Terrence Johnson emphasizes its roots in the Black Church ("Black Lives Matter and the Black Church"), whereas Pinn highlights its humanistic elements ("How Black Lives Matter Challenges Twentieth Century Models of Protest"). "Berkley Forum: Religion and Black Lives Matter," October 31, 2016, https://berkleycenter.georgetown.edu/forum/religion-and-black-lives-matter.

12. This is not to deny that market-driven interests also go into the making of BLM music. Protest sells. In addition to that, strong ties between the industry and anti-Black and neoliberal policies exist: for instance, major record labels are primary shareholders in private prisons and thus heavily invested in and complicit with the prison-industrial-complex that has devastated many Black communities (see Daniel Hodgman, "Hip-Hop Pipelines: The Glaring Connection between Commercial Rap and the Private Prison Industrial Complex," *Bonus Cut*, May 1, 2014, https://bonuscut.com/2014/05/01/hip-hop-pipelines-the-glaring-connection-between-commercial-rap-and-the-private-prison-industrial-complex).

13. Christopher J. Lebron, *The Making of Black Lives Matter: A Brief History of an Idea* (New York: Oxford University Press, 2017), xx.

14. Keeanga-Yamahtta Taylor, *From #BlackLivesMatter to Black Liberation* (Chicago: Haymarket Books, 2016), 82.

15. The Movement for Black Lives, "Platform," accessed on Feb 15, 2016, https://web.archive.org/web/20170106083404/https://policy.m4bl.org/platform. The statement has since been revised and updated, demonstrating the movement's dynamism.

16. Pinn, *African American Religion*, 61–62.

17. Pinn, *Terror and Triumph: The Nature of Black Religion* (Minneapolis, MN: Fortress Press, 2003), 158.

18. Pinn, "'Handlin' My Business:' Exploring Rap's Humanist Sensibilities," in *Noise and Spirit: The Religious and Spiritual Sensibilities of Rap Music*, ed. Anthony B. Pinn (New York: New York University Press, 2003), 86–87.

19. In some ways, this is reminiscent of Calvin Warren's take on spiritual versus political hope that Joseph Winters details in his essay in this book, "Death, Spirituality, and the Matter of Blackness." There is a crucial difference though at the very root of the traditions: Afro-pessimists like Warren deem political hope terribly misplaced. However, Black humanism does not preclude the possibility of political and social change even though it does not count on it either. In Black humanism, people's ability to be a source of hope in the world through their actions—regardless the outcome—is the basis for a continued and tragic engagement with the political. Black humanism thus stands in opposition to Afro-pessimism: the humanistic strand leaves

Black humanity unquestioned and engages with *existence* as a mode of being, whereas the Afro-pessimist tradition ontologizes anti-Blackness and locates Blackness forever outside of the realm of the Human. For more on this, see also Lewis R. Gordon, "Critical Exchange: Afro Pessimism," *Contemporary Political Theory* 17, no. 1 (2017): 105–37. Gordon elaborates on the differences between Black existentialist thought and Afro-pessimism in that essay.

20. Fernando Orejuela identifies optimism as an important force in social movements: "Optimism is necessary for healing to happen, even with the anticipation of more death and injustices at the back of our collective minds." Fernando Orejuela, introduction to *Black Lives Matter Music: Protest, Intervention Reflection*, ed. Fernando Orejuela and Stephanie Shonekan (Bloomington: Indiana University Press, 2018), 10. While I would caution against conflating optimism and hope, Orejuela is nonetheless right to point out that BLM activism is driven by a desire for a different tomorrow.

21. Pinn, *African American Religion*, 90.

22. Judith M. Green, *Deep Democracy: Community, Diversity, and Transformation* (Lanham, MD: Rowman and Littlefield, 1999), xi.

23. Green, 135.

24. Cornel West, *Democracy Matters: Winning the Fight against Imperialism* (New York: Penguin, 2004), 68–86.

25. West, 86–101.

26. Patrick J. Deneen, *Democratic Faith* (Princeton, NJ: Princeton University Press, 2005), 9–11.

27. For historical overviews of secular and humanist thought in the Black tradition see Anthony B. Pinn, *By These Hands: A Documentary History of African American Humanism* (New York: New York University Press, 2001); Anthony B. Pinn, *Why, Lord?: Suffering and Evil in Black Theology* (New York: Continuum, 1995); Christopher Cameron, *Black Freethinkers: A History of Africa American Secularism* (Evanston, IL: Northwestern University Press, 2019).

28. Barbara Ransby, *Making All Black Lives Matter: Reimagining Freedom in the Twenty-First Century* (Oakland: University of California Press, 2018), 203.

29. Usher, "Chains," featuring Nas and Bibi Bourelly, by Bibi Bourelly, Paul Epworth, Albert Andre Bowman, Nasir Jones, and Usher, RCA, 2015; Kendrick Lamar, "Alright," by Duckworth, Pharrell Williams, and Mark Anthony Spears, *To Pimp a Butterfly*, Top Dawg Entertainment, 2015; John Legend, "Penthouse Floor," featuring Chance the Rapper, by Stephens Mills Greg Kurstin, and Chancellor Bennett, *Darkness and Light*, Columbia, 2016.

30. Michelle Alexander, *The New Jim Crow: Mass Incarceration in the Age of Colorblindness* (New York: New Press, 2012).

31. A recording of the performance is available on various streaming platforms; see for example Micah Singleton, "Grammys 2016: Watch Kendrick Lamar's stunning performance," The Verge, Feb. 15, 2016, https://www.theverge.

com/2016/2/15/11004624/grammys-2016-watch-kendrick-lamar-perform-alright-the-blacker-the-berry.

32. Jeff Chang, *We Gon' Be Alright: Notes on Race and Resegregation* (New York: Picador, 2016), 166.

33. Many artists of the BLM era center Black history in their works as Phillip Luke Sinitiere also shows in his essay in this book, "Black Lives Matter and American Evangelicalism: Conflict and Consonance in History and Culture."

34. Pinn, *Why, Lord?*, 158.

35. Kendrick Lamar, "Pride," by Duckworth, Steve Lacy, Anna Wise, and Anthony Tiffith, *DAMN*, Top Dawg Entertainment, 2017.

36. Stefano Harney and Fred Moten, "The General Antagonism: An Interview with Stevphen Shukaitis," in *The Undercommons: Fugitive Planning and Black Study*, ed. Stefano Harney and Fred Moten (Wivenhoe, UK: Minor Compositions, 2013), 140.

37. James Baldwin, *The Cross of Redemption*, ed. Randall Kenan (New York: Pantheon Books, 2010), 251.

38. Daniel Arsham and Ben Louis Nicholas, dir., "Chains," Film the Future, 2016, chains.tidal.com.

39. Chang, *We Gon' Be Alright*, 158.

40. George Yancy, *On Race: 34 Conversations in a Time of Crisis* (New York: Oxford University Press, 2017), 56. This is in line with Richard Kent Evans' argument about the centrality of mourning in his essay "MOVE, Mourning, and Memory" collected in this book.

41. West, *Democracy Matters*, 81.

42. See for example Alex S. Vitale, *The End of Policing* (London: Verso Books, 2017).

43. John Legend, "Glory," featuring Common, by Che Smith, John Stephens, Lonnie Lynn, from the *Selma* soundtrack, Columbia Records, 2014.

44. Ransby, *Black Lives Matter*, 2. Taylor takes note of such a revival as well in her discussion of the Combahee River Collective's history and continuing influence and maintains with Demita Frazier that "the point of talking about Combahee is not to be nostalgic; rather we talk about it because Black women are still not free." Keeanga-Yamahtta Taylor, *How We Get Free: Black Feminism and the Combahee River Collective* (Chicago: Haymarket Books, 2017), 14.

45. Beyoncé, *Lemonade* (studio album), Parkwood Entertainment and Columbia Records, 2016; *Beyoncé: Lemonade* (film), Beyoncé and Ed Burke, exec. producers, Good Company and Parkwood Entertainment, HBO premiere April 23, 2016.

46. Chang, *We Gon' Be Alright*, 159.

47. Vincent Lloyd, "Religion, Secularism, and Black Lives Matter: An Introduction," *Immanent Frame: Secularism, Religion, and the Public Sphere*, September 22, 2016, https://tif.ssrc.org/2016/09/22/religion-secularism-and-black-lives-matter.

48. *Beyoncé: Lemonade*, 51:41.

49. *Beyoncé: Lemonade*, 3:07.

50. *Beyoncé: Lemonade*, 47:11.

51. *Beyoncé: Lemonade*, 50:45–51:28.

52. Stef Craps, *Postcolonial Witnessing: Trauma Out of Bounds* (New York: Palgrave Macmillan, 2013), 26.

53. Beyoncé, "Don't Hurt Yourself," featuring Jack White, by Jack White, Beyoncé, Diana "Wynter" Gordon, James Page, Robert Plant, John Paul Jones, and John Bonham, *Lemonade*, Columbia Records, 2016.

54. Zora Neale Hurston, *Their Eyes Were Watching God* (New York: Harper Perennial, 2006), 14.

55. See Alice Walker, *In Search of Our Mothers' Gardens: Womanist Prose* (London: Phoenix, 2005).

56. Rosemarie Garland-Thomson, *Staring: How We Look* (New York: Oxford University Press, 2009).

57. bell hooks, *Black Looks: Race and Representation* (New York: Routledge, 2015), 168.

58. Beyoncé, "Forward," featuring James Blake, by James Blake and Beyoncé, *Lemonade*, Columbia Records, 2016.

59. *Beyoncé: Lemonade*, 43:01.

60. *Beyoncé: Lemonade*, 43:15, 43:37.

61. West, *Race Matters*, 22–23.

62. West, *Race Matters*, 29.

63. Yancy, *34 Conversations*, 265.

64. Chang, *We Gon' Be Alright*, 165.

65. Beyoncé, "Freedom," featuring Kendrick Lamar, by Jonathan Coffer, Beyoncé, Carla Williams, Arrow Benjamin, Kendrick Duckworth, Frank Tirado, Alan Lomax, and John Lomax Sr., *Lemonade*, Columbia Records, 2016.

66. Pinn, *Terror and Triumph*, 159.

67. *Beyoncé: Lemonade*, 51:50–52:32.

68. Toni Morrison, *Beloved* (London: Vintage Books, 2005), 103.

69. Beyoncé, "All Night," by Thomas Wesley Pentz, Beyoncé, Henry Allen, Timothy and Theron Thomas, Ilsey Juber, Akil King, Jaramye Daniels, Andre Benjamin, Patrick Brown, and Antwan Patton, *Lemonade*, Columbia Records, 2016.

70. *Beyoncé: Lemonade*, 52:34.

71. Eddie S. Glaude, *Democracy in Black: How Race Still Enslaves the American Soul* (New York: Crown Publishers, 2016), 236. Italics in original.

72. Brittany Packnett, "How Black Lives Matter Is Resisting Trump," *New Yorker Public Forum*, March 28, 2017, video, 0:38, https://www.newyorker.com/video/watch/how-black-lives-matter-is-resisting-trump.

73. Taylor, *#BlackLivesMatter*, 182–83.

74. Robin D. G. Kelley, "Thug Nation: On State Violence and Disposability," in *Policing the Planet: Why the Policing Crisis Led to Black Lives Matter*, ed. Jordan Camp and Christina Heatherton (London: Verso Books, 2016), 18.

CHAPTER 11

Black Lives Matter and American Evangelicalism

Conflict and Consonance in History and Culture

Phillip Luke Sinitiere

On the September 30, 2017, episode of *Truth's Table*, a Christian theology and culture podcast hosted by three Black women— Michelle Higgins, Christina Edmondson, and Ekemini Uwan— rapper and Christian artist Lecrae (b. 1979, Lecrae Devaughn Moore) appeared as a guest to discuss his recently released album *All Things Work Together*. In a conversation on art, faith, and music, Lecrae described his new project as a "divorce" from white evangelicalism. No longer, Lecrae said, would he maintain in his art a preoccupation with how white Christians might respond to his music. He adamantly refused anymore to center whiteness as a starting point for how he defined and crafted his art. "As far as white evangelicalism is concerned I don't feel any sense of prioritizing [it]. . . . I feel priority to be who God has created Lecrae to be, not who white evangelicalism wants Lecrae to be." Lecrae's admission stirred in evangelical circles. In the *Truth's Table* interview he discussed his mother's "pro-Black" influences through not only teaching him about Angela Davis, but also through some of the literature she gave him to read as a pre-teen, which included W.E.B. Du Bois's *The Souls of Black Folk*, Eldridge Cleaver's *Soul on Ice*, and *The Autobiography of Malcolm X*.[1]

Despite the possession of such a cultural education, he stated that Michael Brown's death in 2014 created a transitional moment—he called it "a shock to my system . . . a jolt"—for his identity as a Black Christian within white evangelicalism. He found disturbing many white evangelicals' dismissive disposition toward Brown's death and tacit rejection of Black life in the era of Black Lives Matter (BLM). In November 2014, three months after Brown's death and in the midst of the Ferguson rebellions, Lecrae asked in a *Billboard* essay, "Why does loving black people equate to hating white people in so many people's minds?"[2] He explains in his memoir *I Am Restored: How I Lost My Religion but Found My Faith* that additional research and study of history, including global travels to Africa, deepened his relationship to Black Christianity. Lecrae tapped further into the writings and speeches of radical evangelical Tom Skinner, for example, and explored the publications of Chanequa Walker-Barnes, James Cone, and Cornel West, among others. An implicit allegiance to white Christianity dissipated and eventually crumbled. "Deconstruction of my faith to ground zero was what I needed to reestablish my faith."[3] Through such a remaking, Lecrae observed, "The God of the oppressed became real to me" and as a result "I am no longer willing to accept Christian expression that refuses to hear voices from the margins."[4]

Lecrae put a finer point on his critical view of American evangelicalism in a foreword he penned for Black evangelical historian Jemar Tisby's 2020 book *The Color of Compromise*. He connected theology and culture through the lens of evangelicalism's history. "My work as a Black hip-hop artist with an audience in white evangelicalism has shown me that tension that exists between Black and white America, specifically when it comes to the history of the white evangelical church in America," he said. "We live in a country centered around whiteness that disregards how the image of God is on magnificent display in nonwhite bodies (and histories and theologies, etc.). If we don't take responsibility for what has happened in America, we're not willing to see the image of God throughout the world."[5]

Reading between the lines, Lecrae's comments targeted the white evangelical culture within which he had operated for many years. Lecrae's question about how whiteness's zero-sum performance operates in American society, specifically its expressions within evangelicalism, and the historical context in which he posed it is a powerful point of entry to think about this chapter's broader subjects: American evangelicalism, art, and BLM.

This essay explores the cultural history and political meaning of Christians in hip hop, especially art that has been made, produced, and circulated during the BLM era, roughly 2013 to 2020. It analyzes the art and aesthetics of three rappers and emcees who identify as evangelical: Propaganda, Sho Baraka, and Jackie Hill Perry. Each of these artists has made music during the BLM era that serves as a lens through which to analyze the contemporary historical moment. In addition, during the same period they have engaged rap and religion through other sites of cultural production (e.g., spoken word, lectures, books, podcasts). This chapter attends to the historical context in which these rappers have made art, and spotlights art produced at the junctures of BLM, race, and the religious culture of Protestant evangelical Christianity. It probes the tensions of how the insurgent art form of rap music challenges evangelicalism's foundational and historical adherence to whiteness, and its hierarchical and often spiritualized assumptions about race and culture. It studies how religion and hip hop aesthetics expose evangelicalism's racial hypocrisy while disclosing how artists envision potential for rearrangements of power and material resources through a possible future of interracial solidarity. It is a story in which conflict and consonance coexist in a complex relationship within history and culture.

This chapter, like Alexandra Hartmann's essay on musical and cultural performance, connects to this volume's aim of spotlighting cultural production created in the BLM era while advancing new perspectives on the movement through an examination of religion, history, and art. As current civil rights scholarship documents, from a historical point of view, the oppressive intersections between

evangelicalism and white supremacy on display during Black freedom struggles produced multiple forms of Black artistic and creative defiance.[6] The rappers this essay focuses on are a contemporary
manifestation of how music and art have worked in tandem in the
Black freedom struggle. They exemplify what Black studies scholar
Reiland Rabaka terms hip hop's "archeological aesthetic" that draws
on Black history to advance artistic, creative visions of liberation.[7]
Furthermore, the artists featured in this chapter connect both past
and present by disclosing what Fernando Orejuela calls a "thematic
soundscape" of the BLM era through the art form of rap music and
hip hop culture.[8]

In this chapter the term *evangelicalism* refers to a historical movement of Protestant Christians who believe in the Bible's spiritual
authority, insist on a conversion experience of personal spiritual
transformation, valorize Jesus Christ as the savior of humanity, and
adopt the imperative to evangelize or spread their message of faith.
Rather than merely a set of beliefs, these convictions present a short
summary of the lenses through which evangelicals over time have
sought to understand the world around them, act on their spiritual
beliefs, and wrestle with the material aspects of a spiritual message
that prizes transcendence. Evangelicals are also people whose orientation to the world in which they live often spiritualizes material
realities in the quest for philosophical certainty about questions
they associate with ultimate meaning. Such beliefs, practices, and
philosophical dispositions have also inhered institutionally over
time through, for example, thousands of denominational expressions, independent ministry organizations, publishing houses, television networks, colleges and universities, and even through the
work of political parties.[9]

The denominational diversity and divergent theological opinion
that exists within evangelicalism means that for this article defi-
nitional clarity requires more specificity. The three emcees whose
work I explore below are all connected to the trend of New Calvinism within American evangelicalism. New Calvinists trace a historical and theological lineage to the Protestant Reformation and the
teachings of John Calvin, a sixteenth-century French Protestant

who emphasized divine power as a dominant concept in understanding the relationship between God and human beings. Calvin's teachings influenced many other like-minded Protestants during the seventeenth and eighteenth centuries, including the English and New England Puritans whose theological and devotional writings New Calvinists prize. Such theological developments over time informed the larger historical movement of Reformed Christianity in the United States, which in the post–World War II period came to encompass numerous evangelicals across countless denominations. In 2009, *Time* magazine's David Van Biema identified the New Calvinists as one of the "10 Ideas Changing the World Right Now." He described the New Calvinist emphasis on "an utterly sovereign and micromanaging deity" that connects to a view of "sinful and puny humanity, and the combination's logical consequence, predestination: the belief that before time's dawn, God decided whom he would save (or not), unaffected by any subsequent human action or decision." A 2014 *Religion and Ethics Newsweekly* profile explored New Calvinism's devotion to an intellectual theology rooted in philosophical ideas and theological certitude. For many years, members of this movement have published books and convened conferences. Denominations started colleges and supported the establishment of seminaries. Most recently, the digital era has produced a proliferation of magazines, online periodicals, and podcasts about theology.[10]

White male evangelicals such as John Piper, the late R.C. Sproul, Michael Horton, Tim Keller, R. Albert Mohler, and John MacArthur, among others, have in the last thirty to forty years served as some of the self-proclaimed leaders within the New Calvinist movement. Active preachers and prolific authors, these individuals not only published analyses of the Bible in the form of commentaries or scriptural studies, they also offered social commentary on social media and through other digital platforms such as podcasts as emerging technologies opened new pathways for communication. As these white New Calvinist leaders gained cultural capital within the movement, particularly in the 1990s and early 2000s, Black Reformed evangelicals such as pastor Anthony J. Carter and philosopher Anthony Bradley began publishing about their experiences as Calvinistic

African Americans. In 2003, for example, Carter edited *Glory Road: The Journeys of 10 African-Americans into Reformed Christianity*, a text that narrated different experiential engagements with New Calvinism. Reflecting the patriarchal dimension of Reformed Christianity, all of the contributors to the volume were men. Like Carter, Bradley used autobiography to describe his embrace of Reformed Christianity; however, he also explored wider philosophical and institutional aspects of Black Calvinism that found historical resonance with earlier figures in the movement such as eighteenth-century poets Phyllis Wheatley and Jupiter Hammon, abolitionist minister Lemuel Haynes, and twentieth century preacher and activist Francis Grimké.[11]

In addition to published books, the Reformed Blacks of America, the Reformed African American Network, which later changed its name to The Witness: A Black Christian Collective, and The Front Porch organized as online communities to offer additional content resources for the Black Calvinist community. Beyond resources for spiritual instruction, authors such as Jemar Tisby (co-founder of The Witness) and Thabiti Anyabwile (a curator at The Front Porch) published books and articles that documented the lives and thought of Reformed Christians of African descent. By the very nature of online communities, these sites featured writings, sermons, and speeches from both men and women. As a result, the work of Black and Reformed women became more central to this strand of the New Calvinist movement. In addition to Higgins, Edmondson, and Uwan's *Truth's Table* podcast mentioned at the chapter's outset, as well as podcasts by Jackie Hill Perry and her spouse, artist Preston Perry (*Thirty Minutes with the Perrys*), and Propaganda and his spouse, scholar Alma Zaragoza-Petty (*The Red Couch Podcast*), books like Austin Channing Brown's *I'm Still Here: Black Dignity in a World Made for Whiteness* and Kristie Anyabwile's *His Testimonies, My Heritage: Women of Color on the Word of God* exemplify critical and emerging voices in the expansion of Black Calvinism.[12]

The appearance of such culturally specific productions within New Calvinism is of historical significance because it indicts the inherent whiteness at the heart of the movement. In other words, the various entities and publications organized to amplify the voices of African American Calvinistic Christians suggests that the embedded whiteness within Reformed Christianity has been conflicted, inhospitable, and unwelcoming to Black people. The historical stakes of such inherent whiteness, and thus anti-Blackness, has profound social and cultural implications. It illustrates what Michael Emerson and Christian Smith termed "the problem of race" in American evangelicalism: racism constituted, and still constitutes evangelicalism's structural and spiritual foundations—what the historian and theological scholar Willie James Jennings dubbed the "Christian imagination."[13] It animates what Anthea Butler called "white evangelical racism" and fueled in part what John W. Compton described as the disappearance of "empathy" within white American Protestantism.[14] And it is bound up with the cultural anxieties of what Robert Jones referred to as "the end of white Christian America," which has been as he aptly put it, "white too long."[15] Yet the creation of cultural content by Black Calvinists reflects historic expressions of resistance and freedom work within African American Christianity that has often recalibrated, renarrated, or reconstituted forms of faith and identity. This chapter uses rap music and hip hop culture created by Black Reformed Christians in the BLM era to examine such complexity and contradiction.

Methodologically, this chapter combines history and ethnography—"ethnolifehistory"—an approach pioneered by cultural studies scholar Daniel White-Hodge. Ethnolifehistory couples the study of lyrical content with documentary evidence, digital data, and oral history. It uses longitudinal aspects of document-based historical analysis alongside ethnography to examine how distinct moments, events, and/or geography in an artist's life shape and reshape his or her hip hop artifacts (e.g., rap, fashion, music videos, album covers, etc.). Ethnolifehistory presents a more "expansive window" into an artist's work, thereby providing the possibility for a "thicker consideration" of the interrelationship of religion, culture, history, and hip hop.[16]

To further contextualize the art of Propaganda, Jackie Hill Perry, and Sho Baraka within American evangelicalism there are key indexes that provide snapshots of opinion about the broader movement's engagement with BLM. *Christianity Today* is one of American evangelicalism's leading periodicals. It has been in print for over half a century, and its print and digital editions, along with its broader media enterprises, effectively cover trends and happenings within the wider evangelical world. More recently, the online publication of a collective called *The Gospel Coalition* has also served as a clearinghouse for popular opinion about Reformed Christianity. A brief historical sampling of how these publishing outlets have addressed race matters related to BLM over time will assist with setting the stage to understand the cultural significance of rap music and American evangelicalism in the contemporary period.[17]

While *Christianity Today* provided general reporting on BLM, in 2016 a writer and pastor named D. A. Horton presented a four-part series that assessed the larger political movement for Black lives, the BLM organization, and its meaning. He offered a prescriptive recommendation about how evangelical Christians should relate to BLM. Horton used his own identity as a Mexican American person with Native American ancestry as a bridge of solidarity with the movement. He pleaded with evangelical Christians to both observe and embrace BLM's "Black-centeredness," especially considering history: how white Christians supported and sanctioned slavery using the Bible and how they practiced white supremacy in social, economic, political, and legal forms of anti-Blackness designed to dehumanize African-descended people for the maintenance of power. According to Horton, the practice of spiritual solidarity should result in "the dedication to long-lasting interpersonal relationships" between Christians assembled as multiracial congregations or collectives.[18] In addition, using a series of Bible verses, he offered a theological rationale for practicing social inclusion across racial and ethnic categories designed to foster a spiritual solidarity of shared belief that dignified rather than dismissed cultural differences.[19] He suggested that while it is likely that evangelicals would differ with BLM in terms of sexual politics—thus announcing the co-existence of evangelicalism's conflict and consonance with the movement—there were a host of ways to proclaim "black lives matter" by "strategically mobilizing

believers (leaders and laity) in local churches to address the broken-
ness found in Black communities by working to renew the broken
systems" including tackling "adequate and affordable housing (in
light of gentrification), broken family structures, crime, education
reform (grassroots to top levels of leadership), food deserts, mass
incarceration, poverty, sex-trafficking, and unemployment."[20] Importantly, Horton emphasized the need for systemic change through the
alteration of resources even in the midst of addressing the necessity
of cultivating cross-racial interpersonal relations. While Horton's
series was far from the only statement *Christianity Today* offered
about BLM, his suggestion about the need for historical knowledge
of the often violent intersection of religion and race, his discussion of the practice of pursuing individual friendships across racial
and ethnic lines, and his commentary on the necessity of structural
changes for more stable race relations mirrored other essays, articles, and blogs the magazine published.[21]

In 2016 *The Gospel Coalition* featured several articles on the BLM
movement specifically. For example, a Black Michigan-based minister Mika Edmondson canvassed Black history and the modern civil
rights movement to elucidate how evangelical churches should relate
to BLM. Like Horton, he drew on scriptures to valorize community
building based around shared spiritual principles. He also critiqued
white resistance to engaging in cross-cultural efforts, and in turn
offered prescriptive practices for everyday life. Within the space of
a congregation, Edmondson wrote that "white suburban men are
called to cry tears with the Black inner-city woman scared to death
her husband is going to be the next Eric Garner, or that her teenage son is going to be the next Trayvon Martin or Tamir Rice. And
if you are so entrenched in your socio-political camp that you can't
shed some tears with Tanisha, something is deeply wrong."[22] Also
like Horton, Edmondson rejected BLM's queer sexual politics and
instead advocated for a what he called a "biblically rooted sexual
ethic," in other words, the politics of straight, cisgender experience
that historically within evangelicalism has centered and privileged
heterosexual relationality as incontrovertibly sacred.[23] Yet on matters of racial injustice his critique targeted the broader evangelical

movement itself. For a Black person committed to their Christian faith and maintaining the importance of African American culture within the larger confines of American evangelicalism in the BLM era, Edmondson commended a "full engagement with the concept [of BLM] and critical engagement with the movement, especially since there's no evangelical alternative to Black Lives Matter. It grieves me deeply to say there's no evangelical movement robustly, consistently, and practically affirming the value of disparaged Black people. So we must be careful how we criticize Black Lives Matter in the absence of an evangelical alternative."[24] Because of evangelicalism's inherent whiteness, which is to say the ways the movement entangles whiteness with its theological perspective and spiritual practice, Edmondson's commentary suggests that his vision of the world and indeed his very survival depends upon centering Blackness in the midst of his commitment to the American evangelical tradition and his intention to foster Christian community.[25] While the stance on racial identity Edmonson advocates gestures in progressive, perhaps even radical directions, a refusal to intersect analysis of race with gender or sexual identity demonstrates how evangelicals place limits on evangelicalism's complete alignment with BLM tenets. It is a position of both conflict and consonance.

By contrast, Michelle Higgins (a co-host of *Truth's Table* mentioned above, and a pastor and activist with St. Louis-based organization Faith for Justice), is an evangelical woman of color whose capacious conception of justice is less interested in circumscribing the movement's relationship to BLM. In a high-profile speech in 2015 at an evangelical conference called Urbana—an address toward which many evangelicals reacted with hostility—Higgins explained how centering Black dignity actually magnified evangelicalism's religious claims about allegiance to biblical teachings and maximized the movement's stated practice of dependence on God. She commented that if evangelicals, and particularly white evangelicals, reckon fully with an uncomfortable historical record of how the evangelical church's practice of racist hate and racist policies has gravely imperiled Black life, then application of Jesus' teaching about love of God and neighbor to which evangelicals claim fidelity would generate the conviction that all Black lives, not just unborn Black lives, or straight, cisgender Black lives, matter. The utterance of Black lives matter, Higgins remarked, contrasts with what many white evangelicals believe about BLM. It is "not a mission of hate. It's not a mission to bring about incredible anti-Christian values and reforms to the world. Black Lives Matter is a movement on mission in the truth of God because what lives matter demands that we face the facts" of the evangelical church's racist history of rejecting Jesus' teachings on generous love toward the outcast, the battered, and the bruised. In other words, she said that being motivated by Jesus' message of abundant love to ensure the survival of all Black lives could translate into the survival of everyone, regardless of theological opinion or denominational affiliation, for example.[26]

This subtle but important pivot Higgins made advocated for a religious perspective that favors the daily practice of recognizing all Black lives as centerpieces of divine creation instead of an emphasis on doctrinal agreement as the primary threshold for advocacy or allyship. It is a religious practice that doesn't seek to gain power to horde it or wield it in retaliation, but an evangelical spiritual principle that aims to redistribute power in the interest of the greatest number of people. As a member of the Presbyterian Church in America (PCA) denomination, which is in the New Calvinist orbit, Higgins prized theological sophistication; therefore, in her speech she did not aim to contrast doctrine with practice. She refused to live confined by evangelicalism's theological and philosophical double bind that often forces evangelicals of color to constrain politics to either race, or gender, or sexuality, depending upon a particular situation. As a Black evangelical woman, Higgins' outlook understands interlocking oppressions in ways that require forms of improvisational, creative survival inspired to foreground the flourishing of all Black life despite the lack of doctrinal alignment or theological synchronicity across an entire group. Practically speaking, on an issue that has bitterly divided evangelicals of all racial backgrounds, she accented adoption as part of a pro-life outlook instead of solely taking an antiabortion position. "We are too busy withholding mercy from the living so that we might display a big spectacle of how much we want mercy to be shown to the unborn," she said of pro-life white evangelicals who emphasize antiabortion politics. If all Black lives matter to evangelicals, Higgins contends, then they must matter from the cradle to the grave.[27]

This account of Higgins' speech does not demonstrate a historical resolution to the conflict and consonance with which evangelicals relate to BLM. Rather, it illustrates some of the political and humanistic stakes for evangelicals of color who continue to reside within a severely frayed evangelical movement birthed in and often bolstered by whiteness instead of the movement's stated goal of godliness.

A brief survey of how selected evangelical publications and evangelical intellectuals and activists have grappled with BLM's historical emergence and cultural importance demonstrates how some evangelicals find themselves in conflict theologically with BLM's intersectional politics. By contrast, how BLM dignifies Blackness has proved central for some evangelicals of color who align with the movement. As the articles and illustrations above demonstrate, part of evangelical political solidarity with BLM also comes from how central historical understanding is to the movement's politics because Black evangelicals reject the whiteness of American religious nationalism. While this dynamic of conflict and consonance speaks to the complexity of how religion and race—in this case specifically evangelical Christianity and race—have operated historically, these indexes of racial opinion derived from evangelical culture and history offer helpful context for understanding the art and aesthetic creativity of Christians in hip hop, especially the ways Propaganda, Jackie Hill Perry, and Sho Baraka factor Black history into their musical endeavors.

The category of "Christian rap" emerged in the 1980s with artist Stephen Wiley's release of the song "Bible Break." While hip hop's history dates to the 1970s in New York City, it quickly impacted all of US society as it gave voice to proletarian experiences in predominately nonwhite, but also interracial, communities. Wiley's upbringing in Oklahoma, his experiences in the African Methodist Episcopal Church, and eventual connection to the prosperity gospel teachings of white ministers like Kenneth Hagin and Black clergy like the late Frederick K. Price placed him in religious, multiracial settings that shaped the future expansion of Christian rap's history.[28]

As hip hop developed in the 1990s and thereafter, Christian rap has operated as a cultural force and creative space within American evangelicalism that mixed race, ethnicity, and gender with religion, theology, and categories of belief. In recent years a group of emcees loosely organized in a segment of gospel hip hop labeled "Reformed rap" or "Calvinist hip hop" has linked to the New Calvinist tradition. White evangelicals constitute the core of New Calvinism, but Reformed rappers speak and perform at New Calvinist meetings and conferences. In addition, these artists use sermon snippets from white Calvinist preachers such as John Piper in their songs. While some New Calvinists may not fully appreciate the nuanced relationship of gospel hip hop to hip hop's history more generally, the theological nature and depth of Reformed emcees proves attractive to evangelicals from the standpoint of scriptural literacy, theological reflection, and identity formation. Record labels such as Reach, Lamp Mode, and Humble Beast have produced the albums of Reformed rappers, and social media through Twitter and Instagram assist in distributing the music and message of Calvinist hip hop. Reformed rap is a cultural site in which contemporary evangelicalism's past and present have commingled in creative and paradoxical ways. The cultural performance of Reformed rap spotlights evangelicalism's inherently racialized character and its active support of segregation and cultural separation. Artists deploy word play, creativity, and a lyrical craft that scripturalizes a sonic resistance to evangelicalism's attempts at racial exclusivity in efforts to promote the promise of interracial community rooted in theological unity and cultural diversity. Reformed rap theologizes cultural diversity and doctrinal specificity even as it speaks back to evangelicalism's racialized fractures and fissures. Contextually, the artist Lecrae is probably the most visible name in this camp; however, Propaganda, Jackie Hill Perry, and Sho Baraka have been part of this cultural and theological orbit during their careers.[29]

Atlanta-based Reformed rapper and spoken word artist Jackie Hill Perry expressed her alignment with the teachings of New Calvinism through her publications and with her inaugural 2014 album *The Art of Joy*. Specifically, she drew on the teachings of white New

Calvinist pastor John Piper in her song "The Argument." A central feature in Piper's theological concept of "desiring God" describes an affective satisfaction in Jesus Christ as an aspect of faith, what Perry calls "obedient delight." Hill cited Piper's direct influence in her album. She commented that the question *The Art of Joy* answers is, "What does it look like when God is our joy, when God is our satisfaction, and what does it look like when he's not?" In the album's opening track "The Argument," Hill makes the connection explicit by stating, "if pleasure is our aim, then we'll find it when our God is who our target is." She translates the connection further when she says that "it's actually finding pleasure in the treasure that was buried and resurrected."[30]

The art and creative expression through which Perry offers her ideas comes from the emotional edge aesthetic performance brings to spaces of culture and history. Perry says that the art forms of poetry and rap music can impact at an affective register. She further comments that such creative expressions through wordplay and literary innovation have the potential to transform the imagination and translate new ideas into resonant social action. If art is about creative expression, then art has the potential to remake or recreate the world in which people wish to live.[31]

While Perry's music adopts a New Calvinist grid through which she addresses life and culture, it also explores issues of state violence against Black people along with African American history. Her art doesn't spiritualize responses to state violence with merely prayers and thoughts—although she does find such internal postures meaningful as a practice of faith—in alignment with BLM it seeks to name the white supremacy that forms the foundation of the nation's anti-Black structures. She aims to strike a balance between spiritual sensibility and analysis of social structures.[32] For instance, her song "The Solution" from *The Art of Joy* cosigns BLM's focus on dismantling the carceral state. Perry descries the injustice of mass incarceration ("Justice system sicker than the intervention given to individuals with limited images") while alluding to surveillance culture in a police state ("Take an aerial shot of my block / see the Glock of an officer pop a kid / that how it is in the ghetto metropolis / way before the introduction of stop and frisk").[33] Similarly, her 2018 record *Crescendo*, released four years after *The Art of Joy* targeted some of the anti-Black state violence that took place in the intervening years. While it is a record that addressed theological questions and Christian practices of expressing faith in God, it is also an album written in the context of increasing hostility against Black bodies emboldened by a more visible and seemingly resurgent white nationalism and in conjunction of the swelling significance of BLM and the Movement 4 Black Lives.

As a Reformed rapper, Hill invokes spirituality and prayer in response to the weight of Black death while speaking clearly and cogently about the reality of suffering, especially considering how over 81 percent of white evangelicals voted for Donald Trump. Strikingly, these are the same people from the evangelical cloth with whom Perry has spoken, preached, and performed. She therefore speaks from a place of personal conflict with evangelicalism's anti-Blackness and from a religious and theological consonance with the movement. "It's hard to pray and say the name of what 81 invited but who will listen?" Hill asks in the song "No Ways Tired." She then relates an insidious white supremacy emanating from the White House to mass incarceration:

> This prison system is lynching my babies
> His bail is higher than what put him inside and it's crazy
> Is he a colleague from Rikers Island with violence
> Or maybe he gotta die to be safe.

She replies, "And I'm still alive, let us pray."[34]

In the track "Maranatha" Perry commented on recent history related to BLM. For example, she alluded to Walter Scott's 2015 murder in South Carolina ("What's the price to find the rifle that / emptied out inside the back and called it freedom") and then addressed the arrest, apprehension, and eventual death of Sandra Bland that took place only a few months after Scott. "Man could you ever pray for God to come back before the bullet came?" Perry asked incredulously in relation to the #SayHerName hashtag. She then invoked

Bland's case, "Did you want have to die for us to say your name /
Sandra you took the blame / We still hangin' onto every word you
said."[35] The layered meaning of the line "hangin' onto every word
you said" alluded to Perry's former residence in Chicago, the alleged
cause of Bland's death (the medical examiner ruled her cause of
death as asphyxiation, meaning she took her own life by hanging
herself), and the imagery of lynching. Conversely, the reference to
Bland's words highlight the "Sandy Speaks" videos Bland recorded
and posted to her Facebook page in early 2015 just before she died.[36]

The work of Atlanta emcee, filmmaker, activist, and writer Sho Baraka
lands an equally direct punch to evangelicalism's racial divisions, while
his projects display interracial engagement through intellectual culture.
New Calvinism informs the theological references in Baraka's music, as
it does for Perry, even though his art opts for more frequent historical
references than hers. For example, Baraka's 2013 record *Talented Xth*
adopted its album title from a famous phrase on racial progress coined
by W. E. B. Du Bois and channels Malcolm X through the configura-
tion of the album art. Aesthetically, the album's cover visualizes "Talented Xth" with text from the "Talented Tenth" essay as background.
Furthermore, Baraka's references to Malcolm X throughout the record
reconfigure the album cover's "X" to function as an artistic provoca-
tion that symbolizes resistance to white supremacy, an aesthetic Black
fist raised for the listener to see, learn, and understand.[37]

In an album produced in the context of BLM's rise to significance, Baraka challenged white indifference to Black pain and criticized his Anglo audience for failing to appreciate the wide diversity
of Black life. Baraka also pushed back against evangelical culture for
dichotomizing creativity by forcing Black Christian rappers to make
a choice between theology and art instead of letting art do its work
of exploring and exposing truthful and raw perspectives about the
world. "I know God is sovereign and I should pray about it," he raps
in reference to Calvinistic teaching on a track called "Jim Crow," "but
a man won't stop if it increases his profits. . . . So instead of truth
they'd rather be duped / I guess they want me to make more songs
for youth groups." In the same song Baraka stated, "I am the invisible man," echoing Ralph Ellison's book of the same title.[38]

Lyrically, *Talented Xth* explored the concept of double consciousness, and the record took a deep dive into history with explorations of slavery, Reconstruction, Jim Crow, capitalism, segregation, integration, class consciousness, and education, among many other topics. The song "Jim Crow" addresses the subject of its title, especially as it relates to being Black in predominantly white Christian spaces, what he likens to "swimming through bleach." To "Wash my brain from some of the things that race taught," Baraka draws on historical references that center Black history in an international framework ("I am the invisible man . . . from an invisible land") from the vantage point of Du Bois's work ("Ain't much Booker T when you look at me / But a whole lot of Du Bois making noise."). "Jim Crow" connects history to present societal conditions. "Yeah I got a consciousness, but I'm still in touch / Cops got my hands in the air, so I ain't feeling much," Baraka proclaims. "Lookin' for protection, all I can see is tyrants / I'm fighting them coons and thugs, some racists and Don Imus." Similarly, the opening track called "Bethesda" alludes to current affairs through a historical lens ("Police got rap sheets so ya kids getting / Hit after hit video in the crowd and still not enough evidence / I'm on my Harriet Tubman maybe my Sojourner / More like Martin Luther the King and Nat Turner").[39]

Baraka's interracial sensibilities continued on his 2016 Humble Beast Records release *The Narrative*. Part of this record's inspiration materialized around the time that BLM started. Baraka undertook a careful reexamination of Black history and cultural study that produced both *Talented Xth* and *The Narrative*. He recalled, "I had a meeting with a professor, a theologian and an African American gentleman who challenged me and kind of saw how I wrote. He challenged me to stop reading, this may sound crazy, so much Christian stuff and said you need to read more sociology if you are really trying to connect with the pain of people and the struggle of people. A lot of these Christian writings don't really do that."[40] This led to Baraka delving further into writers like Du Bois and Douglass and creating art inspired from a wider culture stream. If his 2013 record channeled Du Bois, then *The Narrative* drew on Douglass more explicitly. As on his 2013 record, Baraka's carefully crafted album cover art and record title specified history in the service of art: his pose in a tuxedo along with an Afro invoked Frederick Douglass while *The Narrative* alluded to Douglass's most famous writing. "I'm brave, I'm unchained, I'm Frederick Douglass with a fade," he said on the record's second track "Soul, 1971." Further investing the record with historical sensibility, he coupled each song title with a date, a significant year either in his life personally or to make a larger point about Black history in light of the contemporary era. For example, the opening track "Foreward, 1619" comments on the origins of slavery in North America while speaking back to slavery's afterlife through a narrative of freedom, circa 2016.[41]

An autobiographical song, "Road to Humble, 1971," explained divine grace from a Calvinistic viewpoint, "I was glad that the Lord found me, because he was never lost / Once blind, but now I see more than I ever saw," while simultaneously alluding to a multicultural imagination that combines the thought and literary creativity of Black and white thinkers and artists.

> So, now I mix a little Augustine with Du Bois
> A little Selassie I mix it with Mahalia's joy
> A C. S. Lewis mind with some Phillis Wheatley art
> A little Sojourner spirit, with a King David heart.

In the New Calvinist movement, the story of King David depicts dramatic conversion and symbolizes divine power to overcome obstacles; fifth-century African Christian intellectual Augustine is a popular author, as is the early twentieth-century British writer C. S. Lewis. Baraka included an additional autobiographical element in the song "Foreward" when he stated, "I'm from the west, between Cornel and Kanye," a reference to his origins in California as well influences from the well-known Christian ethicist and philosopher and the hip hop mogul.[42]

Like *Talented Xth*, *The Narrative* translates Baraka's theological convictions creatively into verse and upbraids evangelical Christians for remaining silent in the face of anti-Black actions that imperil the lives of African-descended people. In addition, the historical context of the BLM era in which Baraka made *The Narrative* further put evangelical Christianity in his cultural crosshairs, especially the increasing inflections of Christian nationalism. "I hear disturbing things come from so-called 'Christians,'" Baraka observes on "Maybe Both, 1865." "Quick to justify a man's death / Because of a criminal record or how a man dressed / Thugs I guess." He then moves into a historical exposition about the visibility of Black death at the hands of state officials ("True flaw, America kills and hides behind the law / They purchase this land with violence, but never count the cost / Put a dollar to your ear, you can hear the moaning of a slave / America the great was built off the labor that they gave"). Such a strain of white supremacist revisionist history, Baraka continued, rendered "Jefferson and Washington [as] great peace pursuers / But John Brown was a terrorist and an evil doer."[43]

"Road to Humble" also lists as sources of intellectual and spiritual formation African American scholar W. E. B. Du Bois, Ethiopian leader and Pan-African and Rastafari figure Haile Selassie, and female artists such as singer Mahalia Jackson, eighteenth-century poet Phyllis Wheatley, and nineteenth-century abolitionist Sojourner Truth. By spanning time periods and traversing geographical boundaries, Baraka's song signals to his white evangelical listeners the importance of a cross-cultural intellectual heritage that shapes an interracial religious disposition to engage society. While this is a way for Baraka to call out his intellectual influences, the performative dimension of the art also speaks to white listeners who engage the music. "Road to Humble" also performs an aesthetic callback to his 2013 song "Bethesda" in its specific invocation of Sojourner Truth and C. S. Lewis and its reference to literary figures more generally where Baraka mentions the Harlem Renaissance and Zora Neale Hurston. Yet mixed within this lyrical recollection are contemporary concerns about state violence against African Americans ("I'm on my Oscar Grant and invisible children / Jena Six, Rakeem Boyd, I am Bobby Tillman"). Other tracks on *The Narrative* comment about contemporary society, including the song "Here, 2016," which address the death of Tamir Rice, and "Profhet, 1968," where he reimagines civil rights history in service of freedom and liberation for African-descended people ("I dream of Angela and Martin in the morning marching / Bringing hope to the homeless, the widows, and the orphans").[44]

Historical references coupled with Baraka's literary sensibilities as a rapper distinguish his art from Jackie Hill Perry. Yet simultaneously the New Calvinist theological conceptualizations that frame his orientation to culture align their perspectives. Los Angeles–based spoken word artist and rapper Propaganda reflects such viewpoints himself.

Like his artistic comrades discussed above, Propaganda draws insights from history, colonialism, and European theology, as well as his experiences as a classroom teacher and his interracial marriage to a Mexican American woman, to fuel his art as a Reformed rapper. His radical roots also come from his father, a Vietnam veteran and a Black Panther. As a young person his family exposed him to the philosophy of Marcus Garvey, the work of Cesar Chavez, the story of Nat Turner, and the historical accounts of figures like Malcolm X and Angela Davis. In the context of BLM and BLM-era art, Propaganda described how his revolutionary consciousness stirred most passionately with the death of Eric Garner. He found it difficult to cope with, yet in consulting with community elders he received wisdom for the road ahead. He recalled that they reminded him that the fight for justice is long and difficult, that the Bible supported justice, and that community-based love and solidarity offered the truest form of existential sustenance. He translated his life experience, creativity, and the community knowledge he had acquired into the art form of his music.[45]

Propaganda's cultural background and faith position has produced work that traverses cultural boundaries and fiercely holds his evangelical comrades accountable for the larger ways the movement seeks to spiritualize materialize conditions and blunt the hard edges of its complicity in cultures of injustice. He has often turned to history to make connections between current conditions in light of historical change over time. An early example of this materialized in a 2012 song titled "Precious Puritans" from his project *Excellent*. The track illustrates a form of hip hop's righteous reckoning at the intersection of American evangelicalism's art, identity, religion, and culture. Propaganda opens the song by proclaiming that he will "take care of some in-house issues," by which he meant the song will confront Reformed evangelicalism's racism and racialized thought that valorizes Puritan theology without regard to the historical context of its exclusionary structure. Flipping the script, Propaganda asks, "You know they were chaplains on slave ships, right?" and continues with a direct line of questioning that connects to indigenous history: "Would you quote Columbus to Cherokees? Would you quote Cortez to Aztecs?" From these interrogatives, Propaganda states, "Their fore-destined salvation contains a contentment in the stage for which they were given which is to be owned by your forefathers' superior image-bearing face / Says your precious puritans." These statements contextualize the origins of Puritan theology by connecting the Reformation-era doctrine of divine election and the Protestant emphasis on evangelization with the onset of colonialism, the birth of racialized capitalism, the transatlantic slave trade, and the practice of chattel slavery in North America. Against the backdrop of this historical framework, the song interrogates the foundations of American exceptionalism, critiques how colorblindness perpetuates racism, blasts Reformed theology's entanglement with the Confederacy, and questions the artistic depiction of Jesus as white. After such structural critiques of US religious history, Propaganda individualizes his theological claim that "God really does use crooked sticks to make straight lines, just like your precious puritans."[46]

Propaganda's song "Andrew Mandela" from his 2017 record *Crooked* connects the racist history he chronicled in "Precious Puritans" with a more recent political landscape of nineteenth-century America and twentieth-century South Africa. *Andrew* refers to Andrew Jackson while *Mandela* refers to Nelson Mandela. Referencing the ways his art uses history in unflinchingly creative ways, in the track Propaganda says,

> I take shots at your sacred cows
> I dance with skeletons in closets
> I point at elephants in the room
> And make a mockery of heroes.

With regard to South Africa, the song laments Mandela's incarceration and the debilitating nature of colonialism while it pays tribute to his fortitude and analysis of apartheid ("It ain't fair, but you called hate a cancer / Said love was the answer / And gladly took 10-25 with your fist high / Refused to accept death until the end of apartheid.") Turning to the 1800s, the track condemns Andrew Jackson's racist ways through the Trail of Tears ("When you write your own rules, you could never lose . . . now we got a destiny to manifest"). "Oh, God forgive me for my brash delivery," Propaganda says,

> But I remember vividly what Lewis and Clark did to me
> His face is on our currency, the struggle is real
> A man whose legacy is literally a trail of tears.[47]

The invocation of Nelson Mandela and Andrew Jackson from the horizon of the current BLM era makes the historical connection to slavery and slavery's afterlife explicit. Propaganda adopts hip hop's insurgent art form to center blackness in ways that both celebrate revolutionary diasporic culture and "point at elephants in the room" to comment on white supremacy's deadly legacy.

A song called "Cynical" from the *Crooked* project offers a final example of how Christians and hip hop invoke BLM-era related critiques of white evangelicalism and white religious nationalism. The track offers condemnation and critique through a series of interrogative engagements. "Where were you when we were dying?" Propaganda asks. "Flying to Trump rallies, sipping the finest wine and / . . . Why you ain't march on Selma? / . . . Why do you love your guns more than our sons? / Why you patriots first? Why you worshipping the flag?" The song also referenced Donald Trump's anti-immigrant rhetoric and critiqued the evangelicals who parroted such nativist Christian nationalism. Finally, the song moves from complicity with forms of injustice to the absence of Christian solidarity, in other words the act of historical erasure and the adoption of a white theology that blinds white evangelicals to the sacramental nature of Christian community ("Why when you take communion, it don't remind you of your union?").[48]

Conclusion

This chapter uses hip hop culture and rap music—specifically Christians in hip hop—to examine the relationship between American evangelicalism and BLM. It is a relationship fraught with both conflict and consonance. On the one hand, the reality of American evangelicalism's racialization means that its entire history is one enmeshed with the scripturalization of white supremacy; on the other hand, its emphasis on the Bible presents an equally important history during which evangelicals have marshaled scriptural support in the service of racial and economic justice. The "problem of race," as the subtitle of Michael Emerson and Christian Smith's book *Divided by Faith* (2000) describes it, renders a movement that struggles to reconcile power, subjectivity, and community while wrestling with the function of spirit and matter. BLM's materialist origins and its insurgent disruption of cultural, social, and political binaries, especially regarding gender and sexuality, not to mention capitalism, have vexed evangelicals who remain wedded to the complex entanglements of conservative theology, cultural power, faith in free market economics, and the allure of progressive politics.

By exploring art of Christians in hip hop that has been made, produced, and circulated during the BLM era, this chapter attends to the historical context in which art is made and spotlights art produced at the junctures of BLM, race, and the religious culture of Protestant evangelical Christianity. It probes the tensions of how an insurgent art form challenges evangelicalism's hierarchical (and often spiritualized) assumptions about race and culture, and how hip hop aesthetics expose evangelicalism's racial hypocrisy while disclosing the potential for rearrangements of power and material resources and a possible future of interracial solidarity. Due to history's unpredictability, it is not a predetermined future; however, the dialectic of conflict and consonance between evangelicalism and BLM suggests that the aesthetic imagination of Christians in hip hop will remain a site of fascinating, contradictory, and complex contingency and cultural production.

NOTES

I thank Edward Carson and Timothy Welbeck for feedback and illuminating comments on a previous version of this chapter.

1. Michelle Higgins, Christina Edmondson, and Ekemini Uwan, "Facts about Lecrae," September 30, 2017, in *Truth's Table*, produced by Joshua Heath, podcast, 50:26, https://www.truthstable.com/season-1.

2. Lecrae, "Lecrae on Ferguson: 'The System We Have in Place Has Biases,'" *Billboard*, November 26, 2014, https://www.billboard.com/articles/columns/the-juice/6327837/lecrae-ferguson.

3. Lecrae, *I Am Restored: How I Lost My Religion but Found My Faith* (Grand Rapids, MI: Zondervan, 2020), 55.

4. Lecrae, *I Am Restored*, 56–57.

5. Lecrae, foreword to *The Color of Compromise: The Truth about the American Church's Complicity in Racism* by Jemar Tisby (Grand Rapids, MI: Zondervan, 2020), 9–11.

6. Recent studies of white religious resistance to Black freedom struggles consulted for this chapter include Curtis J. Evans, "White Evangelical Protestant Responses to the Civil Rights Movement," *Harvard Theological Review* 102, no. 2 (2009): 245–73; Michael O. Emerson and Jason Shelton, *Blacks and Whites in Christian America: How Racial Discrimination Shapes Religious Convictions* (New York: New York University Press, 2012); Stephen R. Haynes, *The Last Segregated Hour: The Memphis Kneel-Ins and the Campaign for Southern Church Desegregation* (New York: Oxford University Press, 2012); Carolyn Renée Dupont, "White Protestants and the Civil Rights Movement in Kentucky," *Register of the Kentucky Historical Society* 113, Nos. 2 & 3 (Spring/Summer 2015): 543–73; and Carolyn Renée Dupont, *Mississippi Praying: Southern White Evangelicals and the Civil Rights Movement, 1945–1975* (New York: New York University Press, 2015).

7. Reiland Rabaka, *Hip Hop's Inheritance: From the Harlem Renaissance to the Hip Hop Feminist Movement* (Lanham, MD: Lexington, 2011), 216.

8. Fernando Orejuela, introduction to *Black Lives Matter and Music: Protest, Intervention, Reflection*, ed. Fernando Orejuela and Stephanie Shonekan (Bloomington: Indiana University Press, 2018), 3.

9. Scholarship on evangelicalism's history is expansive. Most helpful for my definition is Randall Balmer, *The Making of Evangelicalism: From Revivalism to Politics and Beyond* (Waco, TX: Baylor University Press, 2010); *Mine Eyes Have Seen the Glory*; David Bebbington, *Evangelicalism in Modern Britain* (London: Unwin Hyman, 1989), 2–3; Mark Noll, *American Evangelical Christianity: An Introduction* (Malden, MA: Blackwell, 2001), 7–108; Douglas A. Sweeney, "Evangelicals in American History," in *The Columbia Guide to Religion in American History*, ed. Paul Harvey and Edward J. Blum (New York: Colum-

bia University Press, 2012), 122–35; Molly Worthen, *Apostles of Reason: The Crisis of Authority in American Evangelicalism* (New York: Oxford University Press, 2013); and Timothy Gloege, *Guaranteed Pure: The Moody Bible Institute, Business, and the Making of Modern Evangelicalism* (Chapel Hill: University of North Carolina Press, 2017), epilogue.

10. David Van Biema, "The New Calvinism," *Time*, March 12, 2009, http://www.time.com/time/specials/packages/article/0,28804,1884779_1884782_1884760,00.html; Collin Hansen, *Young, Restless, Reformed: A Journalist's Journey among the New Calvinists* (Wheaton, IL: Crossway, 2008); Drew Angerer, "Evangelicals Find Themselves in the Midst of a Calvinist Revival," *New York Times*, January 3, 2014, http://www.nytimes.com/2014/01/04/us/a-calvinist-revival-for-evangelicals.html; "The New Calvinism," *Religion and Ethics Newsweekly*, April 4, 2014, http://www.pbs.org/wnet/religionandethics/2014/04/03/april-4-2014-new-calvinism/22607; Brad Vermurlen, *Reformed Resurgence: The New Calvinist Movement and the Battle over American Evangelicalism* (New York: Oxford University Press, 2020). In a previous publication, I explored the New Calvinist movement's relationship to the prosperity gospel movement; this paragraph draws from Phillip Luke Sinitiere, *Salvation with a Smile: Joel Osteen, Lakewood Church, and American Christianity* (New York: New York University Press, 2015), chapter 8.

11. See Anthony J. Carter, *On Being Black and Reformed: A New Perspective on the African-American Experience* (Phillipsburg, NJ: Presbyterian and Reformed, 2003); Anthony J. Carter, Kenneth Jones, and Michael Leach, *Experiencing the Truth: Bringing the Reformation to the African-American Church* (Wheaton, IL: Crossway, 2008); and Anthony J. Carter, ed., *Glory Road: The Journeys of 10 African-Americans into Reformed Christianity* (Wheaton, IL: Crossway, 2009).

12. Reformed Blacks of America maintains a web presence (reformedblacks.org), however in 2019 the Reformed African American Network rebranded and became The Witness: A Black Christian Collective. See its website, https://thewitnessbcc.com, as well as Richard Clark, "The Witness is Building a Community for Christian Outsiders," *Christianity Today*, September 23, 2019, https://www.christianitytoday.com/partners/witness/calling/witness-is-building-community-for-christian-outsiders.html.

13. Willie James Jennings, *The Christian Imagination: Theology and the Origins of Race* (New Haven, CT: Yale University Press, 2011); Willie James Jennings, "Can White People Be Saved?: Reflections on the Relationship of Missions and Whiteness," in *Can "White" People Be Saved?: Triangulating Race, Theology, and Mission*, ed., Love L. Sechrest, Johnny Ramírez-Johnson, and Amos Yong (Downers Grove, IL: IVP Academic, 2018), 27–43; Willie James Jennings, *After Whiteness: An Education in Belonging* (Grand Rapids, MI: Eerdmans, 2020).

14. Anthea Butler, *White Evangelical Racism: The Politics of Morality in America*

(Chapel Hill, NC: Ferris and Ferris, 2021); John W. Compton, *The End of Empathy: Why White Protestants Stopped Loving Their Neighbors* (New York Oxford University Press, 2020).

15. Robert P. Jones, *The End of White Christian America* (New York: Simon and Schuster, 2016); Robert P. Jones, *White Too Long: The Legacy of White Supremacy in American Christianity* (New York: Simon and Schuster, 2020).

16. Daniel White-Hodge, "Methods for the Prophetic: Tupac Shakur, Lauryn Hill, and the Case for Ethnolifehistory," in *Religion in Hip Hop: Mapping the New Terrain in the US*, ed. Anthony B. Pinn, Monica R. Miller, and Bernard "Bun B" Freeman (New York: Bloomsbury Academic, 2015), 24–37. I deployed this methodology in a previous essay on religion, culture, and rap music; see Phillip Luke Sinitiere, "Skipp Coon: Race, Religion, and Black Radical History in Hip Hop," in *Beyond Christian Hip Hop: A Move Towards Christians and Hip Hop*, ed. Erika Gault and Travis Harris (New York: Routledge, 2020), 162–78.

17. While the limitations of space do not allow me to address how the progressive evangelical magazine *Sojourners* has addressed BLM, readers can find multiple articles by searching the magazine's archives on sojo.net. For a historical perspective on this periodical's engagement with racial justice, see David R. Swartz, *Moral Minority: The Evangelical Left in an Age of Conservatism* (Philadelphia: University of Pennsylvania Press, 2012), 26–46; Brantley W. Gasaway, "'Glimmers of Hope': Progressive Evangelicals and Racism, 1965–2000," in *Christians and the Color Line: Race and Religion after Divided by Faith*, ed. J. Russell Hawkins and Phillip Luke Sinitiere (New York: Oxford University Press, 2014), 72–99; Brantley W. Gasaway, *Progressive Evangelicals and the Pursuit of Social Justice* (Chapel Hill: University of North Carolina Press, 2014), 75–100.

18. D. A. Horton, "Viewing Black Lives Matter—Part 1," *Christianity Today*, February 4, 2016, https://www.christianitytoday.com/edstetzer/2016/february/viewing-black-lives-matter-part-1.html; D. A. Horton, "Viewing Black Lives Matter—Part 3," *Christianity Today*, February 18, 2016, https://www.christianitytoday.com/edstetzer/2016/february/viewing-black-lives-matter-part-3-horton.html.

19. D. A. Horton, "Viewing Black Lives Matter—Part 2," *Christianity Today*, February 11, 2016, https://www.christianitytoday.com/edstetzer/2016/february/viewing-black-lives-matter-part-2.html.

20. D. A. Horton, "Viewing Black Lives Matter—Part 4," *Christianity Today*, February 25, 2016, https://www.christianitytoday.com/edstetzer/2016/february/viewing-black-lives-matter-part-4-da-horton.html.

21. See, for example, Natasha Sistrunk Robinson, "Dear White Brothers and Sisters: Why #BlackLivesMatter Matters to You," *Christianity Today*, December 8, 2014, https://www.christianitytoday.com/amyjuliabecker/2014/december/dear-white-brothers-and-sisters-why-blacklivesmatter-must-m.html; "Michelle

Higgins: 'I Am a Worshiper' First and Foremost," *Christianity Today*, November 23, 2016, https://www.christianitytoday.com/ct/2016/november-web-only/michelle-higgins.html; Hope E. Ferguson, "Taking the Charleston Shooting Personally," *Christianity Today*, June 2015, https://www.christianitytoday.com/women/2015/june/taking-charleston-shooting-personally.html; "Jemar Tisby: It's Never Too Soon to Talk about Race in Your Church," *The Calling* (podcast), *Christianity Today*, July 13, 2016, https://www.christianitytoday.com/ct/2016/july-web-only/its-never-too-soon-to-talk-about-race-in-your-church.html.

22. Mika Edmondson, "Is Black Lives Matter the New Civil Rights Movement?," *The Gospel Coalition*, June 24, 2016, https://www.thegospelcoalition.org/article/is-black-lives-matter-the-new-civil-rights-movement.

23. Edmondson, "Is Black Lives Matter." On evangelicalism's sexual politics, see among others Amy DeRogatis, *Saving Sex: Sexuality and Salvation in American Evangelicalism* (New York: Oxford University Press, 2015) and R. Marie Griffith, *Moral Combat: How Sex Divided American Christians and Fractured American Politics* (New York: Basic Books, 2017).

24. Edmondson, "Is Black Lives Matter."

25. Mika Edmondson, "Yes, You Are Your Brother's Keeper: The Final Call of MLK," *The Gospel Coalition*, March 22, 2018, https://www.thegospelcoalition.org/article/you-are-brothers-keeper-final-call-mlk.

26. Michelle Higgins, "Michelle Higgins - Urbana 15," December 28, 2015, posted to YouTube by InterVarsity Christian Fellowship USA, on January 26, 2015, https://www.youtube.com/watch?v=XVGDSkxxXco. Journalists documented how evangelical opinion divided over Higgins' speech. See Mark Oppenheimer, "Some Evangelicals Struggle with Black Lives Matter Movement," *New York Times*, January 22, 2016, https://www.nytimes.com/2016/01/23/us/some-evangelicals-struggle-with-black-lives-matter-movement.html; Kevin Porter, "Michelle Higgins Challenges Evangelical Church on #BlackLivesMatter at Urbana 15," *Christian Post*, December 31, 2015, https://www.christianpost.com/news/black-lives-matter-ubana-15-michelle-higgins-challenges-evangelical-church.html.

27. Higgins, "Michelle Higgins - Urbana 15"; Oppenheimer, "Some Evangelicals Struggle."

28. Josef Sorett, "'It's Not the Beat, but It's the Word that Sets the People Free': Race, Technology, and Theology in the Emergence of Christian Rap Music," *Pneuma* 33, no. 2 (2011): 200–217. For this section of the chapter, and part of my discussion of Jackie Hill Perry, Sho Baraka, and Propaganda below, I draw on portions of my article, Phillip Luke Siniatiere, "Interracialism and American Christianity," *Oxford Encyclopedia of Religion in America*, ed. John Corrigan (Oxford University Press, 2018), https://oxfordre.com/religion/view/10.1093/acrefore/9780199340378.001.0001/acrefore-9780199340378-e-499?rskey=TjkZXX&result=6.

29. Van Biema, "The New Calvinism"; Angerer, "Evangelicals Find Themselves"; Brad Vermurlen, "Structural Overlap and the Management of Cultural Marginality: The Case of Calvinist Hip-Hop," *American Journal of Cultural Sociology* 4 no. 1 (2016): 68–106; Travis Harris, "Refocusing and Redefining Hip Hop: An Analysis of Lecrae's Contribution to Hip Hop," *Journal of Hip Hop Studies* 1, no. 1 (Spring 2014): 14–37.

30. Jackie Hill Perry, "The Argument," *The Art of Joy* (Humble Beast Records, 2014). On Perry's music, see David Daniels, "John Piper's Book 'Desiring God' Inspires Jackie Hill-Perry's Album," *Rapzilla*, November 17, 2014, http://www.rapzilla.com/rz/features/interviews/9441-john-piper-s-book-desiring-god-inspires-jackie-hill-perry-s-album. See also her writings on John Piper's website, Jackie Hill Perry, "The Search for Better Pleasure," DesiringGod.org, November 20, 2014, https://www.desiringgod.org/articles/the-search-for-a-better-pleasure; Jackie Hill Perry, "When Temptation Holds Out Pleasure," DesiringGod.org, January 10, 2019, https://www.desiringgod.org/articles/when-temptation-holds-out-pleasure. While this essay does not explore the question of Perry's sexuality because she has not addressed it in direct relation to BLM, readers might consult her memoir for an account about a previous lesbian partnership she had. See Jackie Hill Perry, *Gay Girl, Good God: The Story of Who I Was and Who God Has Always Been* (Nashville, TN: Broadman and Holman, 2018).

31. Jackie Hill Perry, "On Poetry and Rap Music," video, *Gospel Coalition*, February 9, 2018, https://www.thegospelcoalition.org/video/jackie-hill-perry-poetry-rap; Jackie Hill Perry, "What's the Point of Art," at the Gospel Coalition 2017 National Conference, April 4, 2017, audio, *Gospel Coalition*, March 23, 2018, https://www.thegospelcoalition.org/podcasts/tgc-podcast/whats-point-art.

32. Brett McCracken, "Jackie Hill Perry and the 'Crescendo' of Christian Faith," *Gospel Coalition*, May 11, 2018, https://www.thegospelcoalition.org/article/jackie-hill-perry-and-the-crescendo-of-christian-faith.

33. Jackie Hill Perry, "The Solution," *The Art of Joy* (Humble Beast Records, 2014).

34. Jackie Hill Perry, "No Ways Tired," *Crescendo* (Humble Beast Records, 2018).

35. Jackie Hill Perry, "Maranatha," *Crescendo* (Humble Beast Records, 2018).

36. On Bland's videos, see Phillip Luke Sinitiere, "Religion and the Black Freedom Struggle for Sandra Bland," in *"The Seedtime, the Work, and the Harvest": New Perspectives on the Black Freedom Struggle in America*, eds. Reginald K. Ellis, Jeffrey Littlejohn, and Peter Levy (University Press of Florida, 2018), 197–226.

37. This paragraph on Sho Baraka and the two that follow draws from the section of a previously published essay of mine in which I discuss Baraka's specific engagement with the writings of Du Bois; see Phillip Luke Sinitiere,

"'Hold Sacred Strong and Purposeful Art': W. E. B. Du Bois and Poetry," *Phylon* 56, no. 1 (Summer 2019): 156–79.

38. Sho Baraka, "Jim Crow," *Talented Xth* (Lions & Liars Music, 2013).

39. Sho Baraka, "Bethesda," *Talented Xth* (Lions & Liars Music, 2013).

40. Tony Cummings, "Sho Baraka: The Radical Rapper Determined to Continue The Narrative," *Cross Rhythms UK*, October 21, 2016, http://www. crossrhythms.co.uk/articles/music/Sho_Baraka_The_radical_rapper_ determined_to_continue_The_Narrative/59216/p1; Author conversation with Sho Baraka, Atlanta, Georgia, February 23, 2018.

41. Sho Baraka, "Soul, 1971" *The Narrative* (Humble Beast, 2016). See also, Matthew Teutsch, "The Black Intellectual Tradition and Hip-Hop," *Black Perspectives*, September 20, 2017, https://www.aaihs.org/the-black-intellectual-tradition-and-hip-hop.

42. Sho Baraka, "Road to Humble, 1979," *The Narrative* (Humble Beast, 2016).

43. Sho Baraka, "Maybe Both, 1865," *The Narrative* (Humble Beast, 2016).

44. Sho Baraka, "Here, 2016" and "Profhet, 1968," *The Narrative* (Humble Beast, 2016).

45. Meagan Clark, "Propaganda Speaks: On His New Album, Justice, and Faith," Journey through NYC Religions, October 16, 2013, http://www.nycreligion. info/propaganda-speaks-album-justice-faith; Jason "Propaganda" Petty, "Romanticizing Revolution," *King Movement* (blog), October 7, 2016, http://www. kingmovement.com/blogs.

46. Propaganda, "Precious Puritans," *Excellent* (Humble Beast Records, 2012). Predictably, this song created a firestorm of controversy with the Reformed evangelical community that revealed conflict along lines where race and theology intersected, a larger point that Reformed rappers examine in their music. See Thabiti Anyabwile, "The Puritans Are Not That Precious," *Gospel Coalition* (blog), October 2, 2012, https://blogs.thegospelcoalition.org/thabitianyabwile/2012/10/02/the-puritans-are-not-that-precious; Anthony B. Bradley, "Puritans and Propaganda," *UrbanFaith*, October 2012, https://urbanfaith. com/2012/10/puritans-and-propaganda.html; Owen Strachan, "Reflecting on Propaganda's Fiery 'Precious Puritans' Rap Song," *Thought Life* (blog), September 26, 2012, http://www.patheos.com/blogs/thoughtlife/2012/09/ reflecting-on-propagandas-fiery-precious-puritans-rap-song.

47. Propaganda, "Andrew Mandela," *Crooked* (Humble Beast Records, 2017).

48. Propaganda, "Cynical," *Crooked* (Humble Beast Records, 2017).

Contributors

IMAN ABDOULKARIM is a PhD student in religious studies at Yale University. Her research interests include Black women's contributions to Islamic religious knowledge, Muslim ethics, Black feminist intellectual history, and transnational activism. She was a 2017–2018 Fulbright Postgraduate scholar at the Centre for the Study of Islam in the UK at Cardiff University, where she also completed her MA. Iman formerly served as a contributor and editor for *Azizah Magazine*, the first Muslim women's lifestyle magazine in North America.

CHRISTOPHER CAMERON is a professor of history at the University of North Carolina at Charlotte. He was the founding president of the African American Intellectual History Society. Cameron received his BA in history from Keene State College and his MA and PhD in American History from the University of North Carolina at Chapel Hill. His research and teaching interests include early American history, the history of slavery and abolition, and African American religious and intellectual history. Cameron is the author of *To Plead Our Own Cause: African Americans in Massachusetts and the Making of the Antislavery Movement* and *Black Freethinkers: A History of African American Secularism*. He is also the co-editor of *New Perspectives on the Black Intellectual Tradition*. His research has been supported by the Gilder Lehrman Institute of American History, the Massachusetts Historical Society, the American Philosophical Society, and the American Council of Learned Societies.

MARJORIE CORBMAN is an assistant professor in the Department of Theology and Religious Studies at Molloy College in Rockville Centre, New York. She defended her dissertation, on the influence of the Nation of Islam on early Black Theology's portrayal of God's anger and judgment, in the Department of Theology at Fordham University in February 2020. Her MA research at the School of Oriental and African Studies (SOAS) at the University of London (receiving her degree in 2012) focused on interactions between Christian and Muslim theologies in a colonial context. Broadly speaking, her research focuses on the multireligious history of social movements in modern American history, with particular attention to Muslim, Jewish, and Christian interreligious encounters and confrontations. In addition, she is interested in political theology, religion and violence, and theologies of anger and suffering. Her theological pursuit is also deeply informed by her time spent living and working at a Catholic Worker community in Chicago and as a member of organizing and activist communities in Boston.

MATTHEW J. CRESSLER is an associate professor of religious studies and affiliate faculty in African American studies at the College of Charleston. His writing on religion, race, and US Catholicism includes *Authentically Black and Truly Catholic: The Rise of Black Catholicism in the Great Migrations* (NYU Press, 2017), "'Real Good and Sincere Catholics': White Catholicism and Massive Resistance to Desegregation in Chicago, 1965–1968" (*Religion and American Culture* 30, no. 2), and "Centering Black Catholic Religio-Racial Identity, Revealing White Catholicism" (*Journal of the American Academy of Religion* 88, no. 2). He co-authored the Religion News Service series "Beyond the Most Segregated Hour" with journalist Adelle M. Banks, which won a Wilbur Award from the Religion Communicators Council. You can connect with him on Twitter @mjcressler.

RICHARD KENT EVANS is a historian of American religion. He is currently visiting assistant professor of religion at Haverford College. He is the author of *MOVE: An American Religion* (Oxford University Press, 2020). Evans is currently writing an intellectual and cultural history of "religious madness," a cluster of psychiatric diagnoses premised on the idea that some forms of religious experience had the potential to be contagious forms of insanity. He received his PhD in North American religions from Temple University in 2018.

ALEXANDRA HARTMANN holds a PhD in American studies and is currently a postdoctoral researcher and lecturer of American literature and culture at Paderborn University in Germany. Her dissertation, entitled *A Fragile Hope: The Black Humanist Tradition in Anti-Racist Literature*, focuses on Black Humanism in twentieth- and twenty-first-century African American literature. It explores literary works from a philosophy of race perspective and embodiment theories. While her dissertation manuscript is in preparation for publication, she has published essays on anti-racism, white privilege, and complicity. She has held research appointments at Washington University in St. Louis and Harvard University.

KERRY PIMBLOTT is a lecturer in international history at the University of Manchester with interests in anti-racism, social movements, and the African diaspora experience. Pimblott holds a PhD in history from the University of Illinois at Urbana-Champaign and a BA in American studies from King's College in London. Her recent publications include *Faith in Black Power: Religion, Race and Resistance in Cairo, Illinois* (University of Kentucky Press, 2017) and chapters in *The Pew and the Picket Line: Christianity* (University of Illinois, 2016) and the *Oxford Handbook on Religion and Race in American History* (Oxford University Press, 2018). Committed to meaningful community-based research and anti-racist pedagogy and activism, Pimblott is a co-founder of the Race, Roots & Resistance Collective and a member of the Northern Police Monitoring Project and Resistance Lab, a Greater Manchester collective against state violence.

PHILLIP LUKE SINITIERE is a professor of history at the College of Biblical Studies, a predominately African American school located in Houston's Mahatma Gandhi District. He is also the scholar in residence at UMass Amherst's W. E. B. Du Bois Center. A scholar of American religious history and African American studies, his recent books are *Protest and Propaganda: W. E. B. Du Bois, The Crisis, and*

American History (University of Missouri Press, 2014), *Salvation with a Smile: Joel Osteen, Lakewood Church, and American Christianity* (NYU Press, 2015), and *Citizen of the World: The Late Career and Legacy of W. E. B. Du Bois* (Northwestern University Press, 2019). Sinitiere has received research funding from the Lily Endowment, the Houston Public Library, Rice University's Center for Engaged Research and Collaborative Learning (CERCL), the Society for Values in Higher Education, the American Sociological Association, and the Andrew W. Mellon Foundation.

ALEX STUCKY received his PhD in American studies from the University of Kansas in 2019. His dissertation, *White Liberalism in Black Comics: Metaphorical Marginalization and the Displacement of America*, discussed the role of black superheroes and their relation to black political movements during the 1970s. His research primarily focuses on how white comic book authors use superpowers and other fantasy narratives to discuss socio-political movements.

CAROL WAYNE WHITE is Presidential Professor of Philosophy of Religion at Bucknell University, specializing in poststructuralist philosophies, process philosophy and theism, religious naturalism, science and religion, and critical theory and religion. Her books include *Poststructuralism, Feminism, and Religion: Triangulating Positions* (2002); *The Legacy of Anne Conway (1631–70): Reverberations from a Mystical Naturalism* (2009); and *Black Lives and Sacred Humanity: Toward an African American Religious Naturalism* (2016), which won a Choice Award for Outstanding Academic Titles. White has published numerous essays in philosophy of religion and on religious naturalism; her work in philosophy and critical religious thought has also appeared in *Zygon: The Journal of Religion and Science*, *The American Journal of Theology and Philosophy*, *Philosophia Africana*, and *Religion and Public Life*. White has received international awards and national fellowships, including an Oxford University Fellowship in Religion and Science, a Science and Religion Grant from The John Templeton Foundation, and an NEH Fellowship.

JOSEPH WINTERS is an associate professor at Duke University in religious studies and African and African American studies. He holds secondary appointments in English and gender, sexuality, and feminist studies. His interests lie at the intersection of African American religious thought, black literature, and critical theory. His research examines the ways Black literature and aesthetics develop alternative configurations of the sacred, piety, (Black) spirit, and secularity. Winters's first book, *Hope Draped in Black: Race, Melancholy, and the Agony of Progress* was published by Duke University Press in 2016. He is currently working on a second manuscript, tentatively titled *Disturbing Profanity: Hip Hop, Black Aesthetics, and the Volatile Sacred.*

Index

CPSIA information can be obtained
at www.ICGtesting.com
Printed in the USA
LVHW092153171121
703677LV00006B/188